UNDER CONSTRUCTION
PARDON THE MESS

UNDER CONSTRUCTION

PARDON
THE MESS

A Collection of Family-Building Thoughts
Compiled by VIOLA WALDEN
Introduction by CURTIS HUTSON

SWORD of the LORD
PUBLISHERS
P.O. BOX 1099, MURFREESBORO, TN 37133

SWORD OF THE LORD PUBLISHERS

ISBN 0–87398–854–X

Printed and Bound in the United States of America

Introduction

UNDER CONSTRUCTION: Pardon the Mess was compiled with women in mind, but anyone—man, woman, boy or girl—will surely find it enjoyable reading. The 200 pages are filled with poems, one-sentence sermons, humorous and serious stories, with many pictures to illustrate the articles.

The busy housewife will find much good advice in this volume. The young lady looking forward to marriage will find much good counsel. A mother trying to raise children in this day and age will find good instruction, encouragement and examples.

The reading of this book will sometimes bring a laugh, at other times a tear. But whether through laughing or crying, it will cause one to think, to do some soul-searching and, we trust, often make some needed corrections.

Philippians 1:6 states, "...he which hath begun a good work in you will perform it until the day of Jesus Christ." As long as we are in this flesh, God will be working on us. Occasionally, changes and corrections are needed.

A. J. Gordon once prayed, "Be thorough with me, Jesus; be thorough." Every Christian could appropriately wear a sign that reads: PLEASE BE PATIENT WITH ME; GOD ISN'T FINISHED WITH ME YET. That is what the author had in mind when she added the subtitle, "Pardon the Mess"!

Miss Viola Walden, a faithful assistant, has done a remarkable job in compiling these hundreds of items, with pictures to illustrate them.

This book will prove a valuable addition to any Sunday school teacher's library. Ladies who teach or speak to other ladies will find here much helpful information. And preacher, you will refer to it time and time again for material to use in your own teaching and preaching.

Charles Spurgeon once said that illustrations in a sermon are like windows in a house—they let the light shine in. This book is filled with windows that will let the light shine in on a lot of good Bible teaching and preaching.

We recommend it to any who want to do a better job in communicating with people.

Buy a copy and give it to your own Sunday school teacher or preacher. How grateful that one will be to have this valuable addition to his/her library!

We pray that this book will be a blessing to all who read it.

CURTIS HUTSON
March, 1994

A Wife, Man's Inspiration

No one can so inspire a man to noble purposes as a noble woman. No one can so thoroughly degrade a man as a wife of unworthy tendencies. While in the case of Jezebel we have an illustration of wifely ambition employed in the wrong direction, society and history are full of instances of wifely ambition gloriously triumphant in the right direction.

All that was worth admiration in the character of Henry VI was a reflection of the heroics of his wife Margaret.

Justinian, the Roman emperor, confesses that his wise laws were the suggestions of his wife Theodora.

Andrew Jackson, the warrior and President, had his mightiest reenforcement in his plain wife, whose inartistic attire was the amusement of the elegant circles in which she was invited.

Washington, who broke the chain that held America in foreign vassalage, wore for forty years a chain around his own neck, that chain holding the miniature likeness of her who had been his greatest inspiration, whether among the snows of Valley Forge or amid the honors of the presidential chair.

Pliny's pen was driven through all its poetic and historical dominions by his wife.

Pericles said he got all his eloquence and statesmanship from his wife.

De Tocqueville, whose writings will be potential and quoted while the world lasts, ascribes his successes to his wife: "Of all the blessings which God has given me, the greatest of all in my eyes is to have lighted on Maria Motley."

Martin Luther says of his wife, "I would not exchange my poverty with her and all the riches of Croesus without her."

Isabella of Spain, by her superior faith in Columbus, put into the hand of Ferdinand, her husband, America.

John Adams, President of the United States, said of his wife, "She never, by word or look, discouraged me from running all the hazards for the salvation of my country's liberties."

Thomas Carlisle spent the last years of his life in trying by his pen to atone for the fact that during his wife's life he never appreciated her influence on his career and destiny. The literary giant woke from his conjugal injustice and wrote the lamentations of Craigen-puttock and Chyne Row.

A whole Greenwood of monumental inscriptions will not do a wife as much good as one plain sentence like that which Tom Hood wrote to his living wife: "I never was anything until I knew you."

—T. DE WITT TALMAGE

Criminals are home-grown.

—J. Edgar Hoover

PATCH-WORK MARRIAGE

I got my marriage out today
* To look at it again,*
I hadn't looked in quite a spell—
* Just do it now and then.*

It's so much like a patchwork quilt,
* With patches not a few!*
Some patches large, some patches small,
* Some patches old, some patches new.*

Each patch brings back to memory
* Some unkind word or deed,*
By which we've learned to give and take,
* And love with greater heed.*

I pray the time will never come
* When we patch it up no longer,*
For it seems that where the patches are,
* The fabric is much stronger.*

—Bill Ashworth, in *Home Life*

A college graduate was asked which books had helped him the most thus far in life.

"That's easy," he said, "Mom's cookbook and Dad's checkbook!"

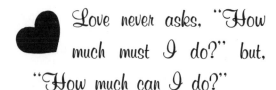

Love never asks, "How much must I do?" but, "How much can I do?"

"Where's Mother?"

When Father came from work at night,
  Before he'd wash his hands and face
Or hang his hat upon the peg,
  His glance would wander 'round the place,
And if dear Mother's sunny head
  Was not within his vision's ken,
He'd search for her from room to room—
Upstairs and down and all—and then
He'd stop and ask,
        "Where's Mother?"

But if he found her in her chair,
  He'd putter off about the lot
And pick a mess of early greens
  Or fix a chicken for the pot;
He'd mend a fence or set a hen
  Or do some other homely chore,
With only now and then a glance
  Toward the half-open kitchen door
That seemed to ask,
        "Where's Mother?"

When Mother left us sorrowing,
  He followed her within a day;
And while we laid white flowers around
  His smooth-brushed hair, as white as they,
We could but think that when the light
  And beauty of that wondrous place
Burst on his newly-quickened gaze,
  He must have raised an eager face
And simply asked,
        "Where's Mother?"

—Author Unknown

An aged gentleman remarked:

"Once I was young but now am old, and I've never seen a girl unfaithful to her mother that ever came to be worth a one-eyed button to her husband.

"If one of you boys ever comes across a girl with a face full of roses who says as you come to the door, 'I can't go with you for thirty minutes, for the dishes are not washed,' you sit right down on that doorstep and wait for that girl! Because some other fellow may come along and marry her, and right there you have lost an angel. Wait for that girl and stick to her like a burr to a mule's tail."

—*The Christian World*

† † †

FIRST "FIRST LADY" WHO REFUSED

The first "First Lady" to go counter to the social custom of serving champagne and other wines at formal White House functions was the wife of President Rutherford B. Hayes, who, in fact, refused to serve any kind of alcoholic beverages.

"I have young sons," she said, "who have never tasted liquor. They shall not receive, from my hand, or with the sanction that its use in my family would give, their taste of what might prove their ruin. What I wish for my own sons, I must do for the sons of other mothers."

A Good Prescription

Dr. Karl Menninger was asked at a forum once what one should do if he felt a nervous breakdown coming on. The famous psychiatrist said, "If you feel a nervous breakdown coming on, lock up your house, go across the railroad tracks, find someone in need, and do something for him."

"Marriage is forever... and ever...and ever!"

Whether we like it or not, when we marry, we must look at it as permanent. God has given us no alternative. The field has been narrowed down. A person must learn to live with this one whom he has married.

> *A woman who creates and sustains a home and under whose hands children grow up to be strong and pure men and women, is a creator second only to God.*

Pass on the Praise

"You are a great little wife, and I don't know what I would do without you." And as he spoke he put his arms about her and kissed her, and she forgot all the care in the moment.

And, forgetting it all, she sang as she washed the dishes and sang as she made the beds, and the song was heard next door, and a woman there caught the refrain and sang also, and two homes were happier because he had told her that sweet old story—the story of the love of a husband for a wife.

As she sang, the butcher boy who called for the order heard it and went out whistling on his journey, and the world heard the whistle, and one man hearing it thought, "Here is a lad who loves his work, a lad happy and contented."

And because she sang her heart was mellowed; and as she swept about the back door, the cool air kissed her on each cheek, and she thought of a poor old woman she knew, and a little basket went over to that home with a quarter for a crate or two of wood.

So, because he kissed her and praised her, the song came and the influence went out and out.

Pass on the praise.

A word and you make a rift in the cloud, a smile and you may create a new resolve, a grasp of the hand and you may repossess a soul from Hell.

PASS ON THE PRAISE!

—*Heart Blessings*

Lord, Let It Be Me!

A virtuous woman is known by her deeds,
A rose by the wayside surrounded by weeds;
A cup of cold water on desert of sand,
A cloud in the sunset, a jewel in the hand.

She's far above rubies or diamonds that glow,
Her spirit is quiet, so gentle and low;
A breath of fresh air when a storm blows on past,
For Christ living through her will make her work
*   last.*

A virtuous woman's a keeper at home,
She's blest by her children; she does love her own;
Her life spent for others, a candle burned low,
Becomes like the sunset's last soft fading glow.

That virtuous woman I pray I may be,
That rose by the wayside, Lord, let it be me;
That cup of cold water on desert of sand,
That cloud in the sunset, that jewel in the hand.

        —Angela Poole, *The Baptist Bulletin*

A fable tells about a bear whose cubs asked, "Mother, which foot shall we put forward first?"

She answered, "Shut up and walk!" Some are so careful about how to walk by faith that they never walk.

A Heaven . . .

A Heaven where we didn't have anything to do but sit by the side of crystal seas and pearly streams and gaze forever on the eternal beauty and dazzling effulgence about us would be too ghostly. It would be too senseless and insipid. That'll do for some old monk or idle dreamer, but I wouldn't want to go there.

I read the other day the Epitaph of a Tired Woman:

"Here lies a poor woman who always
    was tired,
For she lived in a place where help
    wasn't hired.
Her last words on earth were, "Dear
    Friends, I am going
Where washing ain't done, nor sweeping,
    nor sewing;
And everything there is exact to my
    wishes,
For where they don't eat, there's no
    washing of dishes.
I'll be where loud anthems forever are
    ringing;
But having not voice, I'll get rid of the
    singing.
Don't weep for me now, don't weep for
    me ever;
For I'm going to do nothing forever and
    ever."

But that's not Heaven. There is going to be something doing in Heaven all the time. And that sort of a Heaven would soon become monotonous even to a poor tired woman like that, although she may not think so now, and she would soon be asking the Lord for something to do.

Just what work you'll have to do, what errands you'll have to run, what ministries of love you'll have to perform, and just what studies He'll illumine your mind for, I do not know, but Heaven is not a place of idleness whatever else it is.

        —*William Edward Biederwolf*

Anger Never Pays

When I have lost my temper
*   I have lost my reason, too.*
I'm never proud of anything
*   Which angrily I do.*

When I have walked in anger
*   And my cheeks are flaming red,*
I have always uttered something
*   That I wish I hadn't said.*

In anger I have never done
*   A kindly deed, or wise,*
But many things for which I know
*   I should apologize.*

In looking back across my life
*   And all I've lost or made,*
I can't recall a single time
*   When fury ever paid.*

        —UNKNOWN

Just Things

"Dear Thief . . . ," the letter in the *Evening Tribune* began. The writer explained that she spotted a man stealing something heavy from her garage, but ". . . we had so much stuff in the garage that we could not tell what it was that you took." (Mrs. Smith did not necessarily want the stolen things returned, but she wanted to report the loss, and the police could not make out a report until she knew what was stolen). ". . . **Until we finally miss what it was you took, we can't report it missing: if we can't report it stolen, we can't claim our loss and deduct it from our income tax. So would you, just as a token of your appreciation, send us an itemized list of what you stole and its approximate value so we can turn it in to our tax man?"**

This is a commentary on human nature! Most of us have so many things that we cannot keep inventory of what we have nor miss it when it's gone! How much better to lay up our treasure in Heaven, "where thieves do not break through nor steal." Heaven will keep a good inventory of what we send on ahead.

There is the story of a lady who never spoke ill of anybody. "I believe you would say something good even about the Devil," a friend told her.

"Well," she said, "you certainly do have to admire his persistence."

How Far Is It Called to the Grave?

How far is it called to the grave?
The boy looked up from his play,
To the grave . . . to the grave?
I've not heard of the grave,
It must be far away!
Naught he knew of the silent tomb,
Naught he knew but his play and prayer;
Yet the time to go had almost come,
His feet were almost there,
Were almost there, were almost there!

How far is it called to the grave?
The lover looked up with a smile,
How far? from the golden land of love,
It must be many a mile!
He could not see that his darling

With the bridal flowers in her hair,
As he gave her the wedding token,
Was almost . . . almost there,
Was almost there, was almost there!

How far is it called to the grave?
The mother looked up with a tear,
The rose in her cheek grew pale and white,
Her heart stood still with fear.
How far? O 'tis close to the hearthstone,
Alas for the baby feet,
The little bare feet that, all unled,
Are going with step so fleet,
And they're almost there, they're almost there!

How far is it called to the grave?
It is only a life, dear friend,
And the longest life is short at last,
And soon our lives must end.
But there's One who arose from the grave,
Who ascended triumphant on high,
With our trust in Him we'll know no sting,
Tho' low in the grave we lie,
And we're almost there, we're almost there!

—Anonymous

Finding a Good Wife

And as they rode off into the sunset the prince promised her his love, his riches and his castle in the clouds if only she would be his.

She agreed.

Later, after the wedding, they discussed the running of the kingdom. "The King, my father, is old; and my blessed mother, the Queen, has long been gone; and the castle is in terrible disarray," explained the Prince. "It needs the hand of a fine woman like yourself to straighten its many rooms and dust its many nooks and light its many fires and clean its many chimneys and sweep its many corridors and feed its many occupants and visitors. Then we shall have many sons so that they may run the kingdom long after I am gone.

"I can only hope that, when they come of age, they will be as lucky as I in finding a good wife."

And with that, they kissed; **and the Prince lived happily ever after.**

A Baby—

§ *That which makes the home happier,*
Love stronger,
Patience greater,
Hands busier,
Nights longer,
Days shorter,
Purses lighter,
Clothes shabbier,
The past forgotten,
The future brighter.

—Marion Lawrence

A Husband's Lament

I never knew how much she was to me;
I never knew how patient she could be;
I never realized until she went away
How much a woman helps a man each day.
And, oh! I never knew how thoughtless I
Had been at times, until I saw her die.
I never knew the crosses that she bore
With smiling patience, or the griefs that tore
Upon her heartstrings as she toiled away:
I only saw her smiles and thought her gay.
I took for granted joys that were not so;
I might have helped her then but didn't know.
I see her life was bounded by regret;
I might have done much more for her had I
But known her sorrows, or had thought to try;
But now that I'm alone, at last I see
How much of pain her smiling hid from me.
I never knew how much I leaned upon
That little woman till I found her gone,
How much her patience, gentleness and cheers
Had meant to me through all those early years,
How many little things she used to do
To smooth my path. Alas, I never knew!

—Edgar A. Guest

A parent's life is the child's copy-book.

—W. S. Partridge

† † †

Home is the place where the great are small and the small are great.

*   *   *

Granny's Glasses

A little boy said to his playmate, "When I get old, I want to wear glasses just like Granny's because she can see much more than most people. She can see good in a person when everyone else sees their bad. She can see what a fellow meant to do even if he didn't do it. I asked her one day how she could see so good, and she said it was the way she learned to look at things when she grew older. When I get older, I want a pair of glasses just like Granny's so I can see good, too."

Evidently Barnabas, about whom we read in the book of Acts, had a pair of Granny's glasses. When the Apostle Paul did not want to take John Mark on the second missionary journey because he had turned back the first time, Barnabas took Mark, and he turned out well.

How different our world would be if we all wore a pair of Granny's glasses! I would look for the good in you, and you would look for the good in me, and lives would be so much more pleasant.

At times, we are like the buzzard that likes to dwell upon what is rotten and ugly, when we should be like the hummingbird that looks for what is sweet and beautiful.

I dare you to try on a pair of Granny's glasses!

Forgive Me, Lord

Today upon a bus, I saw a lovely maid with golden hair. I envied her—she seemed so gay—and I wished I were as fair.

When suddenly she arose to leave, I saw the cruel braces as she hobbled down the aisle; a victim of polio was she.

But as she passed—a smile! O God, forgive me when I whine. I have two straight feet. The world is mine!

And when I stopped to buy some sweets, the lad who sold them had such charm. I talked with him. He said to me, "It's nice to talk with folks like you. You see," he said, "I'm blind."

O God, forgive me when I whine. I have two eyes. The world is mine.

Then walking down the street, I saw a child with eyes of blue. He stood and watched the others play. It seemed he knew not what to do. I stopped a moment; then I said, "Why don't you join the others, dear?"

He looked ahead without a word, and then I knew he could not hear. O God, forgive me when I whine. I have two ears. The world is mine!

With feet to take me where I'd go, with eyes to see the sunset's glow, with ears to hear what I should know—O God, forgive me when I whine. I'm blessed indeed. The world is mine.

—*Author Unknown*

Why Do You Suppose He Married You?

You probably have wondered this a good many times.

There was a reason. The usual reason is that you made him feel different from what any other girl ever did. Perhaps it was the perfume you wore, maybe the way you walked, or the way you wrinkled your nose. You gained his attention. You stirred his imagination, built up his male ego, gave him a sense of belonging.

Don't shift gears now. The same things in you that were attractive to him before marriage should be used now to hold him.

When a Vancouver librarian retired, her colleagues presented her with a beautiful silver bracelet bearing this inscription: "Shhhhhhh."

Mother-Love

Abuse cannot offend it; neglect cannot chill it; time cannot affect it; death cannot destroy it. For harsh words it has gentle chiding; for a blow it has beneficent ministry; for neglect it has increasing watchfulness.

Oh, appreciate a mother's love. If you could only look in for an hour's visit to her, you would rouse up in the aged one a whole world of blissful memories.

What if she does sit without talking much; she watched you for months when you knew not how to talk at all.

What if she has ailments to tell about; during 15 years you ran to her with every little scratch and bruise, and she doctored your little finger as carefully as a surgeon would bind the worst fracture.

You say she is childish now; I wonder if she ever saw you when you were childish.

You have no patience to walk with her on the street; she moves so slowly. I wonder if she remembers the time when you were glad enough to go slowly.

—T. DeWitt Talmage

"SHOULD YOU GO FIRST"

Should you go first and I remain
  To walk the road alone,
I'll live in memory's garden, dear,
  With happy days we've known!
In spring I'll wait for roses red,
  When fades the lilac blue,
In early fall when brown leaves fall
  I'll catch a glimpse of you!

Should you go first and I remain
  For battles to be fought,
Each thing you've touched along the way
  Will be a hallowed spot!
I'll hear your voice, I'll see your smile,
  Though blindly I may grope,
The memory of your helping hand
  Will buoy me on with hope!

Should you go first and I remain
  To finish with the scroll,
No length'ning shadows shall creep in
  To make this life seem droll!
We've known so much of happiness,
  We've had our cup of joy,
And memory is one gift of God
  That death cannot destroy!

Should you go first and I remain,
  One thing I'd have you do:
Walk slowly down the path of death,
  For soon I'll follow you!

I'll want to know each step you take,
  That I may walk the same,
For someday down that lonely road,
  You'll hear me call your name!

Albert Kennedy Rowswell
(Appeared in *Congressional Record*, June 9, 1941)

Dumb Teachers!

Little Betty was about to be promoted to the Primary Department from the nursery school—and she wasn't a bit happy about it. Her teacher tried to tell her how nice it would be; but Betty, who did not want to give up her teacher, responded, "I wish you knew enough to be my teacher in the Primary Department!"

A Place to Go
By Mariana L. Brierton

A middle-aged man known as a playboy died suddenly while attending a party. The doctor summoned to the scene examined the formally attired man—white tie, tails and all. Someone at the party volunteered the information needed: name of deceased, age and address. When the doctor asked the man's religious preference, the response was, "He was an atheist."

"What a pity!" replied the doctor sadly. "All dressed up and no place to go."

As believers in Christ Jesus, we know there *is* "a place to go." Nothing and no one can alter our assurance of that heavenly destination. The Lord promised He has a beautiful place especially for us; that there are "many mansions." He also said, "And if I go and prepare a place for you, I will come again, and receive you unto myself; that where I am, there ye may be also" (John 14:3).

We are preparing ourselves, too. Not with fancy clothes or white-tie finery, but with pure and expectant hearts.

However, "a place to go" is a most inadequate expression of our belief in a resurrected Lord. Peter Marshall once said he knew someday he would have to stand listening to a recital of his past sins. During this "judgment listing," though, Jesus would come over to him, put a strong, steady arm around his shoulders and say, "Yes, it's true; but I have taken care of all that for Peter."

We not only have a place to go that is perfect and indescribably wonderful, but Someone to meet who is perfection and love everlasting.

The Christian is different. We are *already* seated "together in heavenly places in Christ Jesus" (Eph. 2:6). Our Lord has risen and ascended "far above all principality, and power, and might, and dominion." Therefore, our duty is to live *experientially* where we already dwell *positionally!*

As someone has said, "Many men see only a hopeless end; the Christian rejoices in endless hope." Indeed . . . the hope of a place prepared by the Lord Himself, an angelic welcoming party at the gates of Heaven. We'll never know the tragedy of "all dressed up and no place to go."

—From *Evangelical Beacon*

Bible on Woman's Attire

God thought womanly attire of enough importance to have it discussed in the Bible.

Paul the apostle, by no means a sentimentalist and accustomed to dwell on the great themes of God and the resurrection, writes about the arrangement of woman's hair and the style of her jewelry. Moses, his ear yet filled with the thunder at Mount Sinai, declares that womanly attire must be in marked contrast with masculine attire. Infraction of that law excites the indignation of high Heaven.

Just in proportion as the morals of a country or an age are depressed is that law defied. Show me the fashion plates of any century, from the time of the Deluge to this, and I will tell you the exact state of public morals.

—*T. DE WITT TALMAGE*

An Advantage List for Children

To the Editor:

I want my children to have all the advantages I can give them, such as—

—having to earn their own allowance by running errands, cutting lawns, learning to sew and to keep their own room straight.

—being proud to be clean and decent.

—standing up and standing proud when our country's flag goes by.

—being kind to all younger children and polite to elder friends and relatives, addressing them as "sir" and "ma'am."

—having to earn their own way in the world and knowing they have to prepare for it by hard work, hard study and sacrificing some of the pleasure and ease that their friends may get from too-indulgent parents.

—giving their respect to policemen, letting them know they're behind them one hundred percent.

—being a student, unselfish, honest, forgiving and conscious at all times respecting their teacher as a parent.

These are the advantages I want my children to have, because these are the things which will make them self-respecting, self-reliant and successful, with the opportunity to overcome obstacles through prejudices of men. Remembering God is no respector of persons, neither shall they.

Mrs. Carrie Bartlet
(From *Nashville Tennessean*)

I heard about a boy who wanted to know how wars started, so he asked his dad.

"Well," said Dad, "suppose America quarreled with England and—"

"But," interrupted the mother, "America must never quarrel with England."

"I know," said the father, "but I'm only taking a hypothetical instance."

"You are misleading the child," protested the mother.

"I am not!" shouted the father.

"Never mind," put in the boy, "I think I know how wars start!"

—From *Maranatha*

Have you ever heard a conversation like this:

"When I was at the lake, I caught a fish that went over three pounds!"

"Now, Henry, you know that fish only weighed two pounds and a half. Why do you want to sit there and lie?"

"As I was saying, here I was trying to get that twenty-three-inch fish in without a net...."

"Now, Henry, when are you going to start telling the truth? That fish wasn't a bit over eighteen inches."

Many an otherwise good marriage has been ruined by a sharp-tongued wife. Such "tongue-lashing" is almost a form of capital punishment to a man.

PRAYER and POTATOES

An old woman sat in her old
armchair
With wrinkled visage and dishev-
eled hair
And hunger-worn features.
For days and for weeks her only
fare
As she sat there in her old armchair
Had been potatoes.
But now they were gone, of bad or
good,
Not one was left for the old lady's
food
Of those potatoes.
And she sighed and said, "What
shall I do,
Where shall I send, and to whom
shall I go
For more potatoes?"
Then she thought of the deacon
over the way,
The deacon so ready to worship
and pray,
Whose cellar was full of potatoes;
And she said, "I'll send for the
deacon to come.
He'll not mind much to give me
some

Of such a store of potatoes."
So the deacon came over as fast as
he could,
Thinking to do the old lady some
good,
But never thought once of potatoes.
He asked her at once what was her
chief want.
And she, simple soul, expecting a
grant,
Immediately answered, "Potatoes."
But the deacon's religion didn't lie
that way—
He was more accustomed to preach
and to pray
Than to give of his hoarded
potatoes.
So not hearing, of course, what the
old lady said,
He prayed for wisdom, for patience
and grace;
But when he prayed, "Lord, give
her peace,"
She audibly sighed, "Give
potatoes."
The deacon was troubled, knew not
what to do.

'Twas very embarrassing to have
her act so
About those tarnal potatoes.
So ending his prayer, he started for
home,
But as the door closed behind him
He heard a deep groan, "Oh, give
to the hungry . . . potatoes."
And that groan followed him all the
way home.
In the midst of the night it haunted
his room . . .
"Oh, give to the hungry . . .
potatoes."
He could bear it no longer;
He arose and dressed;
And from his well-filled cellar, tak-
ing in haste
A bag of his best potatoes,
Again he went to the widow's lone
hut.
Her sleepless eyes she had not yet
shut.
So entering he poured on the floor
A bushel or more from his goodly
store
Of choicest potatoes.
The widow's heart leaped up for
joy.
Her face was haggered and wan no
more.
"Now," said the deacon, "shall we
pray?"
"Yes," said the widow, "now, you
may."
So he kneeled him down on the
sanded floor
Where he had poured his goodly
store,
And a prayer the deacon prayed
Had never before his lips assayed.
No longer embarrassed, but free
and full,
He poured out the voice of a liberal
soul.
And the widow responded a loud
"Amen!"
But said no more of potatoes.
And would you who hear this sim-
ple tale
Pray for the poor and, praying,
prevail?
Pray for peace and grace and
spiritual food,
For wisdom and guidance; for all
these are good;
But don't forget the POTATOES!

Try Losing! It's Fun! Don't always try to get your own way. Deliberately lose sometimes. The way to get your own way more often is to give in to the other party.

Wife, you must never demand your mate to be less than a man. Mr. Milquetoast or Mousey Milford may be great comic strip characters, but they make poor husbands. Make sure your husband reserves the right to feel that he is still king of the home.

Is Abortion Murder?

A mother stepped into the doctor's office carrying a bright and beautiful baby a year old. Seating herself near her family physician, she said, "Doctor, I want you to help me out of trouble. My baby is only one year old, and I have conceived again, and I do not want to have children so close together."

"What do you expect me to do?" asked the physician.

"Oh, anything to get rid of it for me," she replied.

After thinking seriously for a moment the doctor said, "I think I can suggest a better method of helping you out. If you object to having two children so near together, the best way would be to kill the one on your lap, and let the other one come on. It is easy to get at the one on your lap, it makes no difference to me which one I kill for you. Besides, it might be dangerous for you if I undertook to kill the younger one."

As the doctor finished speaking he reached for a knife and continued by asking the mother to lay the baby out on her lap and turn her head the other way.

The woman almost fainted away as she jumped from her chair and uttered one word, "Murderer!"

A few words of explanation from the doctor soon convinced the mother that his offer to commit murder was no worse than her request for the destruction of the unborn child. In either case it would be murder. The only difference would be in the age of the victim.

—*Old Faith Contender*

"No Occupation"

She rises up at break of day,
   And through her tasks she races.
She cooks the meal as best she may
   And scrubs the children's faces.
While schoolbooks, lunches, ribbons, too,
   All need consideration,
And yet the census man insists
   She has "no occupation."

When breakfast dishes all are done,
   She bakes a pudding, maybe;
She cleans the rooms up one by one,
   With one eye watching Baby.
The mending pile she then attacks
   By way of variation,
And yet the census man insists
   She has "no occupation."

She irons for a little while,
   Then presses pants for Daddy;
She welcomes with a cheery smile
   Returning lass and laddie.
A hearty dinner next she cooks—
   No time for relaxation;
And yet the census man insists
   She has "no occupation."

For lessons that the children learn
   The evening scarce is ample.
To "Mother, dear!" they always turn
   For help with each example.
In grammar and geography
   She finds her relaxation;
And yet the census man insists
   She has "no occupation."

—Author Unknown

The Clock

The clock of life is wound but once,
  And no man has the power
To tell just when the hands will stop,
  At late or early hour.
To lose one's wealth is sad indeed.
  To lose one's health is more.
To lose one's soul is such a loss
  That no man can restore.

—39 people died while you read this short poem. Every hour 3,420 go to meet their Maker. You could have been among them. Sooner or later you will be. Are you ready?

Living One Day at a Time

Did you know that there are at least two days in every week that we should never worry about, two days that should always be kept free from fear and apprehension?

One of these days is *yesterday* with its mistakes and cares, its faults and blunders, its aches and pains. Why worry about *yesterday* since it has already passed beyond our control? Only God could turn back the shadow on the sundial and reverse the process of time. There is no blessing or benefit to be obtained through needless worry over the mistakes of a day that has passed into eternity. All the money in the world cannot bring back *yesterday*. We cannot undo a single act once performed; we cannot erase a single word that was written or spoken—*yesterday* is gone.

The other day that we should not worry about is *tomorrow* with its possible adversaries, it burdens, its greater problems and its increased dangers. It is a settled fact that most of those things pertaining to *tomorrow* are beyond our immediate control. *Tomorrow's* sun will rise, if God so wills, either in splendor or behind a mask of clouds. Therefore, until it does, we have no stake in *tomorrow*—for it is yet unborn.

This leaves only one day—*today*. Any man can fight the battles of just one day. It is only when you and I add the burdens of those two awful eternities—*yesterday* and *tomorrow*—that we break down. It is not the experience of *today* that drives men mad. It is remorse or bitterness for something which happened *yesterday* and the dread of what *tomorrow* may bring.

'Therefore, do not worry about *tomorrow*, for *tomorrow* will worry about itself. Each day has enough trouble of its own' (Matt. 6:34).

—Selected

Sad! Sad! But so true. Don't let it happen to you!

✳ Suppose

Over the foaming tub of suds
  The washerwoman sang,
And through the quiet of the house
  Its reverberations rang.

An anxious Christian called to ask
  How she could sing God's praise
While she was poor and destitute,
  And dark the future days.

"Suppose that you should lose your job,
  Suppose you're taken ill,
Suppose you fall and break your arm,
  Then, who would pay the bill?"

"Stop where you are," the laundress said;
  "Supposing is all wrong;
Cast out supposing from your mind,
  Try praising God with song."

"I trust the Lord and sing His praise
  And never suppose sorrow;
And each time I wake to find
  A brighter day tomorrow."

—Charles F. Smith

TEMPTED & TRIED

I followed her for several blocks,
　But I was afraid to pass
Because first she'd slow to a creep
　And then step on the gas.

With each block my patience ebbed,
　And finally in disgust,
I pulled around in an attempt to pass
　And leave her in the dust.

Then, sure enough, it happened,
　When our cars were neck and neck,
She swung left without a glance
　And caused an awful wreck.

My car was smashed, my face cut,
　My nerves were all ajar;
And when the dust had passed away,
　I walked up to her car.

I asked why she had chosen to turn,
　Without a single sign,
Or why she didn't look around
　To see who was behind.

With innocent smile she turned to me,
　And this excuse did give,
"You should have known I'd turn here,
　Since this is where I live!"

　　　　　　　—From *Selah*

> It took the old-time mother less than a minute to dress for dinner because all she had to do was take off her apron.

The Rearward Look

A pastor, having temporary financial difficulties, said to his wife, "Dear, please cut down on expenditures, especially for clothes, until our finances improve."

Some days later the wife came home regaled in a beautiful new dress! Eyeing it with mingled feelings, he said, "It's surely pretty; but, Honey, I asked you not to buy any clothes for awhile. Remember?"

She replied, "Yes, dear, but when I was in the store I saw this lovely dress, and Satan tempted me!"

"Now, Honey, you know the Bible answer to such a situation. You should have said, 'Get thee behind me, Satan!'"

Disarmingly, she replied, "I did that, dear, but when Satan got behind me, he said that *it looks beautiful from the back, too!*"

Happy is the household when potentially explosive situations are defused and given a humorous turn!

Painting Now the Picture

When my hair is thin and silvered,
　and my time of toil is through;
When I've many years behind me,
　and ahead of me a few:
I shall want to sit, I reckon,
　sort of dreaming in the sun,
And recall the roads I've traveled
　and the many things I've done.
I hope there'll be no picture
　that I'll hate to look upon,
When the time to paint it better
　or to wipe it out, is gone.
I hope there'll be no vision
　of a hasty word I've said
That has left a trail of sorrow,
　like a whip welt sore and red.
And I hope my old age dreaming
　will bring back no bitter scene
Of a time when I was selfish,
　or a time when I was mean.
When I'm getting old and feeble,
　and I'm far along life's way,
I don't want to sit regretting
　any bygone yesterday.
I am painting now the picture
　that I'll want someday to see;
I am filling in a canvas
　that will soon come back to me.
Though nothing great is on it,
　and though nothing there is fine,
I shall want to look it over
　when I'm old, and call it mine.
So I do not dare to leave it
　while the paint is warm and wet,
With a single thing upon it
　that I later will regret.

　　　　　　　—*Author Unknown*

A mother said to her children, "Mind your manners; they may come back in style someday."

Music-ing the Plants

Over two years Mrs. Dorothy Retallack carried on a series of experiments in the laboratory of Temple Buell College. The experiments consisted of the simple placing of plants before the radio, exposing them to the various types of music.

The reactions were almost unbelievable. Three hours of rock music a day shrivelled young squash plants, flattened philodendron and crumpled corn in less than a month. Mrs. Retallack wondered what the same rock music was doing to teenagers.

—*Sawdust Trail*

HOME—a world of strife shut out, a world of love shut in.

HOME—a place where the small are great, and the great are small.

HOME—the father's kingdom, the mother's world, and the children's paradise.

HOME—where we grumble the most and are treated the best.

HOME—the center of our affection, round which our hearts' best wishes twine.

HOME—the place where our stomachs get three square meals a day and our hearts a thousand.

—*Charles M. Crowe*

Cheerful Resolve

I've reached my threescore years and ten,
The Bible limit; so what then?
I've still ten fingers, all my toes,
See with my eyes, scent with my nose;
Should I bring walking to a stop—
All my activities let drop?
Have I delayed my flight too long,
Or should I go on with a song?
For still I love to laugh and joke
And play at games with friendly folk;
Perhaps the good Lord wants me here—
Thinks maybe I can spread some cheer,
In all this time of want and gloom,
Feels that there still is lots of room
For greetings gay and laughter sound;
So maybe I'll just linger 'round!

—*Anna H. King*

A Mother's Creed

Lord, who am I to teach the way
To little children, day by day,
So prone myself to go astray?

I teach them knowledge, but I know
How faint they flicker and how low
The candles of my knowledge glow.

I teach them power to will and do,
But only now to learn anew
My own great weakness through and through.

Lord, if their guide I still must be,
Oh, let my little children see
Their mother leaning hard on Thee.

—Copied

Marriage Not a Mission Field

Mark Twain, the well-known American humorist, fell in love with Miss Olivia Langdon. "Livy," as he called her, grew up in a Christian home and held firm religious convictions. Mark Twain made no profession of faith, although he appeared to have been touched by Livy's life.

Mark Twain and Olivia Langdon were married. Early in their marriage, Mark regularly asked a blessing at mealtime and joined in family worship, but this did not last.

One day Twain announced, "Livy, I don't believe in the Bible."

Bit by bit, Mark Twain's lack of faith worked like a cancer on his wife's spiritual life.

Later, during a period of pressing sorrow, he tried to strengthen Livy by saying, "Livy, if it comforts you to lean on the Christian faith, do so." But his wife could only reply, "Mark, I can't. I haven't any!"

Marriage is not a mission field. God never called you into marriage to convert your partner. Marriage strains under the burden of an unshared faith. Not only will you harm the person with whom you join your life, but you will harm yourself if your partner is not a Christian. Too much is at stake to ignore God's command.

—Extract

Be Faithful in the Little Things

I love to do the things my hands
Can find to do.
I cannot sing a solo sweet,
But I can fill an empty seat
And listen with devoted care
While someone lifts his heart in prayer.

I cannot play the organ grand,
But I can clasp a stranger's hand
And smile and say a word of cheer.
Who knows, it may dispel a fear
And help that one upon his way,
If I can just the right word say.

I cannot preach a sermon great;
But when the offering they take,
I can be honest with my Lord
And freely give of my small hoard.
And I can bring a flower fair
So God's own house will look less bare.

These little things that I can do,
Seem, oh, so small and far too few;
But if I'm faithful to them all,
When His dear voice to me shall call,
I'll say, "Here, Lord," and all I bring
Is faithfulness in little things.

—Roselyn C. Steere

"I Ain't Dead Yet!"

My hair is white and I'm almost blind,
The days of my youth are far behind,
My neck's so stiff, can't turn my head—
Can't hear half that's being said.
My legs are wobbly, can surely talk!
And this is the message I want you to get:
I'm still a-kickin' and I ain't dead yet.

I've corns on my feet and ingrowing nails—
And do they hurt! Here language fails.
To tell you my troubles would take too long.
If I tried you surely would give me the gong.
I go to church and Sunday school, too,
For I love the story that is ever new.
And when I reach the end of my row,
I to my heavenly home will go.
Then, when I leave this house of clay,
If you listen closely, I'm apt to say,
"Well, folks, I've left you, but don't forget,
I've just passed on, but I ain't dead yet!"

(Written by a 94-year-old woman)

Anything Your Little Hurt Desires

"I'm not starting an argument!" the wife tells her husband. "This is the same one you started yesterday!"

We nurture and pamper our "hurts" long after they should have recovered and been discharged. When we finally discharge them as cured, they keep coming back to the out-patient department as ambulatory patients for periodic checkups. We look them over carefully. "Say ahhhhhh," we say. "Ahhhhhh," they say. And we pop them into the intensive-care unit and hover over them day and night happy to be keeping a close check on them again...

The desire to strike back is ingrown. It has to be pulled up by the roots and put on the altar. And the roots are deep, for they've been growing since we were children. One little boy (a true story), smarting after his dad had tanned his hide, finished his prayers with blessings for everybody in the family down to the dog—with one exception. Then he turned to his dad. "I suppose you noticed you wasn't in it."

—*Ethel Barrett*

Be Patient, for the Potter Is Not Finished

Be patient—
For the Potter is not finished
With me yet.
Many blemishes
Must be smoothed away
By His skillful hands.
A useful vessel
I can become
Only when I am filled
With His love.

Be patient—
For the Potter is not finished
With me yet.
He will mold
Into me
Love and joy,
Patience and kindness,
Gentleness
And self-control.

Be patient—
For the Potter is not finished
With me yet.
Many faults and blemishes,
Many selfish motives
Destroy my usefulness.
Be patient,
For the hands of the Potter
Are full of love.

—*Martha Yeargin Norris*

It's a Special Reducing Diet for You Heavy Weights

"Monday: Breakfast, weak tea. Lunch, 1 boullion cube in ½ cup diluted water. Dinner, 1 pigeon thigh and 2 oz. prune juice (gargle only).

"Tuesday: Breakfast, scraped crumbs from burnt toast. Lunch, 1 doughnut hole (without sugar). Dinner, 2 jelly fish skins and 1 glass dehydrated water.

"Wednesday: Breakfast, boiled out stains from tablecloth. Lunch, ½ dozen poppy seeds. Dinner, bee knees and mosquito knuckles sauteed with vinegar.

"Thursday: Breakfast, shredded eggshell skins. Lunch, bellybutton from naval orange. Dinner, 3 eyes from Irish potato (diced).

"Friday: Breakfast, 2 lobster antennae and 1 guppy fin. Lunch: 1 guppy fin. Dinner, jellyfish vertebrae a la book binders.

"Saturday: Breakfast, 4 chopped banana seeds. Lunch, broiled butterfly liver. Dinner, fillet of soft shell crab slaw.

"Sunday: Breakfast, pickled hummingbird tongue. Lunch, prime ribs of tadpole and aroma of custard pie plate. Dinner, tossed paprika and clover leaf (1) salad."

Oh, well.

Statistics show that men who kiss their wives goodbye in the morning live five years longer than those who don't. So some of you men had better pucker up before you tucker out.

He Got Them All in the Fold

He was a man in a world of men,
No greater in stature than they;
A man with a million common needs,
Humble enough to pray.
He made no name for the world to own,
He amassed no amount of gold,
But no child left his house unwon for Christ—
He got them all in the fold.

Some men have boasted their sons were great,
Or their sons were wise or strong,
Their daughters were polished and beautiful
Or they have written a song,
Or they have excelled in some realm of life
And their story oft will be told;
But this man saw his children kneel and pray.
He got them all in the fold.

Some laughed at the way he went to church,
Dragging the kids by the hand.
Some said, "Oh, wait a little while—
When they're older they'll understand!"
But he took them early to hear the Word,
He prayed they would Christ behold;
He prayed right on 'til they found the Lord—
He got them all in the fold.

When the books are at last unsealed,
All things are so clearly known,
We shall learn how futile are wealth and fame,
Or the pomp of a kingly throne;
The victories won by such struggle and strain
Will leave us barren and cold;
He'll be the greatest whose small child prays—
He got them all in the fold.

—Louis Paul Lehman

THE CURE FOR CRIME IS NOT THE ELECTRIC CHAIR BUT THE HIGH CHAIR

—*J. Edgar Hoover*

Character of Face Decided by Character of Soul

The character of the face is decided by the character of the soul. The main features of our countenance were decided by the Almighty, so we cannot change them; but under God, we decide whether we shall have countenances beneficial or baleful, sour or sweet, wrathful or genial, benevolent or mean, honest or scoundrelly, impudent or modest, courageous or cowardly, frank or sneaking.

In all the works of God, nothing is more wonderful than the human countenance. Though the longest face is less than twelve inches from hairline of the forehead to the bottom of the chin, and the broadest face is less than eight inches from cheek bone to cheek bone, yet in that small compass God hath wrought such differences that the billions of the human race may be distinguished from each other by their facial appearances.

The face is ordinarily the index of character, the throne of emotions, the battlefield of the passions. It is the catalogue of character, the map of the mind, the geography of the soul.

And while the Lord decides before our birth whether we shall be handsome or homely, we are, by the character we form, deciding whether our countenances shall be pleasant or disagreeable.

This is so much so that some of the most beautiful faces are unattractive because of their arrogance or deceitfulness. And some of the most rugged and irregular features are attractive because of the kindness that shines through them.

Accident or sickness or scarification may veil the face so that it shall not express the soul; but in the majority of cases, give me a deliberate look at a man's countenance, and I will tell you whether he is a cynic or an optimist, a miser or a philanthropist, noble or dastardly, good or bad.

—*T. DE WITT TALMAGE*

Let's Rewrite the Marriage Vows

There I was, walking slowly down the aisle to the lovely strains of Lohengrin's wedding march. I was wearing the most beautiful bridal dress and veil any doting parents could give their only daughter. The church was artistically decorated, and I held in my arms an exquisite bouquet of roses. Tim stood at the altar, tall, handsome and happy. Warm bursts of excitement and love flooded my whole being as he took my arm at the front of the church.

Then in quiet, sober tones the pastor commenced to speak. After a brief message on the importance of love in the husband-wife relationship, he began to pronounce the wedding vows.

That was when it happened. All at once I realized what I was doing—the commitments I was making. The unreasonableness of it shook me. The horror of it gripped my heart and filled me with fear.

The pastor was saying, "Beth, will you take Tim to be your wedded husband, to live together according to the ordinances of the church in the holy estate of matrimony? Will you obey him, serve him, love him, honor him, and keep him in sickness and health, in poverty and wealth, and **forsaking all others** keep **yourself** only for him as long as you both shall live?"

All at once I knew I shouldn't say, "I will." All at once a thousand reasons why I should say "no" flooded through my mind. Any one of a dozen things could happen to Tim in the first twenty-four hours of our married life which would make the next forty years a living nightmare. Why hadn't I thought of this before—why was I making such irrational promises to any man?

But there I was, and what should I do but say, "I will"?

The pastor then asked me to repeat the following words after him, "I, Beth, take you, Tim, to be my wedded husband, to have and to hold from this day onward, for better, for worse, for richer, for poorer, in sickness and health, to love, cherish, and obey till death . . . . "

I blacked out at that point. Several of the women uttered muffled screams as I sank to the floor. It was all a fake on my part, but it looked real. I had to have time to either change or rethink the wedding vows.

As Tim tenderly lifted me in his arms and carried me out of the church, I heard the pastor say, "Friends, I'm sorry about this, but I'm sure Beth will be all right in a few hours. She has been working hard and is, no doubt, overly tired. We will complete the wedding in the home of her parents when she is feeling better. Perhaps it will be just as well for it to be a private ceremony."

As Father, Mother and I sat around the breakfast the next morning, I started the conversation. "I'm terribly sorry about yesterday," I said. "I know you were disappointed and even mortified, but I had to do something about those wedding vows. They have to be changed. It's not right to ask any girl to make such promises to any man. I'm supposed to love Tim as long as I live more than I love you or anyone else on earth, regardless of what happens to him or of what he turns out to be."

My father couldn't hold in check his horrified reaction. "Beth, if you marry Tim or any other man whom you do not love enough to make such promises gladly—you are not my daughter."

Mother's reaction was more restrained. She said, "I see your point, Beth. There are many things which could happen to either you or Tim which would produce some real hardships and problems in your married life. Perhaps it would be well if we re-wrote the marriage vows."

With pencil in hand, Mother began to write: "I, Beth, take you, Tim, to be my wedded husband, to have and to hold as long as you are well and strong, to forsake when sickness comes along, to love and cherish when I feel like it, to obey when it is to my advantage, to serve as long as you maintain a living standard commensurate with my desires, and forsaking all others, I will keep myself for thee only, until a better man comes along."

"Stop it!" I snapped.

"Yes, dear," Mother replied, then added: "There is one thing more unreasonable than getting married within the unqualified bonds of sacred matrimony—that is, to get married apart from a love which wholeheartedly accepts those bonds."

"I guess you're right," I stammered. "It would be foolish to get married if your wedding vows were filled with 'ifs' and 'buts.' I wouldn't want Tim's promises to me filled with conditions."

"Daddy and I have enjoyed 24 wonderful years together," interrupted Mother. "It was our unqualified love for and unconditional commitment to one another which have made our married life delightful."

(Continued)

All at once I wanted to enter into that same supremely happy entanglement my parents had been enjoying for so many years. A telephone call to Tim—repentance, tears, forgiveness, and a mutual unqualified confession of love for one another brought it about. And how lovely it is to be Tim's wife—how exciting to love him, honor him, and keep myself only for him!

There was a time when I thought the claims of Christ were horribly unreasonable. I rebelled against such demands as—"If any man come to me, and hate not his father, and mother, and wife, and children, and brethren, and sisters, yea, and his own life also, he cannot be my disciple" and, "So likewise, whosoever he be of you that forsaketh not all that he hath, he cannot be my disciple" (Luke 14:26,33). These verses insist on unconditional commitment to Jesus Christ. They make no allowances for "ifs" and "buts." They didn't look fair.

But now I see it all. True discipleship cannot be conditional. It's the old story about having to love God with all the heart, soul, mind and strength. Just as divided loves and loyalties ruin a marriage, so they will render our relationship with the Lord fruitless, which I suppose is just another way of saying, "If He's not Lord of all, He's not Lord at all."

—From *The King's Business*

*   *   *

Do you old-timers remember "In the Gloaming," "Love's Old Sweet Song," "Just a Song at Twilight," or, "Let Me Call You Sweetheart"?

Go to a music store and try to buy an album with such songs. You can't find them. There will be stacks of rock records and all the demonic perversions of popular music in abundance, but nowhere can you find the beautiful songs of a day when love lyrics were based on romance, not on sex.

"It's a Matter of Rank"

During World War II, Brigadier General Theodore Roosevelt, Jr., was waiting at an airport for a plane. A sailor stepped to a ticket window and asked for a seat on the same plane, explaining, "I want to see my mother; I ain't got much time."

The indifferent young thing at the ticket window was not impressed. "There's a war on, you know," she exclaimed.

At this point, General Roosevelt stepped to the window and told her to give the sailor his seat. A friend spoke his surprise, "Teddy, aren't you in a hurry, too?"

"It's a matter of rank," came the reply. "I'm only a general; he's a son!"

—James Keller in
One Moment, Please

■   ■   ■

What Would Be Your Name?

The Indians used to give their babies only temporary names. They waited until the boys and girls grew older and had earned some kind of name. Thus some good girl was named *Bluebird, Snowflower, Spring Wind, Sunshine,* or something else which showed how people felt about her.

Some boys, when they grew old enough to join in the hunt were named *Brown Bear, Running Wolf, Black Eagle,* or *Thunder Stone.*

Suppose boys and girls were left nameless today until they grew at least to junior age and had earned some name for themselves. Some boys might be called *Helping Hand, Brave Lad, Great Heart, Faithful,* or *Mouth of Truth.* There are girls who might be called *Sunny Smile, Blue Flower, Hope.*

There are, however, a few boys and girls who might not have such delightful names. There are some who might have to be called *Scowler, Shirk, Unreliable,* or *Cheat.*

What would be *your* name?

The Lights of Home...

Are you weary and discouraged—
  Loved ones gone; life's hopes all fled?
Look, beloved, there before thee
  Lights of Home shine just ahead!

As the traveler journeying homeward
  Sees afar the welcome light
Like a beacon set to guide him
  Through the darkness of the night;

Though thy heart is ofttimes weary;
  Though thy stumbling footsteps stray;
He who loves thee, lives to keep thee—
  Guides thee onward toward the Day.

Soon the journey will be ended—
  God's own voice will bid thee come!
Rest and welcome shall enfold thee,
  Once within the realms of Home!

HOME! Where love that never ceaseth,
  Hath for thee "a place prepared."
There where angels wait to serve thee—
  There shall joys with Him be shared.

Set this "Blessed Hope" before thee,
  Ever cheering through the gloom;
Shining with celestial brightness,
  See ahead, the "lights of Home."

—Eleanor M. Tucker

The Ten Best Dressed Women

1. The woman whose modesty adorns her.
2. The woman who clothes herself in good works.
3. The woman who does not garb herself with tattling and gossip.
4. The woman who refuses to wear the garment of idleness, but stays busy.
5. The woman whose warmth is generated by an inner love for others.
6. The woman who dresses that she may not be a stumbling block to younger women, or men of any age.
7. The woman whose feet are shod with the preparation of the Gospel of peace.
8. The woman who sparkles, not with jewelry, but with her love for her family.
9. The woman who drapes herself with chasteness and fidelity.
10. The woman whose best suit is her love for Christ and His church.

What You Wear Says a Lot
(Read Isaiah 3:16-26)

What you wear not only says a great deal about you, but it also influences you. The clothing and jewelry worn by the wealthy women of Israel revealed pride, moral looseness, and rebellion against God. That's why Isaiah pronounced severe judgment on them.

A restaurant owner said in a "Dear Abby" letter that he has observed the difference clothing makes in behavior. When teenagers enter his establishment in bermudas, short skirts, and jeans, they "act rowdy and eat like pigs." But when they come in the evening wearing pretty dresses and suits, "they behave like ladies and gentlemen."

This phenomenon was confirmed by an incident in a Pittsburgh area high school. Sixty-nine students were suspended for refusing to dress properly. School authorities noticed that during the two weeks they were absent, the number of students needing discipline declined noticeably. The custodians were amazed at the change in their workload. There was far less debris in the building and in the schoolyard. When the suspended students returned properly dressed, their conduct improved and their grades climbed from a D average to a C!

We are all image-bearers of God. We are not junk! As God's creatures we are responsible to Him. When we look like slobs, we deny the dignity of our personhood. When we dress modestly, we please our Lord and reflect His purity. Yes, what we wear says a lot. It has an impact on ourselves as well as others.

O Lord, we would please You in all
  that we do,
In word and in deed we would always
  be true;
And may we reflect in our manner
  and dress
Devotion to Jesus, whose name we
  confess.

—Lifted from *The Burning Bush*

A godly woman sure should be
A Sarah to her lord,
A Martha to her company,
A Mary to the Word.

—Spurgeon

Sober Facts About That Darling Little Baby!

The Minnesota Crime Commission came to this frightening and factual conclusion which young parents would do well to note:

"Every baby starts life as a little savage. He is completely selfish and self-centered. He wants what he wants when he wants it: his bottle, his mother's attention, his playmate's toy, his uncle's watch. Deny him these wants, and he seethes with rage and aggressiveness which would be murderous were he not so helpless.

"He is dirty. He has no morals, no knowledge, no skills.

"This means that all children—not just certain children—are born delinquent. If permitted to continue in the self-centered world of his infancy, given free rein to his impulsive actions to satisfy his wants, every child would grow up a criminal, a thief, killer, rapist."

> ### Today's unchurched child is tomorrow's criminal.
> —J. Edgar Hoover

*   *   *

CHILDREN ARE HAPPIER WHEN PARENTS REQUIRE OBEDIENCE.

"Have You Grown?"

We stood the children, straight
    and tall,
By last year's marks upon the
    wall.
Another year! How soon they go,
And see how fast the children
    grow!
And then we thought of how
    God's Word
Says, "Grow in grace and in the
    Lord."
And as we knelt with God alone,
He asked us gently, "Have *you*
    grown?

"Now let me get this straight. You **did** do your homework, but you made it into a paper airplane and it was hijacked to Cuba?"

"Iva Footen-mouth"

"Well, really, Henry. All I said was that, if I had a voice like hers, I'd enter the next hog-calling contest. How was I to know that was her husband sitting in front of me? I tried to whisper. Anyhow, that didn't give him the right to turn and glare like that—right in the middle of the service.

"Some people are just too sensitive for their own good. Remember that very large woman I was talking to after church? I said she had a very pretty face. Then I asked if she had heard of the new weight reduction spa in the neighborhood. I was starting to tell her about this other woman I knew who had had marvelous results there, when she just walked off. I mean, she didn't even let me finish what I was saying! I was only trying to be helpful. 'Speak the truth in love,' the Scriptures say.

"Like the last time I taught junior church, I mentioned to the pianist how I dreaded those terrible Digby boys in my class. They really are a handful, you know, so rambunctious. Sometimes it's all I can do to make them behave.

"Well, just as I was saying this, Mrs. Digby herself walked right up behind me. But then everything I said was true. And the Bible says, 'Lie not.' It's her fault if she happens to walk up at the wrong time. And if the boys had behaved in the first place, there wouldn't have been a problem.

"That's all I was trying to do last Sunday when I told the guest speaker in Sunday school that I was certainly glad to have someone speaking to us who knew his Bible so well. But Mr. Smith—that's our regular teacher—looked at me so funny. He almost seemed offended.

"Well, like Paul said in Galatians 1:10, 'If yet pleased men, I should not be the servant of Christ.' Still, Henry, I don't understand why some people are so touchy. I was only trying to make a little conversation."

PARENTS WONDER WHY THE STREAMS ARE BITTER WHEN THEY THEMSELVES HAVE POISONED THE FOUNTAIN.

"I'm so grateful for my first-aid training," exclaimed the girl. "Last night there was an accident right in front of my house. An old man was knocked down by a car and was bleeding all over. He was moaning something awful. That's when my first-aid training came in handy. I remembered to put my head between my knees to keep from fainting."

"Mom's Just Perfect"

A small boy invaded the lingerie section of a big California department store and shyly presented his problem to a woman clerk. "I want to buy my mom a present of a slip," he said, "but I don't know what size she wears."

"Is she tall or short, fat or skinny?" asked the clerk.

"She's just perfect," beamed the small boy.

So she wrapped up a size 34 for him.

Two days later, Mom came to the store herself—and changed it to a 52.

—*The Saturday Review*

"I heard...."

"They say...."

"Everybody says...."

"Have you heard...?"

"Did you hear...?"

"Isn't it awful...?"

"People say...."

"Did you ever...?"

"Somebody said...."

"Would you think...?"

"Don't say I told you...."

"Oh, I think it's perfectly terrible...."

The Shady Dozen

> EVERYONE CAN GIVE PLEASURE IN SOME WAY. ONE PERSON MAY DO IT BY COMING INTO A ROOM, ANOTHER BY GOING OUT.

A lady walked into a supermarket in a desperate attempt to get supper ready quick and asked one of the grocery clerks, "Do you have anything quicker than instant?"

◆◆◆◆

The minister asked a group of children in a Sunday school class, "Why do you love God?" He got a variety of answers, but the one he liked best was from a boy who said, "I don't know, sir. I guess it just runs in our family."

✳ ✳ ✳

It Feels Good to Be Thanked

"Central" was tired, her head ached; she had just succeeded, after repeated efforts, in getting the number eagerly wanted by a woman—and here the woman was calling again! *Can't that woman be quiet a minute?* she soliloquized while she reiterated, "Number, please?" trying not to speak crossly.

"Central," said a pleasant voice, "I want to thank you for taking so much trouble to get me that last number. You are always very kind and obliging, and I do appreciate it."

The surprise was so great, so overwhelming, that Central could only murmur confusedly, "I—oh, yes, ma'am." Nothing like this had happened before.

Suddenly her headache was better; suddenly the day was brighter; suddenly, too, there came a lump in her throat, and she reached for her handkerchief. It felt so good to be thanked.

—*The Sunday School Times*

ALL THINGS FOR GOOD

"All things for good." Oh, word of sweet assurance,
  Calming all fear and bidding sorrow cease;
The promise of a Father's sure performance,
  Which stills the heart's unrest and whispers "Peace."

"All things for good." Oh, trust Him then completely;
  Leave with the Lord the planning of the way;
The path, which seems to thee so strangely ordered,
  Shall terminate in Heav'n's eternal day.

"All things for good." There is not one exception,
  For He who promised also will fulfill;
His hand controls; His Word, all things obeying,
  Works out the purpose of His perfect will.

"All things for good." The clouds of earth shall vanish,
  The heavenly light shall shine upon thy ways,
Chasing the gloom and turning grief to gladness,
  The sighs of sorrow into songs of praise.

"All things for good." Oh, troubled heart, believe it,
  Though now His ways thou canst not understand;
Christ shall reveal to thee each hidden meaning,
  And thou shalt prove that all in love was planned.

"All things for good." Then wait the full unfolding
  Of all His thoughts and purposes towards thee;
In the full radiance of Heaven's undimmed splendor
  The glory of His working thou shalt see.

—Ruth Thomas

The Prodigal Mother

A certain man had a wife and three children. The wife, becoming dissatisfied with housekeeping and coveting the money being earned by her neighbors, said to her husband, "Husband, secure for me the Social Security number that falleth to me, and divide unto me a portion of thy trousers...."

With a reluctant heart the husband granted her desire and divided his wardrobe. Not many days later the wife donned slacks and, with tool box under her arm, waved good-bye to the children, took her journey into a far country and there secured a man's job in a factory. She made big wages, but she associated with the wicked and listened to the vulgar stories that they told.

There was a mighty spiritual famine in that land, and she grew lean in her soul. The children, turned loose at the mercy of the neighbors, soon forgot that they had a mother; but the husband remembered the duties of a wife and wished that his wife would return to her home.

The husband dined on cold lunch meat, while the wife tried in vain to fill her stomach with the husks of the cheese crackers that fell from the canteen vendor's machine. And no man gave unto her the respect due unto a lady.

One day at rest period as she sat engulfed in cigarette smoke and smutty stories, she came to herself. She said to herself with remorse, "Here I sit, surrounded by vulgarity, and sacrificing the respect due a lady. At home is a deserted husband, while my children roam the streets unrestrained. The money I make seems small compared to peace of mind and soul."

In vain she tried to smother her conscience with the thought that she was contributing to the family's economic welfare. So she said to herself, "I will arise and go to my husband and will say unto him, 'Husband, I have sinned against Heaven and neglected my family in a terrible way. I am no more worthy to be called thy wife, nor the mother of thy children. Make me as thy hired housekeeper.'"

So she gathered her tools together and started home. And when she was yet a long way off, the husband saw her and clasped her in his arms. And the wife said, "Husband, I am no more worthy to be called thy wife, nor the mother of thy children."

But the father said to the children, "Run and bring hither a dress and the best apron. Put shoes on her feet, and rush to the meat market and get a steak of the fatted calf, and let us have a warm meal once more. For this your mother was lost, and is found."

So they rejoiced and made merry.

—Maranatha

"Hello! Is this the welfare department?"

"Yes. What can I do for you?"

"I need a new crib for my baby."

"What is the baby sleeping in now?"

"The box my color TV came in."

◄ ►

COURTESY IS CONTAGIOUS—LET'S START AN EPIDEMIC!

■ □ ■

A broken home is the world's greatest wreck.

THE

LORD'S

POTATOES

There I sat, quietly hunched back on my heels in the semidarkness of the potato bin, an empty bucket beside me.

While Papa and Mama's religious discussion continued at the head of the cellar steps, my childish mind was hassling with a piece of theology I hadn't encountered before.

It had all started when Mama called: "Bonnie, go down cellar and bring up a bucket of potatoes for the preacher." As I opened the cellar door, she reminded me to "pick out the big ones because they are for the Lord!"

At this point Papa entered with new instructions: "Take them as they come, big and small alike."

Experience had taught me that, in a situation like this, I was on my own. Solemnly I weighed the question.

Mama always gave her best to the Lord: the choicest vegetables; the plumpest fryers; the squarest, sweetest bricks of yellow butter. And she was thoroughly convinced that each gift found its way into His hand. It only sojourned on the parsonage table.

The Lord also received His portion first. Always.

Each time I see a dark brown Hershey cocoa can, I smile and bless the Lord a little! Mama kept the "Lord's money" in an old cocoa can safely tucked away behind a row of pickle jars on the top bank of our homestead cellar.

Whenever there was "an increase of the fields or the kine or the flocks," Mama would carefully count out the Lord's tithe first and place it in the cocoa tin.

The 40-mile trip to town for church was a luxury during those days of depression and drought in eastern Montana. Only occasionally could we afford to attend.

One of the highlights on those rare Sunday mornings in the early 1930s was to watch Mama kneel by the cellar door, nimbly reach for the cocoa can, and count out the "Lord's money" for the church offerings.

Dozens of times I descended and ascended those cellar steps, reverently glancing at that cocoa can. I would no more rob the offering plate than steal a nickel of its contents!

My mother's love for God's Word had soon taught her the legal requirements for giving. God had spelled them out clearly in His law: "The first of the firstfruits of thy land thou shalt bring into the house of the Lord thy God" (Exod. 23:19). And in Leviticus 22:20: "But whatsoever hath a blemish, that shall ye not offer: for it shall not be acceptable for you."

For Mama, however, legalism was swallowed up by love. Jesus loved her so much! Had He not saved her and filled her with His blessd Holy Spirit? In love and mercy had He not returned two of her children from the brink of death? Softly she heard her Jesus whisper, "If ye love me, keep my commandments" (John 14:15). Her love for Him was reflected in her living and her giving.

Both by word and by example, the tiny little mother with the deep blue eyes taught me many things. Among them was how to give an acceptable gift to Jesus.

We give to Him first! We give to Him our best! But most of all—we give to Him because we love Him!

That's why I hesitated only a few moments before I began filling the bucket with the biggest potatoes I could find.

—*Bonnie Fenton Lavegne*

Picture Death This Way:

We picture death as coming to destroy; let us rather picture Christ as coming to save.

We think of death as ending; let us rather think of life as a beginning, and that more abundantly.

We think of losing; let us think of gaining.

We think of parting; let us think of meeting.

We think of going away; let us think of arriving.

And as the voice of Death whispers, "You must go from earth," let us hear the voice of Christ saying, "You are but coming to Me!"

—*N. Macleod*

Practical Preaching

Some time ago a Hindu woman was converted chiefly by hearing the Word of God read. Because of her newly found faith, she suffered persecution from her husband.

After she had been a Christian for some time, a missionary asked her, "When your husband is angry and persecutes you, what do you do?"

She replied, "Well, sir, I cook his food better; when he complains, I sweep the floor cleaner; and when he speaks unkindly, I answer him mildly. I try, sir, to show him that when I became a better Christian, I became a better wife and a better mother."

Though the husband could withstand the preaching of the missionary, he could not withstand the practical preaching of his wife. She won him to Christ.

Loosen your tongue when angry, and you will make the greatest speech you will ever regret. ———————

Boys flying kites may haul in their white-winged birds:
You can't do that when you are flying words;
Words unspoken fall back dead,
But God can't kill them when they're said!

"And the tongue is a fire, a world of iniquity."—James 3:6.

SUMMER RECIPE
PRESERVED
CHILDREN

Take 1 large field, half a dozen children, 2 or 3 small dogs, a pinch of brook and some pebbles. Mix children and dogs well together. Put them on the field, stirring constantly. Pour the brook over the pebbles; sprinkle the field with flowers; spread over all a deep blue sky and bake in the sun. When brown, set away to cool in the bathtub.

Do You Know What You Have Asked?

Do you know you have asked for the costliest thing
Ever made by the hand above—
A woman's heart and a woman's life,
And a woman's wonderful love?
You require that your mutton shall always be hot,
Your socks and your shirts shall be whole;
I require that your heart be true as God's stars,
And as pure as Heaven your soul.

I am fair and young; but the rose will fade
From my soft young cheek someday;
Will you love me then, 'mid the falling leaves,
As you did 'mid the bloom of May?
If you cannot do this, a laundress and cook
You can hire with little to pay;
But a woman's heart and a woman's life
Are not to be won that way.

—*Elizabeth Barrett Browning*

Let's Play "Manger Scene"

"Let's play 'manger scene.'" It was Christmas morning, and seven-year-old Karolyn had received a life-sized baby doll. Four-year-old Paul was coaxed away from his Tinker Toys to fill the "Joseph" role. Preparation of the manger involved ingenuity and skill that put the talents of a four-year-old to the test. Collecting all the stuffed animals for the residents of the stable consumed considerable time. This was fun! Finally, the props were all in place, and "Mary" laid the baby Jesus in the tissue-paper straw that had been salvaged from the wastebasket.

She hummed the most appropriate tune she could think of, "Away in a Manger" (what matter that the writer lived centuries this side of the manger!). The baby was petted and patted, fed and burped,

dressed and undressed (no swaddling clothes here, another departure from the story).

"Joseph" tried to enter into the spirit of the situation, but he was only in the way. Finally, he retreated to the sidelines and stood on one foot and then the other, too loyal to bolt the scene and return to his Tinker Toys, but terribly impatient with the turn of events that made him only a spectator. In exasperation he blurted, "Mary, put that kid to sleep, and let's get out of here and have some fun." I mused: How often, in real life, we find people whose idea of having fun is to leave Christ out of the picture. As Christians, "Truly our fellowship is with the Father, and with his Son Jesus Christ" (I John 1:3).

—Kathryn Hillen

NAGGING NELLIE NEVER WINS

If you try to change your marriage partner by browbeating, you are sure to lose. More people are changed by love than by yelling. All of us stiffen our defenses when we are yelled at. We may do what we are told for fear of retaliation, but we will hate the person for telling us.

So if you want your own way do not nag—love. Warm affection has changed more of the world's history than all the Spanish Armadas put together. It was love that caused a king to abdicate his throne. It was love that prompted thousands of France's best young men to leave their homes and follow Napoleon across the wilds of Russia. Love changes our loved ones.

The Priceless Picture

A very wealthy man lost his wife when his only child was very young. Then there came into his home a housekeeper to take care of that boy. The boy lived until he was of age, and then he died. The man had no other relatives, and he died heartbroken soon after the boy died. He had no one to whom to leave his enormous wealth, and there was a great question about what would become of his possessions. They could find no will. It looked as though it would all just pass over to the state. At last it was taken over by the state, and they held a sale to dispose of his personal effects and the mansion where he had lived.

The old housekeeper who had brought up that boy from infancy, not having any money of her own, being just as poor as when she began to work for this wealthy man and keep house for him, went to the sale. There was only one thing she wanted. She couldn't buy the furniture; she couldn't buy the expensive rugs; but there was a picture on a wall in that house, a picture of the boy. She loved that boy. He had been a son to her, although she held no relationship to him.

When the picture came to be sold, nobody else wanted it, and she bought it for just a few cents and took it home. It had been hanging on the wall for some time, and she thought she would clean it, take the back out, take the glass out and polish it.

But when she took it apart, some important papers fell out. They were given to a lawyer, who said to the woman, "I guess you have fallen on your feet this time. This man has left all his wealth to the one who loved his son enough to buy that picture."

God will do anything for those who love His Son.

—Pulpit Helps

Molasses smears and mustard streaks

My cookbook, handed down from my mother, is unlike anything seen in these days of loose-leaf cookbooks with shiny paper and colorful illustrations—although no one could say that my cookbook is not colorful!

Some pages bear the red stains of cherry juice and purple reminders of jelly-making. Splotches of hardened dough decorate some pages. Here is a streak of mustard and there a smear of molasses. A gob of peanut butter ornaments the cookie page.

My husband tells me there is plenty of good eating in my cookbook, and he's not referring to the recipes.

I treasure the book because of Mother's pencilled instructions in the margins, although they give the pages an untidy effect.

Alongside the "3 eggs" called for, for instance, she wrote, "Just as good with 2." In another recipe she changed the "2 cups of sugar" to, "Use part honey." Regarding the chili recipe she wrote, "Too hot for Dad." And the chicken soup recipe bears the warning, "Be sure to skim off the fat." Over a casserole recipe appears the word, "Awful!"

My cookbook contains recipes you can't find these days: one for Baptist bean sandwiches; for herring salad; for onion bread; for Annie's upside-down molasses pie; for hot milk cake, lemon curd, Grandpa's cream cabbage salad —all out-of-this-world goodies.

When my neighbor asked to borrow my cookbook, I apologized for its messy appearance.

"So what?" she responded. "It's the recipes I'm going to copy, not the smears."

After she left, I thought, *It's like God's Book which has the recipes for successful lives. There'll be some stains and smears on the pages of our lives as we try and fail and try again, but we can have absolute faith in His recipes. If we follow His instructions, our lives will be fruitful and satisfying.*

—Marjorie Zimmerman
(Must not use without permission)

By Way of Comparison

Any school administrator would have a lot of headaches if he tried to institute the "rules of conduct" in force for teachers in 1915 in a county just north of us. They were:

1. You will not marry during the term of your contract.

2. You are not to keep company with men.

3. You must be home between the hours of 8 p.m. and 6 a.m. unless attending a school function.

4. You may not loiter downtown in ice cream stores.

5. You may not travel beyond the city limits unless you have the permission of the chairman of the board.

6. You may not ride in a carriage or automobile with any man unless he is your father or brother.

7. You may not smoke cigarettes.

8. You may not dress in bright colors.

9. You may under no circumstances dye your hair.

10. You must wear at least two petticoats.

11. Your dresses must not be any shorter than two inches above the ankle.

12. To keep the schoolroom neat and clean, you must: sweep the floor at least once daily; scrub the floor at least once a week with hot, soapy water; clean the blackboards at least once a day; and start the fire at 7 a.m. so the room will be warm by 8 a.m.

—*CONVENTION HERALD*

CHOOSE YOUR WIFE ON SATURDAY RATHER THAN ON SUNDAY, when she is in her workday clothes, and you can better see what she will be in common everyday life. The same advice is put in another form:

When you would select a wife,
  Do not call on Sunday;
If you'd know her as she is,
  Better seek on Monday.

—Spurgeon

Home on Earth, Home in Heaven

One less at home:
The charmed circle broken—a dear face
Missed day by day from its accustomed place,
But cleansed and saved and perfected by grace;
One more in Heaven.

One less at home:
One voice of welcome hushed, and evermore
One farewell word unspoken. On the shore
Where parting comes not, one soul landed more—
One more in Heaven.

One less at home,
Where, cramped in earthly mold
The sight of Christ is dim, our love is cold;
But there, where face to face we shall behold,
Is home and Heaven.

One less on earth—
Its pain, its sorrow and its toil to share,
One less the pilgrim's daily cross to bear;
One more the crown of ransomed saints to wear,
At home in Heaven.

One more in Heaven:
Another thought to brighten cloudy days,
Another theme of thankfulness and praise,
Another link on high our soul to raise
To home and Heaven.

One more at Home,
That home where separation cannot be,
That home where none are missed eternally!
Lord Jesus, grant us all a place with Thee
At home in Heaven.

— Sarah Geraldine Stock

Visiting a family where the father had just died, the preacher asked the young son, "What were your father's last words?"

"He didn't have any," replied the boy; "Mama was with him to the end."

Clean your fingers before you point at my spots.

—Benjamin Franklin

"I Wish I Could Vanish Into Space...and Start Life All Over Again"

George W. Sweeting has told of an experience he had:

"Some time ago I became engaged in conversation with a doctor and his wife. We were waiting to board a plane. After watching several jets climb into the murky darkness, the young woman said, 'I wish I could vanish into space just like that plane and start life all over again.'

"She was young and attractive, obviously a woman of wealth and position, yet her life was filled with regret.

"Why did she want to vanish? Why did she want to escape life and start all over again? Because she was burdened with the weight of sin. She had never experienced the joy of forgiveness. The future was more than she could take.

"Many people today echo the young woman's words of despair. The same desire haunts millions who do not know and live for Christ."

How disquieted we are until we rest in God. And how blessed are those who can say:

> **I came to Jesus as I was,**
> **Weary and worn and sad;**
> **I found in Him a resting place,**
> **And He has made me glad!**

In the bakery department of a Dallas supermarket, a wedding cake was set out for shoppers with the sign:

"He changed his mind. Have a piece of cake on us."

—*Fort Worth Star-Telegram*

NO HITS, NO RUNS, NO ERRORS!

A spinster by the name of Nancy Jones lived in a midwest town. When she died, the editor of the local newspaper could not think of anything good to write about her. Neither could he think of anything bad to write. She had never spent a night in jail or committed a crime.

Going down the street, the editor met the tombstone craftsman of the town. He experienced the same difficulty as the editor concerning Nancy Jones. He could not think of anything newsworthy about Nancy Jones, either good or bad. The editor went back to his office and asked his sports editor what he could say about Nancy. He wrote the following epitaph:

> **Here lie the bones of Nancy Jones.**
> **For her, life held no terrors.**
> **She lived an old maid:**
> **She died an old maid;**
> **No hits, no runs, no errors.**

I understand that if you pass through that midwest town today, you can read these words on her tombstone.

Well, I wouldn't want that said of me! Here is the point: it is a sorry Christian life that is based on "not's," "no's" and "don'ts." Of course, there is a place for the negative, but don't get too heavy on it. I doubt that you can teach well without using the negative at least a little, because we are constantly bombarded with non-Christian and half-Christian ideas. We may have to say, "Not that but this; not that way but this way." Scripture does this constantly.

To get back to my point, the attitude of some is: "We don't smoke and we don't chew, and we don't go with boys that do." Well, we do not become holy by means of the things that we don't do.

Because of sin, we can't just come bursting into God's presence. We need a remedy for sin. This remedy has already been provided in the person of Jesus Christ. Man's greatest problem is sin. It is human to err; but when the eraser wears out before the pencil does, you're overdoing it. Knowing Christ as Saviour, one doesn't need to live or die scared. There is hope not only in this world, but also in the world to come. As Christians, let us give first place to the world to come. We must learn to "come down hard" when the Bible requires it.

What would you like written on your tombstone? What would you like your epitaph to say? I have shared one with you, and I wish to share two others.

For his epitaph, Sir Winston Spencer Churchill, the great World War II leader, proposed the following:

"I am ready to meet my Maker, but whether my Maker is prepared for the great ordeal of meeting me is another matter."

Historians may appreciate the quip more than anyone else. In reality, however, it is an escape hatch, to keep from facing the reality of death. "Laughing it off" won't solve the problem.

The fact is that the grave claims us all, sooner or later. "It is appointed unto men once to die" (Heb. 9:27). The obituary column in every newspaper confirms this statement from the Bible. Yes, we must "go the way of all the earth" and keep our appointment with death. Sin and death go together (Rom. 5:12). Someone said: "All the world is a hospital, and everyone in it is a terminal case." How does that grab you?

George Bernard Shaw once said: "The statistics on death are quite impressive; one out of every one people dies."

The statistics haven't changed in our enlightened generation. It is still one death per person. Here is a clear illustration from God's Word: "Thou shalt come to thy grave in a full age, like as a shock of corn cometh in in his season. Lo this, we have searched it, so it is; hear it, and know thou it for thy good" (Job 5:26, 27). Death is inevitable! To gain eternal life, we must make a choice about Jesus the Lifesaver. When you need to make a choice, and don't make it, that is in itself a choice.

Perhaps you are quite young and seldom think about death. Sixty percent of the population of the United States is under twenty-five years of age. It is a young people's world. The writer would like to appeal to all young people everywhere to consider seriously the Lord Jesus and a complete life of service to Him.

Mark Twain once said: "Always do right; that will gratify some of the people and astonish the rest."

A rich man once said to a Christian: "I'd give everything I have if I had the peace in my heart that you have." The Christian answered: "That is what it cost me."

God knows all about us. For example: He knew when you were going to be born. You may have been a surprise to your parents, but you were no surprise to God. He knows when you are going to die, too, by the way. "Lo . . . we have searched it, so it is; hear it, and KNOW THOU IT FOR THY GOOD."

(over)

No Hits, No Runs, No Errors
(Continued)

The epitaph on another man's tombstone:

"The resting place of a traveler on his way to the new Jerusalem."

For him, the grave was just a resting place on the way to God's Eternal City. I like this one! I especially appreciate the theology behind it. It shows some real insight into God's program of redemption for earth and men.

John the beloved saw, in vision, "The holy city, new Jerusalem, coming down from God out of heaven" (see Rev. 21:1-4). Jesus spoke of Jerusalem as "the city of the great King" (Matt. 5:35).

Make no mistake, friend! The Holy City, the new Jerusalem, that comes down from God out of Heaven at the close of the millennium, is the destiny of every follower of the Lord Jesus.

Someone said: "To know God's Word is the greatest knowledge; to find God's will is the greatest discovery; to do God's will is the greatest achievement."

The writer concurs with that totally. Paul the apostle, it seems, accomplished these goals (II Tim. 4:6-8).

In spite of the gloom of this world with its problems, it is wonderful to know that the future is as bright as the promises of God. Maybe you have a heavy cross today. Perhaps you have some deep water to cross. Remember that the future is just as bright as the promises of God, but remember this also: nothing—including your life—turns out right unless someone makes it his job to see that it does.

Religion today seems to come in every size and shape. It wears many faces. They represent every persuasion, from the straightlaced types to rock opera, with all of the gimmicks of modern evangelism. Religion, moreover, has been so heavily influenced by Madison Avenue that you can shop for it in much the same way in which one shops for clothes or household needs. But where does it all end? That is what I would like to know!

Friend, make sure that you know Jesus Christ in a personal way; make sure that you lay hold on eternal life (I Tim. 6:12) before you go the way of all the earth and keep your appointment with death. Jesus, God's only Son, is the world's only hope, and man's only Saviour. What will be in your epitaph?

—Hollis Partlowe

Did you hear about the father who fainted when his son asked for the garage keys and came out with the lawnmower?

There has always been a sort of natural conflict between man and woman. You can hear it in the husband-and-wife jokes. You may see it in the struggle of the couple next door over who is going to be boss. Even Adam in the Garden tried to push all the blame of the "apple incident" on Eve.

You may find yourself arguing, threatening, shouting or using any of a thousand other means of domineering. Why is this so wrong? It has been proved that 53 percent of all wife-dominated marriages are unhappy.

Men's egos are bruised easily. An aggressive wife can utterly destroy her husband here.

The woman can become dictator of the home. She can run things with an iron hand. When she cracks the whip, her husband will jump through the hoop. She may accomplish this by such methods as nagging, needling or anger.

Do you tell your husband when he should go to church, what time he must go to bed, when to change jobs and when to ask the boss for a raise? In other words, do you rule the roost with an iron hand?

Change your ways! See the difference.

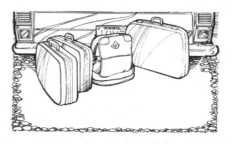

People go on vacations to forget things. When they get there and open their luggage, they find out they have indeed.

Think You're Busy Today?

Grandma on a winter's day, milked the cows, slopped the hogs, saddled the mule and got the children off to school (no bus), did a washing, mopped the floor, cooked a pan of homegrown fruit, pressed Dad's Sunday suit, swept the parlor, made the beds, baked a dozen loaves of bread, split some firewood and brought in enough to fill the kitchen bin, cleaned the lamps and put in oil, stewed some apples she thought might spoil, churned the butter, baked a cake, then exclaimed, "For goodness' sakes, the calves have gotten out of the pen," and went and chased them in again. The fence fixed, she gathered the eggs, closed the stable, went back to the house, set the table, cooked supper, which was delicious, and afterwards washed up all the dishes, fed the cat, mended a basket of socks, sprinkled the clothes, and then opened the organ and began to play, "When You Come to the End of a Perfect Day."

—Emmanuel Baptist News

If the Red Sea is before you, mountains to the left, desert to the right, and the Egyptians are galloping up behind, start praising God, for the situation is ideal. . . for a miracle!

—Peter Allard

On her birthday one lady received this short note from her husband: "To Joanne, my wife, with whom it's as easy to keep in love as to fall in love."

Isn't that sweet!

The epitaph on many tombstones should read: "She might have lived longer if she could have gotten the safety cap off her medicine bottle."

—Red O'Donnell

A BOY IS THE ONLY THING GOD CAN USE TO MAKE A MAN.

Little Hattie's Chair

The day that little Hattie died
　The house seemed strange and
　queer;
The furniture looked different,
　And everything was drear;
We children all would huddle close
　Upon the steps and try
To think of Heaven where she was.
　And then we all would cry.

Then Bobbie sneaked off by himself,
　And we hunted everywhere
Till Father found him in the yard
　In little Hattie's chair;
He was hid behind the lilac bush
　Where she would often play,
And his face was streaked with tears,
　And he called, "Oh, keep away."

But Father kissed him on the head
　And lifted chair and all
And carried him into the house
　And on up through the hall
Until he reached the attic door;
　And we kept following, too,
Because we wondered what it was
　That he was going to do.

He got a hammer and a nail
　And drove it 'way up high,
And said, "Now, children, you may
　kiss
　The little chair good-bye;

But you must never take it down
　And never sit on it"—
And there stood Mother, watching us—
　And we all cried a bit.

One Saturday when Bobbie was
　A-tracking to its lair
A wild beast of the forest,
　He climbed the attic stair—
Quite softly in his stocking feet
　And peeped in through the door,
And there by little Hattie's chair
　Knelt Mother on the floor.

"O Jesus, spare the others—
　And make them pure and good,
Help me to train them carefully
　As a Christian mother should";
Then Bobbie tiptoed down the stairs
　And told us what he'd heard,
And we looked at one another
　But didn't speak a word.

That evening after Father came,
　And we got the songbooks out
And took our turn in reading
　A Bible verse about,
He said he'd heard that we had been
　So very good all day,
But no one told him 'twas because
　Bobbie heard Mother pray.

—*Grace W. Haight*

A housewife was heard to say she didn't want anything expensive for her birthday, just something her husband had made himself—such as money.

• • •

IF YOU LOSE YOUR TEMPER, DON'T LOOK FOR IT.

• • •

Doctor: Tell your wife not to worry about that slight deafness as it is simply an indication of advancing years.

Husband: You tell her.

• • •

Before we leap at any opportunity to criticize our children, we should pause for a moment to remember who raised them.

KEEP A FAIR-SIZED CEMETERY IN YOUR BACKYARD IN WHICH TO BURY THE FAULTS OF YOUR FRIENDS.

—*Beecher*

SOME PEOPLE HAVE AS THEIR MOTTO: "IF YOU CAN'T SAY ANYTHING GOOD ABOUT A PERSON, LET'S HEAR IT."

Stir the Cabbage, Perry

Many an earnest preacher's wife unwittingly handicaps her husband. About the time he gets in his study, she calls, "Perry, will you stir the cabbage?"

She goes on to explain that she is waxing the floor and just can't quit. So Perry pushes aside his book and lumbers off to the kitchen to stir the cabbage. Later, when he resumes his study, she says to him, "Perry, I just must take this pattern across the street to Mrs. Rudy's. Will you keep the baby?"

So Perry, after a minute trying to hold the baby with one hand and Young's Analytical with the other, decides he has tackled the impossible and forsakes the book. When she returns, Perry decides to try to study in that little room behind the choir, really not a study, but just a corner. He steals quietly away.

But in a few minutes she comes to the window, "Perry, you simply must fix that step, or I will break my neck." Perry fixes the step, but Perry comes empty-handed to his pulpit the next Sunday morning. And next year Perry has to move to some other church.

Perry's wife shakes her head in silent wonder, "Why is it that I must go on moving like this?"

Why doesn't someone tell her!

He Could Not Live With Her

 *There is a tradition that Jonathan Edwards, third president of Princeton and America's greatest thinker, had a daughter with an ungovernable temper. But, as is so often the case, this infirmity was not known to the outside world.*

A worthy young man fell in love with this daughter and sought her hand in marriage. "You can't have her," was the abrupt answer of Jonathan Edwards.

"But I love her," the young man replied.

"You can't have her," insisted Edwards.

"But she loves me," replied the young man.

Again Edwards said, "You can't have her."

"Why?" asked the young man.

"Because she is not worthy of you."

"But, she is a Christian, is she not?"

"Yes, she is a Christian, but the grace of God can live with some people with whom no one else could ever live."

Mother's Magic Eyes

My mother had magic eyes, although I did not realize this as a child. In fact, I was quite grown up when I found it out.

As a child I had painted her a scenic picture with a tall birch tree in the foreground. She said it was beautiful. Years later, I noticed that the tree was thick where it should have been straight.

Another time I embroidered her a pincushion which had on it the one word "Mother." The stitches were far-spaced and not too even. The eyelet holes were rather large.

I know now why she could say my handiwork was beautiful. She saw not with her natural eyes, but with the magic eyes of love. She saw not the crooked tree with its odd-shaped branches, but the child at work, painstakingly painting her love. She saw not the crooked stitches, the uneven pattern, but rather the needle-pricked finger and the cramped little hand. Her magic eyes looked past the material offering and saw deep into a small heart presenting its gift of love. What wonderful eyes a good mother has!

To a sincere Christian, how like a mother's love is the affection of his Heavenly Father. Looking beyond thoughtless mistakes, careless blunders and imperfect acts of devotion, the Lord sees a humble heart, eager to love and serve Him.

—Selected

ATTENTION, MOTHERS: If you want a few minutes alone and undisturbed, do the dishes!

The Light Never Goes Out

A husband and wife, married many years, had planned to enjoy life and travel. But only a month after he retired, the husband suddenly died.

All of life seemed to end for that widow. And on her husband's tombstone she had engraved the words:

> THE LIGHT OF MY LIFE HAS GONE OUT

But with the passage of time and the encouragement and counsel of friends, her life came alive again. Two years later her pastor joined her in marriage to another good man and watched them as they enthusiastically anticipated building a new life together.

Later she went to her pastor and said, "I'm going to have to change that inscription on my first husband's tombstone."

"No," replied the pastor, "I think all you have to do is add one more line:

> I STRUCK ANOTHER MATCH!

No matter what happens to us, there is always something left to live for. Broken lives can be rebuilt.

To all who have gone through the crushing experience of losing a husband, recommend Catherine Marshall's enormously popular book, *To Live Again*—her own personal story of victory over grief and love's triumph over loneliness.

What do you do when your world caves in? If you have faith in the goodness of God and in His power to change the course of your life, you never give up on life. You know you're a child of God. He promises to walk through life with you. The bottom can never fall out of your life, no matter what happens.

An inscription found on a small gravestone after a devastating air raid on Britain in World War II gained much attention. People thought it must be a famous quotation, but it wasn't. The words were written by a lonely old lady whose pet was killed by a bomb:

> **There is not enough darkness in all the world to put out the light of one small candle.**

And we have the light of life!

—M. P. Horban

Even though the tongue weighs practically nothing, it's surprising how few persons are able to hold it.

WHATEVER YOU DISLIKE IN ANOTHER PERSON, BE SURE TO CORRECT IT IN YOURSELF.

Fortunately, there's more to a grapefruit than meets the eye.

Wife: "Did you see that hat Mrs. Jones wore to church?"

Husband: "No."

Wife: "Did you see the new dress Mrs. Smith had on?"

Husband: "No."

Wife: "A lot of good it does you to go to church!"

HAVE YOU HAD YOUR HEART EXAMINED LATELY?

How is your heart? If it's strong, you should be very thankful—and you should take care of it.

Proper rest, good exercise and a correct diet are essential if you wish to keep your heart healthy and live out all the years God wants to give you.

The heart is the most vital organ in your body, and normally it is amazingly strong for its size. Though not as large as your two fists, it pumps 12 tons of blood through 970 miles of arteries and veins every day. What a marvelous machine!

But if the heart is diseased, the trouble can be serious. It can hardly be replaced. Medical science can overcome many heart problems, but heart disease is still America's number one killer. A thousand Americans die of heart attacks every day. Diseases of the cardiovascular system cause over half the deaths in the U. S.

So much for the physical heart. Thank God if you have a good one, and don't abuse it.

But how about the spiritual? The Bible speaks of the heart as the seat of one's affections. Is your heart fixed on the Lord? Have you set your affections on things above—or have you given your love to some less worthy objects? Love is an essential ingredient in happy human relations. Have you noticed how happiness glows when love is shown?

There's power in love—power to make dark skies bright, burdens light and turn sighs into songs.

Love's power will never be measured. Luther Burbank believed love caused his plants to prosper. Nurses find sick babies respond to fond attention.

A woman has more charm and beauty when she feels loved. A man finds his true stature when he is loved. Children develop best where there is an abundance of love.

Hostility melts like ice in spring when love shines through. Love is the catalyst that induces change in any confrontation.

If someone has wronged you, don't wait for him to make amends. Let him know you still love him. The person who initiates the reconciliation is the true Christian. "It's the Jesus thing to do."

If your enemy is hungry, don't gloat. "Feed him," said Jesus.

Self-sacrifice, forgiveness, humility, understanding, respect, sharing, appreciation—these are the elements real love is made of.

Simon the sorcerer had heart trouble, and Simon Peter diagnosed it correctly. "Thy heart is not right in the sight of God," he told him (Acts 8:21).

Let the Holy Spirit examine your heart. It may be a painful experience, but it's the wise thing to do.

If you are unsaved, He sees the heart damage. "The whole head is sick, and the whole heart faint" (Isa. 1:5). Has your heart hardened? Is there pride, deceit and wickedness? These diseases take their toll.

But there is hope. God offers to give you a new heart in place of the sinful one, and to write His laws upon it, if you pray, "Wash me throughly from mine iniquity, and cleanse me from my sin. . . . Create in me a clean heart, O God; and renew a right spirit within me" (Ps. 51:2, 10).

Hearts that are "hardened through the deceitfulness of sin" may be mended. Hearts that are "overcharged with. . .cares of this life" may be rededicated in preparation for Christ's return.

May the Lord direct our hearts "into the love of God, and into the patient waiting for Christ" (II Thess. 3:5).

—R. C. Cunningham
Used by permission

So live that you would not mind giving the family parrot to the village gossip.

—*Irish Digest*

Sign in a florist shop: "Caution! Forgetting Your Wife's Birthday May Be Hazardous to Your Health."

Service is the rent we pay for the space we occupy in the world.

IF GOD SENDS US ON STONY PATHS, HE WILL PROVIDE US WITH STRONG SHOES.

—*Alexander Maclaren*

Can You Remember?

(1) When riots were unthinkable?

(2) When you left front doors open?

(3) When socialism was a dirty word?

(4) When ghettos were neighborhoods?

(5) When the Flag was a sacred symbol?

(6) When criminals actually went to jail?

(7) When you weren't afraid to go out at night?

(8) When taxes were only a necessary nuisance?

(9) When a boy was a boy, and dressed like one?

(10) When a girl was a girl, and dressed like one?

(11) When the poor were too proud to take charity?

(12) When the minister actually preached the Gospel?

(13) When clerks and repairmen tried to please you?

(14) When college kids swallowed goldfish, not acid?

(15) When songs had a tune, and the words made sense?

(16) When young fellows tried to join the Army or Navy?

(17) When people knew what the Fourth of July stood for?

(18) When you never dreamed our country could ever lose?

(19) When a Sunday drive was a pleasant trip, not an ordeal?

(20) When you bragged about your hometown and home state?

(21) When everybody didn't feel entitled to a college education?

(22) When people expected less and valued what they had more?

(23) When politicians proclaimed their patriotism, and meant it?

(24) When everybody knew the difference between right and wrong?

(25) When things weren't perfect—but you never expected them to be?

(26) When you weren't made to feel guilty for enjoying dialect comedy?

(27) When our Government stood up for Americans, anywhere in the world?

(28) When you knew that the law would be enforced and your safety protected?

(29) When you considered yourself fortunate to have a good job, and proud to have it?

(30) When the law meant justice, and you felt a shiver of awe at sight of a policeman?

(31) When you weren't embarrassed to say that this is the best country in the world?

(32) When America was a land filled with brave, proud, confident, hard-working people?

—*Americanism Educational League*

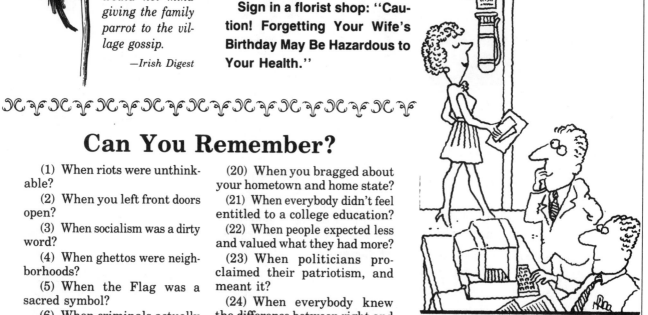

KNEES

I think that I shall never see
A thing as ugly as a knee.
A knee above whose gnarled and
    knotty cress
A mini hemline comes to rest.
Or one that's even worse than
    that,
That's covered with repulsive fat.

A knee that doth in summer wear
Nothing at all, but is quite bare.
A knee behind whose flex
    remains
A nest of blue and broken veins.

Some knees continue to perplex.
How can they form a perfect X?
While in another set one sees
A pair of true parentheses.
Fools may write lines like these,
But bigger nuts display their knees.

On his dining room wall Augustine had written these words:

"He who speaks evil of an absent man or woman is not welcome at this table."

"All right, men, let's straighten out this line!"

Farewell

I've been here long and long enough;
  I'm ready now to start.
I have my ticket in my hand,
  Impatient to depart.
There are loved ones waiting There for me;
  They left so long ago.
I am so anxious, like a child,
  And time does go so slow.
Why must I stay in this old house—
  Its timbers old and weak?
The window panes are cloudy,
  And the walls all groan and creak.
Oh, please, Lord, hurry for my soul!
  I long to come to Thee.
I've known You well, these many years.
  Ah, now Your face I see.
Farewell, dear ones, and do not grieve.
  Come, smile and cheer me on.
For victory is mine today,
  And Heaven has begun.

—Dorris Gainder

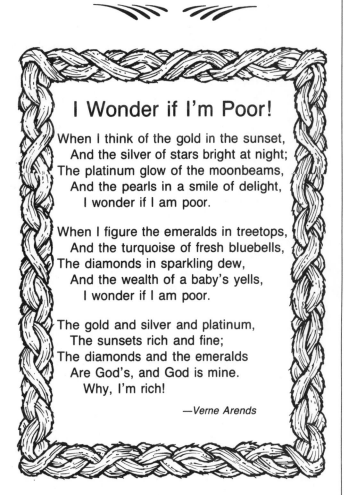

I Wonder if I'm Poor!

When I think of the gold in the sunset,
  And the silver of stars bright at night;
The platinum glow of the moonbeams,
  And the pearls in a smile of delight,
    I wonder if I am poor.

When I figure the emeralds in treetops,
  And the turquoise of fresh bluebells,
The diamonds in sparkling dew,
  And the wealth of a baby's yells,
    I wonder if I am poor.

The gold and silver and platinum,
  The sunsets rich and fine;
The diamonds and the emeralds
  Are God's, and God is mine.
    Why, I'm rich!

—Verne Arends

When the Modern Tide Struck Our Home

I will never forget when the modern tide struck our home.

My sister weighed one hundred pounds. She was an artist, nervous and temperamental and all that kind of stuff that we had to watch out for. She was an artist, while we had to make our own living. She got music and some other ideas in her head and came home from college the first year.

That morning after breakfast, when we had prayer, she rose sweetly and excused herself and went upstairs.

She "got by" with it that morning, but Father "took note of it"; and the next morning when she excused herself, he said, "Sit still!"

"But really," she pouted, "I don't care to stay."

"That doesn't make any difference—stay!"

"I think a person should have some liberty in religion," she answered.

"You can have all the liberty you please in religion," Father told her, "but I run this house; I paid for your grub; I bought the clothes you have on; I paid for your education. Sit down quietly while a father who loves you reads and prays."

My big brother came home one day. He had made money for himself; he had a big fat cigar in his mouth and smoked it awhile on the back porch. Father came out, reached out his hand, took the cigar and, throwing it into the garden, said, "Don't smoke them around here anymore!"

"I would like to know what right you have to throw that cigar out," Brother complained.

"You know my idea," Father answered. "This is my house. I am raising boys and making a specialty of it, and you don't get by with that kind of stuff. When you are working for a man he can tell you where to smoke in his office or in his warehouse. I am running this house. God gave me the command to do so."

"I'll go somewhere else," my brother threatened.

"I am sorry: I love you," Father replied quietly, "but if you want the cigar worse than you do the home, you can go."

He went away three weeks and came back and said, "Dad, you are right. I submit and will play the game according to the rules."

Most people say, "Well, you have to let children have their way."

Is that so? Then good-by to home, to government, to everything—God will not stand for that.

—*Paul Rader*

It's good to have money and the things money can buy; but it's good, too, to check up once in awhile and make sure we haven't lost the things money can't buy.

To an Aspirin Company

Dear Sir:

You manufacture aspirins that relieve suffering, colds and fevers. The mixture used in your tablets makes it possible for people to get out of bed and fight off headaches, muscle spasms and bad nerves.

I have noticed these tablets work wonders on Mondays, Tuesdays, Wednesdays, Thursdays, Fridays—especially well on Saturdays. BUT people who take them on Sundays seem to get no relief. They cannot get rid of their headaches and pains and are not able to attend church on Sundays.

Is it possible for you to examine your tablet and put in it an ingredient that will work on Sundays?

It was a wise man who said that it is important not only to pick the right mate but to be the right mate.

WHEN YOU SING YOUR OWN PRAISE, YOU ALWAYS GET THE TUNE TOO HIGH.

Ladies, have you heard about the new cigarette that is now on the market? Green stamps are given with each pack. When you get 5000 trading stamps, you receive a free cancer operation.

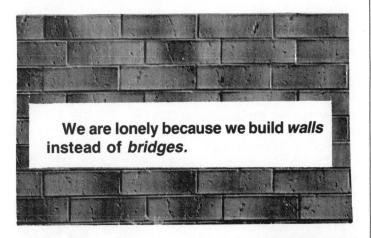

We are lonely because we build *walls* instead of *bridges*.

Paderewski arrived in a small Connecticut town about noon one day and decided to take a walk in the afternoon. While strolling along he heard a piano and, following the sound, came to a house on which was a sign reading:

> MISS JONES. PIANO LESSONS
> 25 CENTS AN HOUR.

Paderewski's Pupil

Pausing to listen he heard the young woman trying to play one of Chopin's nocturnes and not succeeding very well.

Paderewski walked up to the house and knocked.

Miss Jones came to the door and recognized him at once. Delighted, she invited him in; and he sat down and played the nocturne as he only could, afterward spending an hour in correcting her mistakes. Miss Jones thanked him, and he departed.

Some months later he returned to the town, and again he took the same walk.

He soon came to the home of Miss Jones; and, looking at the sign, he read:

> MISS JONES (PUPIL OF PADEREWSKI):
> PIANO LESSONS $1.00 AN HOUR.

So much has been given to me, I have no time to ponder over that which has been denied.

—Helen Keller

"It is a peculiar thing," said an embalmer as he stood by a woman's casket, "but it isn't necessary to tell me she was a Christian. I always know as soon as I see a body; the glory leaves its stamp on the face."

"What! Crying Over Your Lamb, Wifey?"

Mrs. Charles H. Spurgeon must have been a great helpmeet, for Spurgeon referred to her again and again in his writings, and she wrote the most tender feelings toward him in the Autobiography of Charles H. Spurgeon. Often you find her calling him "my beloved."

In the 4-volume set mentioned Mrs. Spurgeon gives us this intimate chapter from her life—and his:

*   *   *

...In the same small room occurred also a touching little scene which I have described in *Ten Years After!* but which cannot be left out of this history, for it has a right to a place here, revealing, as it does, the tenderness of my beloved's heart, while he still consistently put "first things first." He was constantly away from home fulfilling preaching engagements of long or short duration, and these frequent absences were a trial to me, though I kept faithfully to my purpose of never hindering him in his work.

But I remember how, while waiting for his return, late at night, from some distant place, I would tire of the cramped space of the tiny parlor, and pace up and down the narrow passage—dignified by the name of a "hall"—watching and listening for the dear footstep I knew so well, and praying—oh, how fervently—that the Lord would care for his precious life and avert all danger from him as he traveled back by road or rail. I can even now recall the thrill of joy and thankfulness with which I opened the door and welcomed him home.

One morning after breakfast when he was preparing to go out on one of his long journeys, the room looked so bright and cozy that a sudden depression seized me at the thought of its emptiness when he was gone, and the many anxious hours that must pass before I should see him again.

Some tears would trickle down my cheeks, in spite of my efforts to restrain them. Seeing me look so sad, he said, very gently, "Wifey, do you think that, when any of the children of Israel brought a lamb to the Lord's altar as an offering to Him, they stood and wept over it when they had seen it laid there?"

"Why, no!" I replied, startled by his strange question. "Certainly not; the Lord would not have been pleased with an offering reluctantly given."

"Well," said he, tenderly, "don't you see, you are giving me to God, in letting me go to preach the Gospel to poor sinners, and do you think He likes to see you cry over your sacrifice?"

Could ever a rebuke have been more sweetly and graciously given? It sank deep into my heart, carrying comfort with it; and, thenceforth, when I parted with him, the tears were scarcely ever allowed to show themselves, or if a stray one or two dared to run over the boundaries,

Said a teacher to a class of boys in a school in Germany long ago:

"Boys, when I meet you on the street, I am wont to remove my hat in your presence, for who knows but that from this class of boys will come one day a man who will change the course of human history!"

Martin Luther was a boy in that class.

he would say, "What! crying over your lamb, wifey!" and this reminder would quickly dry them up and bring a smile in their place.

And now that I am parted from thee, not for a few days only, as in that long-ago time, but "until the day break and the shadows flee away," I think I hear again thy loving voice saying, "Don't cry over your lamb, wifey," as I try to give thee up ungrudgingly to God—not without tears—ah, no! that is not possible, but with that full surrender of the heart which makes the sacrifice acceptable in His sight.

It's a funny thing but true,
The folks you don't like, don't like you.
I don't know why this should be so,
But just the same I always know
That when I'm sour, friends are few;
When I'm friendly, folks are too.
I sometimes get up in the morn
A-wishin' I was never born,
And then I make cross remarks, a few,
And then my family wishes, too,
That I had gone some other place;
But then I change my little tune,
And sing and smile,
And then the folks around me sing and smile.
I guess it was catching all the while.
It's a funny thing but true,
The folks you like, sure like you.

Now They Know!

A health official came to grade school for a visit and lectured about the dangers of rats and rat infestation. One boy was so impressed, he wrote this note, "We never even knew what a rat looked like until you came here."

A MOTHER IS THE ONLY PERSON ON EARTH WHO CAN DIVIDE HER LOVE AMONG TEN CHILDREN AND EACH CHILD STILL HAVE ALL HER LOVE.

+ + + + +

Where Are Your Good Intentions?

Little Dot was drawing a picture with pen and ink on a paper. It turned out to be a cat without a tail. "Where is the cat's tail?" asked her mother. Little Dot looked puzzled for a moment; then she smiled and said, "Why, it is still in the ink bottle."

Many of our good intentions are like the cat's tail—still in the ink bottle. We need to get our good intentions out and put them to work.

Foreign woman customer (in bank): "I would lika to maka da loan."

Bank official: "You have to see the loan arranger."

Woman: "Who, plizz?"

Official: "The loan arranger."

Woman: "Oh, you mean da one who say 'Hi-Ho Silver'?"

A CHILD IS YOUR SECOND CHANCE.

A lady visiting George Bernard Shaw was surprised not to find any flowers in his home. "I thought you were fond of flowers," she said.

"I am," Shaw replied. "I'm also fond of children. But I don't cut off their heads and stick them in pots around the house."

A secretary declares she heard her boss conduct a telephone conversation without saying a word:

"L.O. O. O.I.C. O.K. U.R.? Y? O.I.C. O.K. B.C.N.U."

Woman driver to cop arresting her:
"But officer, I couldn't slow down while you were going so fast right in back of me!"

+　+　+

SOMETHING GOD CREATED WITHIN US WANTS OUR ARMS AROUND EACH OTHER.

Heart of a Child

Whatever you write on the heart
　of a child,
　No water can wash away.
The sand may be shifted when
　billows are wild,
　And the efforts of time may
　　decay.
Some stories may perish,
　Some songs be forgot,
But this graven record—
　Time changes not.
Whatever you write on the heart
　of a child,
　A story of gladness or care
That Heaven has blessed or
　earth has defiled,
　Will linger unchangeably there.

181 different women are mentioned by name in the Bible.

*　*　*

The easiest way to open a fruit jar is to turn it upside down in hot water. After a minute or two the metal top expands and loosens.

*　*　*

Dry cleaning is not dry. The articles are placed in a washer containing fluid and thoroughly saturated.

The neighborhood kids had congregated in our front yard when a fire truck zoomed past. Sitting on the front seat was a Boxer dog. The children fell to discussing the dog's duties in connection with the fire truck.

"They use him to keep the crowds back when they go to a fire," said a five-year-old girl.

"No," said another, "they carry him for good luck."

The third, a boy about six, brought the argument to an abrupt end. "They use the dog," he said firmly, "to find the fire plug."

"The Hollywood version of the famous quotation," said the Reverend, "seems to be, 'Thou shalt love one, another, and another.'"

Who Is Responsible?

By Mrs. Henry Peabody

At a very beautiful tea, where I felt less at home than at a missionary meeting, I was approached by a charming woman who greeted me cordially and said, "I have been so interested in your prohibition work." I said, with some surprise, "You do not look like a reformer." She was a picture of a leader in social life. "Oh," she said, "I have been the wife of an army officer. I have seen what this thing does to young men."

Then she said, "I was converted to prohibition as a girl, here in the South. I came in one day from the plantation to the county seat. In front of the little store I saw a family in an old wagon with mule team. The woman wore a sunbonnet, had no shoes, and four little children sat on the wagon floor. They were all radiantly happy. I wondered why, and going into the store for my errand found they had driven in to get money for their crop, which the man and wife together had cultivated. It was their only income during the year. The man took them into the store and said to the owner, 'You give her what she wants. I'll be back with the money.'

"So the woman chose, and I waited to see their happiness. They wanted everything, shoes and sheets, sugar and flour, all the things to eat and to wear that they had done without. The kind storekeeper gave the children some candy, and I left them, to go back again later.

"I was delayed, and when I returned the picture had changed. There was tragedy in the woman's voice, but no tears. The children, feeling the changed atmosphere, were crying; and as I came in, the woman said, pointing to the row of bundles ready for her to take home, 'I think you had better put them back; he hasn't come.'

"I could not leave, and waited for the end. Later the old team came up with a drunken man on the seat. He stumbled out, cursing, screaming, and fell across the doorsteps of the store, helpless, beastly.

"Again the woman said, helplessly, 'Put them back.' Every cent was gone; and she lifted the man, with the help of the storekeeper, and carried him to the wagon and herself drove home. I never recovered from the shock and the horror of that drama of life. It made me a prohibitionist."

"This," says Mrs. Peabody, "is the picture we are beginning to forget."

—Woman's Missionary Friend

Life's Journey

Life is like a journey, taken on a plane,
With a pair of travelers at each window pane;
I may sit beside you the whole journey through,
Or I may be seated elsewhere, never knowing you;
But if fate should place me to sit at your side,
Let's be pleasant travelers: it's so short a ride.

"I'll lend you for a little time a child of Mine," He said,
"For you to love the while she lives and mourn for when she's dead.
It may be six or seven years, or twenty-two or three;
But will you, till I call her back, take care of her for Me?
She'll bring her charms to gladden you; and should her stay be brief,
You'll have her lovely memories as solace for your grief.

"I cannot promise she will stay, since all from earth return;
But there are lessons taught down there I want this child to learn.
I've looked the wide world over in My search for teachers true,
And from the throngs that crowd life's lands I have selected you.
Now will you give her all your love, nor think the labor vain,
Nor hate Me when I come to call and take her back again?"

I fancied that I heard them say: "Dear Lord, Thy will be done!
For all the joy Thy child shall bring, the risk of grief we'll run.
We'll shelter her with tenderness, and love her while we may,
And for the happiness we've known forever grateful stay;
But shall the angels call for her much sooner than we've planned,
We'll brave the bitter grief that comes, and try to understand."

—Edgar A. Guest

"How is your son doing in the Army?"

"Very well. They just made him a Court Marshal."

• • •

IT IS UNREASONABLE TO EXPECT A CHILD TO LISTEN TO YOUR ADVICE AND IGNORE YOUR EXAMPLE.

A mother asked a psychologist, "When shall I start training my child?" "How old is he?" she was asked. "Five." The psychologist said, "Madam, hurry home! You've already lost five years!"

A Boy's Tribute to His Mother

A little ragged newsboy had lost his mother. They had kept house together and had been all in all to each other; and now the little fellow's loss was irreparable.

In the tenderness of the boy's affection for his mother, he determined that he would raise a stone to her memory. Obtaining a stone was no easy task, for his earnings were small; but love is strong.

Going to a cutter's yard, he found that even the cheaper class of stones was far too expensive for him. But at length he fixed upon a broken shaft of marble—a part of the remains of an accident in the yard—which the proprietor kindly named at such a low figure that it came within the child's means. There was much yet to be done, but the brave little chap was equal to it.

The next day he conveyed the stone away on a little four-wheeled cart and managed to have it put in position.

The narrator of this story, curious to know the last of the stone, visited the cemetery one afternoon; and he thus describes what he saw and learned:

" 'Here it is,' said the man in charge; and sure enough, there was our monument at the head of one of the newest graves. I knew it at once. *Just as it was when it left our yard,* I thought, until I went closer and saw what the little chap had done. I tell you, boys, when I saw it, something blurred my eyes, so that I couldn't read it at first.

"The little man had tried to keep the lines straight; and evidently he thought that capitals would make the inscription look better and bigger, for nearly every letter was a capital. I copied it, and here it is, but you would have to see it on the stone to appreciate it:

> MY MOTHER
> SHEE DIED LAST WEAK
> SHEE WAS ALL I HAD, SHEE
> SED SHEAD Bee WaITING FuR——

and here, boys, the lettering stopped.

"After a while, I went back to the man in charge and asked him what further he knew of the little fellow who brought the stone.

" 'Not much,' he said, 'not much. Didn't you notice a fresh little grave near the one with the stone? Well, that's where he is. He came here every afternoon for some time, working away at that stone. One day I missed him, and then several days.

" 'Then the man came out from the church that had buried the mother and ordered the grave dug by her side. I asked if it was for the little chap. He said it was.

" 'The boy had sold all his papers one day and was hurrying along the street out this way. There was a runaway team just above the crossing, and—well—he was run over and lived but a day or two. He had in his hand, when he was picked up, an old file, sharpened down to a point, that he did all the lettering with. They said he seemed to be thinking only of that until he died, for he kept saying, "I didn't get it done; but she'll know I meant to finish it, won't she? I'll tell her so, for she'll be waiting for me." ' And, boys, he died with these words on his lips."

When the men in the cutter's yard heard the story of the boy, they clubbed together, bought a good stone, inscribed upon it the name of the newsboy (which they obtained from the superintendent of the Sunday school that the little fellow attended), and underneath it the touching, expressive words:

> HE LOVED HIS MOTHER

When the stone was put up, the little lad's Sunday school mates, as well as others, were present; and the superintendent, in speaking to them, told them how the boy had loved Jesus and tried to please Him.

"Scholars," said he, "I would rather be that brave, loving little newsboy and lie there with that on my tombstone, than to be king of the world and not love and respect my mother."

That newsboy has left a lesson to the world. "Hearken unto thy father . . . and despise not thy mother when she is old."

—Selected

Mother, having finally tucked a small boy into bed after an unusually trying day: "Well, I've worked today from son-up to son-down!"

WHY I QUIT GOING TO SUPERMARKETS

First, let me make it perfectly clear that both of my parents were faithful supermarket goers. They frequented the local grocery haven at least once a week.

Why, I've been in supermarkets from the time I was old enough to be pushed around in a shopping cart! I have fond childhood memories of running the aisles while Mother stopped to squeeze the oranges or to check the meat prices.

But that was a long time ago—before I was old enough to realize how hypocritical grocery stores really are. Now that I see the supermarket for what it really is, I can no longer go there.

For one thing, supermarkets are inconsiderate. In the summer they turn on the air conditioning, and it's too cold. In the winter you have to shop with your coat on. They don't even provide a coatrack!

Neither are there sofas for tired shoppers. You are expected to stand for the entire length of your visit!

The checkout lines can be long and time consuming. I find no inspiration in the boring recital of prices—especially when I have a roast in the oven at home or I'm missing my favorite TV program.

I have found supermarket employees to be an unfriendly lot. The butcher has never come out from behind the counter to shake my hand. The produce manager doesn't even know my name. The checkout girls never send me birthday or anniversary cards. And the store manager didn't even visit me when I was in the hospital!

The people who go to the supermarket are basically selfish. Each seems intent on filling his own cart. No one has ever offered to push my cart for me—which proves one thing: the supermarket has no standard for its clientele. Anyone can go there. I decided I'd rather not be classed with all the social riffraff they allow to come through their doors.

The supermarket has never given me proper recognition. Although I've developed the skill of steering my cart down the aisle without knocking down displays, do you think anyone has ever noticed my talent or expressed appreciation for my expertise? Not once! Nor has the management ever consulted me in any of their decisions. I don't even have a vote in such simple matters as personnel selection!

I suppose my greatest complaint against the supermarkets, however, is their constant plea for money. Every item has a price on it. You can't get out of the building without someone asking for money.

I finally decided the trip to the supermarket just wasn't worth the trouble. I can get as much out of watching food advertisements on TV or reading the recipe section of the newpaper.

Who needs the supermarket?

—Roberta Lashley Bonnici

Soul-Winning Sophie

"Aunt Sophie," a converted washerwoman who was really a soul winner, was accused of talking about Christ to a wooden Indian in front of a cigar store. When some laughed at Sophie for doing this, she replied, "Some people say they saw me talking to a wooden Indian about Christ. I may have done it —my eyesight is not good —but talking to a wooden Indian about Christ is not as bad as being a wooden Christian and never talking to anybody about Jesus."

A woman tried to excuse her bad temper by saying, "It was all over in a minute." Someone replied, "So is a gunshot, but it blows everything to pieces."

DEAD END

Hiram's third wife died. Mary Cornstalk said to her husband, "Sebe, are you going to attend the funeral of Hiram's wife?"

Sebe considered at length and finally ruled, "No, I ain't, honey. I went to Hiram's first wife's funeral. I went to his second wife's funeral, but I ain't going to the funeral for this'n."

"Why not?" Mary demanded.

"Well, sweetheart, it just don't seem right, me acceptin' all of Hiram's invitations, and never havin' nothing like that to invite him back to."

- The thicker our love, the thinner others' faults.

⌐mm⌐

- **What your conscience says is more important than what your neighbors say.**

⌐mm⌐

- Some parents can trace their ancestry back 300 years, but they can't tell you where their children were last night.

✦✦✦✦✦✦✦✦✦✦✦✦✦✦✦✦✦✦✦✦✦✦✦✦✦✦✦✦✦✦

Don't Let Your Clothes Invite...

No guy in his right mind ever starts to paw a perfect lady. The girl who suddenly finds a guy's hands all over her has asked for it in one way or another.

Sometimes it's not in words; it's the way a girl gets herself together. The short, short skirts are a pretty good eyeful when a girl is standing up. When she is sitting down, it's like she is wearing a bikini. No normal guy can look at all that flesh and not get ideas.

Transparent blouses and sweaters and jeans that fit like sausage casings are worn to get guys excited: when a normal guy gets excited, he wants to do more than just look.

So please... give advice, give it to the girls. They are the ones who need it.

The moral of the story is simply this, girls: Don't let your clothes issue any invitations.

—From *Maranatha Messenger*

"Don't Say It!"

Words are peculiar things. By them, one may become loved and admired; may become despised and overburdened, clear on out into dark despair. Words may increase appreciation among acquaintances or drive a wedge between friends. If what you have to say cannot be counted on to do somebody some good, *don't say it!*

The tongue, more devastating than marching armies, more mighty than the mailed fist, more deadly than a serpent's sting, has for all time been man's amazing paradox. Sometimes used both to stir up and reveal sublimest feelings and profoundest thoughts, it is as often employed to the exactly opposite end.

Smite a man with clenched, angry fists; and repentant

words will heal the hurt. But smite him with either cruel or careless words, and for that hurt there is healing alone in the forgetfulness of remote tomorrows. Just *don't say it!*

—D. A. Manker

ONE OF THE MOST DIF-
FICULT INSTRUMENTS TO
PLAY WELL IS SECOND
FIDDLE.

Wife, in case you're thinking, "But I never say a word!" remember most every no-no can be done quite efficiently with the gelid stare, the long-suffering silence, the superior spiritual look, the martyr's sigh, the resigned look, the sweet-patience pattern, and I'll-bear-this-if-it-kills-me syndrome, and various combinations thereof. For the awful truth is, most of us seem bent on doing our best in the worst way.

—Ethel Barrett

Grace to Do Without

My heart rejoices in God's will,
  'Tis ever best—I do not doubt;
He may not give me what I want,
  But gives me grace to do without.

I blindly asked for what I crave,
  With haughty heart and will so stout;
He oft denies me what I seek
  But gives me grace to do without.

He makes me love the way He leads
  And fear is put to route;
With my fondest wish denied,
  He gives me grace to do without.

Oh, blessed, hallowed will of God!
  To it I bow with heart devout;
I will abide in all God's will,
  His way is best, I do not doubt;
He may not give me what I ask,
  But gives me grace to do without.

—Author unknown

A couple stood before the preacher to be married. The boy's hair was as long as the girl's. It was difficult to tell the two apart. So the minister said, "Whichever one you are, take whichever one this is, to be whatever you are going to be."

HOW LONG HAS IT BEEN SINCE YOU read a poem? sang out loud? rubbed your wife's back? put your arms around your kids and said you loved them? spent an afternoon in a hammock? walked in the woods? drank from a spring? played games with the family? called up your mother for no special occasion? took music lessons? stopped at a roadside stand and bought one apple to eat there? stood outdoors looking at the stars and thinking of nothing but the stars? declined a cocktail party to stay at home with your family? went barefoot? read in the bathtub? walked to the store instead of driving? greeted a stranger with a smile? saw a dandelion in your yard without worrying about it? laughed just from the joy of feeling good? made up an absolutely nutty bedtime story for your child?

(If you haven't had the time or the inclination to do some or all of these things for a long time, your life's a bit out of control.)

Who Is at Fault?

A young married couple was contacted and invited to the services of the church. This is the record:

The First Call: "We are going to start as soon as the baby gets old enough to come."

One Year Later: "Yes, we promised, but the baby's in that stage where she cries a lot. I don't get anything out of the services, and I know she disturbs other people. When she gets older . . . ."

Three Years Later: "I know you think we are awful, but we're not coming to church because Julie doesn't want to go. Why do you think she is different from the other children her age?"

Eleven Years Later: "I'm so glad you called. I want you or some of the elders to see if you can talk to Julie. She is running around with the wrong crowd. Perhaps if the church would provide some kind of entertainment for the young people, she might get interested."

Two Years Later: "Yes, Julie is married. They were awfully young, and he is not a member of the church, but we hope it works out."

Ten Years Later: "Well, Julie has finally married a man who can give her the better things of life. This is her third husband, but she couldn't get along with the others. I had hopes that this one would become a member of the church, but the preacher preached a sermon on marriage and divorce, and he says he will never attend that church again. There must be something wrong with that church, or else it would have had a better influence on Julie. Maybe they need to change preachers. I don't know . . . ."

LORD, IS IT I?

—Anonymous

★ ★ ★ ★

IT NOW COSTS MORE TO AMUSE A CHILD THAN IT ONCE DID TO EDUCATE HIS FATHER.

A man once asked an attractive older lady, "And exactly what is your age?"

She responded, "Can you keep a secret?"

"Yes," he said.

To which she replied, "So can I."

I Must Get Home by Night

As I look back across the years,
* I see myself again:*
A little girl away from home
* With darkness closing in.*
As soon as shadows streaked the sky
* With dying shades of light,*
My only thought was getting home
* Before the coming night.*
No other place in all the world
* Could even half compare*
To being home, secure and safe
* With loved ones gathered there.*

Well, many years have hastened by,
* And things are not the same.*
The old home place stands empty now,
* For God has made a claim;*
My loved ones still await my step
* But on a farther shore.*
The lights of home have shifted now,
* As Earth prepares for war.*
Strange shadows move across our land.
* I smell the stench of sin.*
I find myself away from home
* With nighttime closing in;*
And how I long for home tonight!
* Almost the darkness turns;*
Almost I see the shoreline, Lord;
* And how my spirit yearns!*
I long for home! My final home!
* For sunrise without blight.*
It's growing dark so very fast!
* I must get home by night!*

—Mary Mason

Two long-haired teenage sons gave their father a surprise birthday gift—a box filled with their sheared locks and a card which read: "Dear Dad: Forgive us our past tresses."

—*Detroit Free Press*

Out of the depth of sorrow came this hymn

From those who have known shadowed days and nights of trial have come rich melodies to touch many troubled hearts.

Blindness came to George Matheson, an English clergyman. Upon losing his sight, he wrote to his fiancé to release her from their engagement. Her reply showed a ready acceptance of release. She was not willing to share her life with a blind man.

He understood and accepted her attitude; yet his disappointment was deep. His sorrow was measured by the degree of love he had for her. Out of the depth of his sorrow came the hymn that has blessed multitudes of hearts these many years:

O Love that wilt not let me go,
I rest my weary soul in Thee;
I give Thee back the life I owe,
That in Thine ocean depths its flow
　　May richer, fuller be.

O Light that follow'st all my way,
I yield my flick'ring torch to Thee;
My heart restores its borrowed ray,
That in Thy sunshine's blaze its day
　　May brighter, fairer, be.

O Joy that seekest me through pain,
I cannot close my heart to Thee;
I trace the rainbow through the rain,
And feel the promise is not vain
　　That morn shall tearless be.

O Cross that liftest up my head,
I dare not ask to fly from Thee;
I lay in dust life's glory dead,
And from the ground there blossoms red
　　Life that shall endless be.

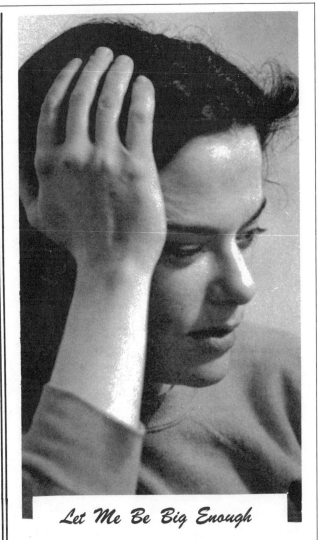

Let Me Be Big Enough

Let me be big enough, Lord, this I pray,
Let me be big enough, just for today;
　Let me not nurse a slight,
　Keep me turned toward the right,
　　Let me be brave to know,
　　Hurts serve to make me grow,
And on the morrow again I will say,
"Let me be big enough, just for today."

Let me be sweet enough, Lord, this I pray,
Let me be sweet enough, just for today;
　Sweet to unravel life's tangled knot,
　Sweet for whatever may be my lot,
　　Sweetness enough to show
　　All the world's good I know,
And on the morrow again I will say,
"Let me be sweet enough, just for today."

Let me be big enough, Lord, this I pray,
Let me be sweet and big, just for today;
　For these I need, O Lord;
　Hold me in right accord;
　　Thus may my love abound
　　For each and all around,
And on the morrow again I will say,
"Let me be big and sweet, just for today."

—*Annette Fowler*

NOW, FREDERICK, YOU KNOW WE DON'T PLAY BASEBALL ON THE DAY OF REST!

A child who does not hear about religion at his mother's knee is not likely to hear about it at any other joint.

When asked what was his greatest ambition, a small boy replied, "I think it is to take Mother away from the dinner table and wash her face."

© DG 1992

Mothers, Take Note!

One Sunday I was entertained in the farm home of a member of a rural New York church. I was impressed by the intelligence and unusually good behavior of the only child in the home, a four-year-old boy.

Then I discovered one reason for the child's charm.

The mother was at the kitchen sink, washing the intricate parts of the cream separator when the little one came to her with a magazine. "Mother," he asked, "what is this man in the picture doing?"

To my surprise, she dried her hands, sat down in a chair and, taking the boy in her lap, she spent ten minutes answering his questions.

After the child had left I commented on her having interrupted her chores to answer the boy's questions, saying, "Most mothers wouldn't have bothered."

"I expect to be washing cream separators for the rest of my life," she told me, "but never again will my son ask me that question!"

Husband: *"In our six years of marriage we haven't been able to agree on anything."*
Wife: *"It's been seven years, dear."*

"OPENED BY MISTAKE" applies more often to mouths than to mail.

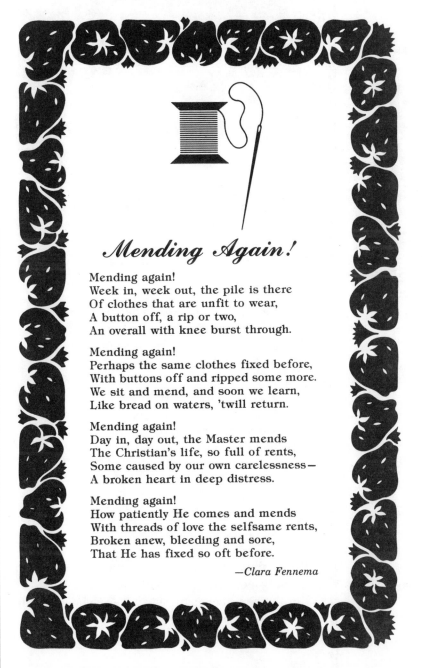

Mending Again!

Mending again!
Week in, week out, the pile is there
Of clothes that are unfit to wear,
A button off, a rip or two,
An overall with knee burst through.

Mending again!
Perhaps the same clothes fixed before,
With buttons off and ripped some more.
We sit and mend, and soon we learn,
Like bread on waters, 'twill return.

Mending again!
Day in, day out, the Master mends
The Christian's life, so full of rents,
Some caused by our own carelessness—
A broken heart in deep distress.

Mending again!
How patiently He comes and mends
With threads of love the selfsame rents,
Broken anew, bleeding and sore,
That He has fixed so oft before.

—*Clara Fennema*

THE SIN OF WASTE

"Use it up—wear it out—make it do—or do without!" used to be the motto of the careful American, but times have changed. Wasted food, broken toys and unnecessary luxuries have made destroyers out of us instead of builders.

One business executive accidentally tipped over a wastebasket and was amazed to see the useful items that fell out of it! He found a perfectly good memo pad, a clean envelope, an almost-new pencil and many paper clips and rubber bands. He computed their value at about 6 cents—but then he realized that his company had 2500 wastebaskets in the buildings! If each one contained 6 cents' worth of good materials, this would mean throwing away $150 a day—an annual loss of $36,000!

Jesus said, "Gather up the fragments that remain, that nothing be lost" (John 6:12). It is a sin to throw away that which is still useful, even if it may not be the latest model. We wonder how many missionaries could be supported out of the wastebaskets of Christian people!

(P.S. Wasted *time* is just as sinful. How important it is to use those "spare" minutes for prayer, meditation, reading, etc.)

INSTEAD OF BEING QUESTION
MARKS FOR CHRIST, WE NEED TO
BE EXCLAMATION POINTS!

YOUR HOME IS BUGGED!

Yes, your home is bugged. In every home there are two microphones per child—one in each ear. These highly sensitive instruments pick up the table prayers, the hymns sung, ordinary conversation, incidental remarks, types of language, a variety of words and intensities of sound. These all-absorbing microphones transmit all that they hear to highly impressionable minds. These sounds then become the vocabulary of the child and his basis for action and reaction.

—Copied

Babies

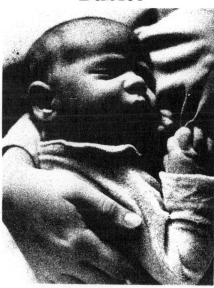

*They're made and sent from Heaven by
  The Father's loving care.
It's up to us to undergird
  And nurture them with prayer.
They don't belong to us, you know,
  Although they bear our name;
They still belong unto the One
  From whom they each one came.
We may not have them very long,
  Or maybe many years.
But in the time allotted us
  They'll share our hopes and fears.*

*We must, by charge, instill those things
  In pliant, childish minds
Which shall endure when all else fails.
  Faith is the tie that binds.
We may not have a lot of wealth
  Nor much of earthly store,
But if we give them faith in God,
  We give them much, much more
Than gold or silver. Things can rust;
  Their value pass away.
But what we give of heav'nly gain
  Shall never know decay.*

—Mary Mason

Keep on Keeping on!

I've dreamed many dreams that never came true.
  I've seen them vanish at dawn,
But I've realized enough of my dreams, thank God,
  To make me want to dream on.

I've prayed many prayers when no answer came,
  Though I waited patient and long,
But answers have come to enough of my prayers
  To make me keep praying on.

I've trusted many a friend that failed,
  And left me to weep alone,
But I've found enough of my friends true blue
  To make me keep trusting on.

I've sown many seeds that fell by the way
  For the birds to feed upon,
But I've held enough golden sheaves in my hands
  To make me keep sowing on.

I've drained the cup of disappointment and pain
  And gone many days without song,
But I've sipped enough nectar from the roses of life
  To make me want to live on.

—Author unknown

Nag, Nag, Nag!

Nagging has sent many a man to destruction and driven some women to despair. You can nag in any language that human lips have spoken. You can nag when your lips are tight shut by lifting the eyebrows, tossing the head or sneering a sneer. It is not confined to sex. It is due to disposition. The one who nags injures himself and is cruel in the extreme to the one attacked. A good, old-fashioned quarrel is preferable. If the continual dropping of water wears away a stone, it is no less true that constant nagging will ruin the best disposition.

If you have a complaint, make it, but don't nag. If you have been injured, say so, but don't nag. If you have a request to make, make it, but stop nagging.

Most people nag when they are tired; some, when they are ill or neglected; others, when they themselves are not right; and some, because of downright, old-fashioned meanness.

Nagging is a sin against yourself, your household, your husband, your wife, your friends. Why not list it with other sins? That is where it belongs. No Christian can be guilty of it and be a true follower of Jesus.

—*Selected*

A THANKFUL OLD LADY:

As an elderly lady with arthritis sat by her window watching the traffic go by, she said, "I don't know what I'd do without it."

Later on she was moved to a room in the rear where she could no longer see the traffic from her window. She commented, "I like this better. The sweetest children play in the backyard next door."

At last she was moved to the slums of the city. To a friend she said, "Come and see my beautiful view—my beautiful view of the sky!"

Heaven grows daily more dear

Oh, hasten the day of Your coming, dear Lord;
I'm weary of living down here.
Life's permanent things are not found on this earth,
And Heaven grows daily more dear.
I'm lonely and homesick; I want to go home.
Somewhere I've an empty abode
Where rust and decay will not ruin or destroy,
And nothing will ever corrode.

Life's permanent things are not found on this earth.
I'm tired of its clamor and din;
My heart is attuned to a far-distant plain
And hopes of Your coming again.
Don't tarry, sweet Jesus; there's smoke in the air;
The sounds of the battle impend.
Your chosen are restless; they wake from their sleep
With stirrings they don't comprehend.

Tomorrow lies shrouded, and yesterday's gone;
Today stands with uncertain eyes.
On tiptoe with wonder I breathlessly watch
Transfixed, with my gaze on the skies.
Oh, hasten that day! Don't tarry so long!
I'm weary of living down here.
Life's permanent things are not found on this earth,
And Heaven grows daily more dear.

—Mary Mason

Sharp Teacher

Down in Jackson, Mississippi, three boys arrived at school late. It was as late as 10:00 a.m. They had been fishing. For their excuse they stated that they were delayed because of a flat tire.

The teacher decided to give them a test immediately, so she had them seated apart from one another. She said, "This test will have only one question, and I will give you thirty seconds to put down your answer." The question was, "Which tire?"

The teacher was pretty sharp. There is no question as to the result of the test. The boys were shown to be liars.

Some psychologists say girls tend to marry men like their fathers. That may explain why so many mothers cry at weddings.

"HOW'S THAT AGAIN?"

"I know you think you understand what you think I am trying to say, but I don't think you understand that what you thought I said is what I really meant."

Bad Easter Egg

The story is told—it may even be true—of a lady pushing her way into church through the Easter crowd who was heard to mutter in exasperation, "You'd think these people who have nothing to do all year but go to church could stay home one day a year and give the rest of us a chance!"

An old farmer, when asked why he had never married, explained, "Well, I'd rather go through life wanting something I didn't have, than having something I didn't want."

INSCRIBED INSIDE A WEDDING RING: *"EACH FOR THE OTHER—BOTH FOR GOD."*

Which Smell Do You Prefer?

A mother leaned down to her small son while repairing his leg and asked, "How do you like my new perfume?"

"Mom," he answered, "I like you better when you're kitchen-flavored."

As the Twig Is Bent...

When Johnny was **six** years old, he was with his father when they were caught speeding. His father handed a five-dollar bill with his driver's license. "It's okay, son," his father said as they drove off; "everybody does it."

When he was **eight**, he was present at a family council, presided over by Uncle George, on the surest means to shave points off the income tax returns. "It's okay, kid," his uncle said; "everybody does it."

When he was **twelve**, he broke his glasses on the way to school. His Aunt Francine persuaded the insurance company that they had been stolen and then collected $27. "It's okay, son," she said; "everybody does it."

When he was **fifteen,** he made right guard on the high school football team. His coach showed him how to block and at the same time grab the opposing end by the shirt so the official couldn't see it. "It's okay, kid," the coach said; "everyone does it."

When he was **sixteen**, he took his first summer job at the supermarket. His assignment was to put the overripe tomatoes at the bottom of the boxes and the good ones on the top where they would show. "It's okay, kid," the manager said; "everyone does it."

When he was **eighteen**, Johnny and the neighbor boy applied for college scholarships. Johnny was a marginal student; his friend was in the upper three percent of his class, but he couldn't play right guard. Johnny got the scholarship. "It's okay, kid," he told his friend; "everybody does it."

When he was **nineteen**, he was approached by an upperclassman who offered test answers for $3. "It's okay, kid," he said; "everyone does it."

Johnny was caught and sent home in disgrace. "How could you do this to your mother and me?" asked his father. "You never learned anything like this at home." His aunt and uncle were also shocked.

If there's anything the ADULT WORLD can't stand, it's a KID WHO CHEATS.

—Jack Griffin
in Reimer Road Church Bulletin

"Divorce creates more problems than it solves."

A husband is upset if he isn't noticed.

Have you heard some husband say, "My wife never notices me. She is always gone from home when I get there!"? Every such complaint is saying, "My wife thinks I am unimportant." Nothing hurts worse than to be ignored. People end up in the divorce courts every day over being late to the concert or burning the toast at the breakfast table. It is the "little foxes that spoil the vines." "She made a fool out of me in public"; or, "She deliberately had liver and onions when she knows I don't like them"—these are ways of saying, "See, my wife doesn't think I am very important."

Ladies, try turning on that charm which won him and see the difference!

Distinguished Mutt

"What kind of a dog you got there, kid?" asked a passerby looking at the nondescript mongrel the boy had at his side.

"He's a German police dog," replied the youngster proudly.

"He surely doesn't look like one," the stranger remarked.

"Course not," said the boy disdainfully, "he's in the secret service."

Think on your own faults the first part of the night—when you are awake, and the faults of others the latter part of the night—when you are asleep.

IF YOU WANT ROSES IN NO-VEMBER, YOU WILL HAVE TO PUT THEM OUT IN THE SPRING-TIME OF LIFE.

—Henry A. Porter

We've got kids who have not yet sprouted long breeches, but they know more about sin and vice than Methuselah.

—Billy Sunday

x x x x

Our teacher was telling us about a new system of memory training being used in some schools today. "It works like this," she said.

"Suppose you wanted to remember the name of a poet—Robert Burns, for instance." She told us to think of him as Bobby Burns. "Now get in your head a picture of a London police-man, a bobby, in flames. See? Bobby Burns!"

"I see what you mean," said the class know-it-all. "But how can you tell that it's not Robert Browning?"

And then there was a lady who ate in a cafeteria where they make coffee the old-fashioned way—they urn it!

She looked exquisite, all in white;
This was her wedding day.
And eyes were misted as she vowed
To honor and obey.
But somehow as I watched the two,
So wonderfully in love,
Another wedding whelmed my soul—
A wedding up above.
I'm wondering if even now
The banquet table's laid
As angels stand in readiness,
Full preparations made,
And if, as Isaac, Jesus walks
Heav'ns fields at eventide,
Awaiting us, expecting us,
His precious blood-washed bride.
Glad maranathas thrill and stir
Our hearts. It can't be long!
I almost hear an angel choir
In measured wedding song.
Here comes the bride! Yes, here she comes,
The bride-church, all in white.
And soon descending from the clouds
Her Bridegroom, her delight!

—Mary Mason

Thank you, dear God,
For all You have given me;
For all You have taken away from me;
For all You have left me.

—Source Unknown

Never Carry a Whistling Bear to Church

By ROBERT W. GRAVES

The pause in the minister's sermon and the stillness of the sanctuary served only to accent the shrill whistle. Before the echo diminished, my head and eyes had darted to my two-year-old son, Michael, who was squeezing his rubber teddy bear. You know the kind, the ones with the two-way whistles—squeeze in and it whistles, let go and it whistles again.

I snatched the toy from Michael, breathing somewhat easier as I strangled the thing. Looking up, I found several people glaring at me. The obviously rattled minister glossed over the incident with some remark about a joyful noise. I slumped into my seat, my face flushed.

As inconspicuously as possible, I tried to catch my wife's attention, hoping for some sympathy. She was seated on the other side of Michael and, to my chagrin, had inched her way down the pew from us.

Traitor, I thought.

Several minutes passed, giving me time to recover my senses. There I was, a grown man, visiting a new church, with a rubber teddy bear compressed between my hands. I could sit through the sermon squeezing teddy and risk the chance of losing my grip, or . . . .

I know. I'll pry the whistle out and be done with it. Then it occurred to me how whistling teddy bears are made these days—safety regulations don't allow for easily removable parts.

Teddy had not inhaled yet, and my brain whirred frantically as Debbie continued to creep down the pew. Noticing that she left her purse behind, I figured I could stuff the toy inside. Trying to be inconspicuous again, I stretched out my leg to hook the strap of her purse with my foot.

Just a little farther, I consoled myself. Then suddenly . . . a seam in my trousers ripped.

I froze. Through the corner of my eye I could see my wife's red face. She was struggling to suppress a burst of laughter. I could hear her choking back the tears. For a moment, I didn't move a muscle.

What am I going to do?

Aided by the expansion in my trousers, I slipped my foot through the

strap and eventually drew the bag within reach. I placed the purse between my knees and unzipped it, thrusting teddy inside and pulling the zipper up to my wrist.

Slowly, I told myself. *Release it slowly.*

Then I discovered how impossible it is to stifle a whistling teddy. No matter how slowly I moved, it would not be denied. I froze again.

Now I was in an even worse predicament. Before, I could squeeze the toy as tightly as I wished. But since air had seeped in, I had to measure my grip—not too hard, not too soft.

This is ridiculous, I thought. *I'll take the bear outside and be done with it.* I didn't care anymore about what the people behind me would think.

Determined this was the thing to do, I reached down to unzip the bag, but the zipper wouldn't budge. There I was—a grown man sitting in church

with a tear in my pants, a teddy bear in my fist and my hand stuck in a woman's pocketbook.

Have mercy! my heart cried. *What next?*

I finally got up and walked down the aisle with my wife's purse dangling from the end of my arm. Reaching the vestibule, I asked one of the more friendly looking ushers, "Which way to the restroom?"

He smiled, looked at the purse and said, "Which one?"

I tried to hide my discomfort. Then a shrill squeak from the bag left the ushers in tears.

I backed my way into the men's room and placed the bag on the vanity. Releasing my grip on teddy allowed him to inhale. I sighed with relief.

—From *Moody Monthly,* February 1983
Mr. Graves is free-lance writer living in Atlanta, GA.

A House Without a Roof

In Scotland a young man was hired to help a farmer. He was given room and board in the farmer's home. But within a few days the young man had quit his job and moved out.

The next day when he met a friend of his in town, the friend immediately asked about his new position and if he enjoyed living in the farmer's home.

"I just quit my job," was the surprised answer he received.

"Was the salary too low?"

"No."

"Was the farmer good to you?"

"Oh, yes. He treated me like a member of his family."

"Then why did you leave?"

"I left because the house had no roof."

In Scotland that means there was no prayer in the home.

How sad to live in a home without prayer, without the Lord and without His holy Word! We must do our best to make our homes Christian homes.

Have You Heard?

GREAT MINDS DISCUSS IDEAS. AVERAGE MINDS DISCUSS EVENTS. LITTLE MINDS DISCUSS PEOPLE.

❧❧❧❧❧❧❧❧❧❧

Whatever parent gives his children good instruction, and sets them at the same time a bad example, may be considered as bringing them food in one hand and poison in the other.

—John Balguy

To marry a woman for her beauty is like buying a house for its paint.

Which Loved Her Best?

"I love you, Mother," said little John;
Then, forgetting his work, his cap went on,
And he was off to the garden swing,
Leaving his mother the wood to bring.

"I love you, Mother," said little Nell;
"I love you better than tongue can tell."
Then she teased and pouted half the day,
Till Mother rejoiced when she went to play.

"I love you, Mother," said little Fan;
"Today I'll help you all I can."
To the cradle then she did softly creep
And rocked the baby till she fell asleep.

Then, stepping softly, she took the broom
And swept the floor and dusted the room;
Busy and happy all day was she,
Helpful and cheerful as child could be.

"I love you, Mother," again they said—
Three little children going to bed.
How do you think that Mother guessed
Which of them really loved her best?

—*Allison*

What can a boy do, and where can a boy stay,
If he is always told to get out of the way?
He cannot sit here, and he must not stand there;
The cushions that cover that fine rocking chair
Were put there, of course, to be seen and admired;
A boy has no business to ever be tired.
The beautiful roses and flowers that bloom
On the floor of the darkened and delicate room
Are not made to walk on—at least not by boys;
The house is no place, anyway, for their noise.

Yet boys must walk somewhere; and what if their feet,
Sent out of our houses, sent into the street,
Should stop 'round the corner and pause at the door
Where other boys' feet have paused oft before;
Should pass through the gateway of glittering light,
Where jokes that are merry and songs that are bright
Ring a warm welcome with flattering voice,
And temptingly say, *"Here's a place for the boys"*?
Oh, what if they should! What if your boy or mine
Should cross o'er the threshold which marks out the line
'Twixt virtue and vice, 'twixt pureness and sin,
And leave all his innocent boyhood within!

Oh, what if they should, because you and I,
While the days and the months and the years hurry by,
Are too busy with cares and with life's fleeting joys
To make 'round our hearthstone a place for our boys!
There's a place for the boys. They'll find it somewhere;
And if our own homes are too daintily fair
For the touch of their fingers, the tread of their feet,
They'll find it, and find it, alas, in the street,
'Mid the gildings of sin and the glitter of vice.
And with heartaches and longings we pay a dear price.
For the getting of gain that our lifetime employs,
If we fail to provide a good place for the boys.

—*Author Unknown*

Just One Day to Fuss

A couple came to me in a revival meeting and said, "We have been married for twelve years. We love each other devotedly. Only one thing prevents our marriage from being an ideal wedlock: *We fuss over trifles!* How childish and unseemly! It is habitual! What can we do to overcome this disruptive evil?"

This situation was different from other marital problems I had ever dealt with. I thought and then came up with a novel plan:

"Suppose you designate one day in the week, say Tuesday, and call it *fuss day* and fuss only on that day."

They agreed. It worked. They began to think: *If we can refrain from fussing six days in the week, we can refrain from fussing seven days in the week.*

Often we can overcome evil habits and besetting sins by surmounting above them a day at the time. God deals with His children on a day-by-day basis: "Give us this day our daily bread" (Matt. 6:11).

A patient with a broken hip asked her doctor, "How long must I lie in this hospital bed?" The wise doctor replied, *"Just one day at a time!"*

Just for today, my Saviour,
Tomorrow is not mine;
Just for today I ask Thee
For light and health divine.
Tomorrow's care I must not bear,
The future is all Thine.

The Grand Old Book

Whenever my heart grows weary
With life's burden and weight of care,
I read for my solace the grand old Book,
Till my soul breaks forth in prayer.

And as I pore o'er the pages,
In the light which the Spirit sheds,
There comes a sweet thrill of devotion
Till meekly I bow my head.

For here I learn the secret
Which the key of promise holds,
And I would not miss communing
For the world and its weight in gold.

And soon I forget life's trials
And cry to be freed from pain,
In weeping and praising and blessing,
Rejoicing again and again.

And I cease to crave for the comforts
I once so longed to possess,
But instead I pray for His Spirit,
That His grace my life may bless.

Worldly minds are seeking pleasure,
Some in folly, some in gold;
But I've found, I've found life's treasure;
In this grand old Book of old.

—Unknown

A diplomatic husband said to his unhappy wife: "But dear, how do you expect me to remember your birthday when you never look one day older?"

I Reared a Criminal

In an issue of the *Ladies' Home Journal* was this article entitled, "I Reared a Criminal"—the true story of a heartbroken mother.

We loved him, but—

His father was too busy to be with him when he was young.

I couldn't bring myself to punish him for misbehavior.

We sided against his teachers when they complained about his work (and conduct) in school.

As he grew up, he would hardly discuss the time of day with us.

He was expelled from school.

We gave him money so he wouldn't steal again.

I wept when the police called and I had to turn my boy over to them. . . . As I watched them search him, my life seemed to end.

She who tells the faults of others to you will tell yours to another at her first opportunity.

"Mother," began little Marge, "what does 'transatlantic' mean?"

"Across the ocean," came the reply.

"But does 'trans' always mean 'cross'?"

"Yes, always," said the mother sternly, "and if you ask me another question tonight, I shall send you straight off to bed."

After a brief silence, however, little Marge braved the threatening storm by remarking: "Then, I suppose 'transparent' means 'a cross parent.' "

A Christian Home

Where family prayer is daily said,
God's Word is regularly read,
And faith in Christ is never dead—
That is a Christian home.

Where father, mother, sister, brother,
All have true love for one another
And no one ever hates the other—
That is a Christian home.

Where family quarrels are pushed aside
To let the love of God abide
Ere darkness falls on eventide—
That is a Christian home.

—Selected

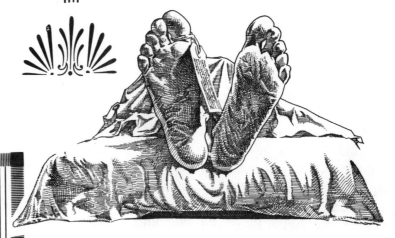

Wit and Wisdom

Too many of us spend money we haven't earned to buy things we don't need just to impress a lot of people we don't like.

A SWITCH IN TIME SAVES CRIME.

Unguided Feet

A certain boy in a Sunday school made things very difficult for his teachers. The last one went to the superintendent and submitted the ultimatum to him, "Either that boy goes or I go! Take your choice!"

The superintendent escorted the boy to the door and said, "There's the street. Go! And don't you ever come back to this Sunday school!"

The boy went into the world and led a life of crime which has possibly never been paralleled in the history of the nation. He left a trail of blood behind him wherever he went. Fabulous rewards were offered for his capture, either dead or alive.

At last, one night, as he emerged from the Chicago theater, a hail of bullets riddled his body.

In one of the Chicago papers a most unusual picture appeared—that showed only the feet of the criminal. In bold type the caption read, **These Are the Feet of John Dillinger,** followed by the searching question, **Who knows where these feet might have gone if someone had guided them aright?**

How essential it is to guide young feet into paths of righteousness. "Let no man despise thy youth" (I Tim. 4:12). And how essential it is for the youths to heed the admonition, "Remember now thy Creator in the days of thy youth, while the evil days come not, nor the years draw nigh, when thou shalt say, I have no pleasure in them" (Eccl. 12:1).

He Knows Us by Name!

Isn't that a blessed thought! The meeting between our Lord and Mary after His resurrection gives us a lovely picture of what that means to us individually who belong to Him. She knew Him when He simply spoke her name—"Mary." It was only one word; but with it came recognition, relief and reassurance. It told her that the very One she had known and loved had not left her desolate but was alive again and had conquered Death.

Our given names are very personal. Sometimes acquaintances of past years forget, and when we meet they do not recall our names. But the Lord Jesus knows everyone who is His, and He never forgets our names. We have His sure word for it: "... The Lord knoweth them that are his" (II Tim. 2:19).

And I can believe that everyone who goes to sleep in Jesus and awakes in His glorious presence doubtless hears Him speak his or her name, as His weeping friend did in the garden, when He said with such love and tenderness, "Mary."

And I don't believe the Lord will welcome "Miss Walden" Home, but that it will be a more personal welcome—

Viola

—*Viola Walden*

Building a Home

The walls of a house are not built of wood, brick or stone, but of truth and loyalty.

Unpleasant sounds, the friction of living, the clash of personalities are not deadened by Persian rugs or polished floors, but by conciliation, concession and self-control.

The house is not a structure where bodies meet, but a hearthstone upon which flames mingle, separate flames of souls which, the more perfectly they unite, the more clearly they shine and the straighter they rise toward Heaven.

Your house is your fortress in a warring world, where a woman's hand buckles on your armor in the morning and soothes your fatigue and wounds at night.

The beauty of a house is harmony.

The security of a house is loyalty.

The joy of a house is love.

The plenty of a house is in children.

The rule of a house is service.

The comfort of a house is in contented spirits.

The maker of a house, a real human house, is God Himself, the same One who made the stars and built the world.

—*Emmanuel Baptist News.*

What is the key that unlocks the door to happiness? Remember that being happy does not always mean getting your own way. Sometimes happiness is the by-product of losing ourselves. The Teacher of Galilee one time said, "Whosoever will save his life shall lose it."

"Mary, Mary, will you marry me?"

Five hundred years ago Maximilian of Austria longed to wed Mary of Burgundy and didn't know how to approach the subject. The perplexed prince took his problem to an older man and asked his advice on how to impress the noble lady.

The old man suggested that Max give his beloved "a ring set with a diamond." The prince followed the advice, had a ring designed and made, and offered it to Mary with proper explanation. Her response was a positive one, and the prince slipped the ring on her finger.

With this incident a beautiful custom was established—for the betrothed and for the jeweler.

Garbage in the Salad

One day as a mother was scraping and peeling the vegetables for a salad, her daughter came to ask her permission to go to a worldly center of amusement. On the defensive, the daughter admitted it was a questionable place, but all the other girls were going, and they did not think it would actually hurt them.

As the girl talked, suddenly she saw her mother pick up a handful of discarded vegetable scraps and throw them into the salad. In a startled voice she cried, "Mother, you are putting the garbage in the salad!"

"Yes," her mother replied, "I know; but I thought that, if you did not mind garbage in your mind and heart, you certainly would not mind a little in your stomach!"

Thoughtfully the girl removed the offending material from the salad, and with a brief "Thank you" to her mother she went to tell her friends she would not be going with them.

If you have spiritual indigestion and have a sick testimony, maybe it's because you have allowed TOO MUCH "GARBAGE IN THE SALAD"!

"God Was Standing By"

Today I did my ironing;
 The stacks were piled real high.
Somehow it seemed no chore at all,
 For God was standing by!

I talked with Him and He with me;
 My iron just fairly flew.
Before I knew it, I looked up;
 The stacks were almost through!

And as I ironed my clothes with love,
 God's love did me enfold;
I knew that God was ironing too
 The wrinkles from my soul!

—Varina C. McWhorter
in *Home Life.*

How a Godly Mother Reared Her 19 Children

What a saintly soul Susannah Wesley was! The mother of nineteen children, including John and Charles Wesley, she dedicated her large brood to God and did not consult child guidance textbooks for guidance as to the preservation from evil in the lives of her children. Here are the Sixteen Rules she laid down, over 200 years ago, for keeping her many sons and daughters in the paths of righteousness.

1. Eating between meals not allowed.
2. As children they are to be in bed by eight p.m.
3. They are required to take medicine without complaining.
4. Subdue self-will in a child, and thus work together with God to save the child's soul.
5. Teach a child to pray as soon as he can speak.
6. Require all to be still during Family Worship.
7. Give them nothing that they cry for and only that which they ask for politely.
8. To prevent lying, punish no fault which is first confessed and repented of.
9. Never allow a sinful act to go unpunished.
10. Never punish a child twice for a single offense.
11. Commend and reward good behavior.
12. Any attempt to please, even if poorly performed, should be commended.
13. Preserve property rights, even in smallest matters.
14. Strictly observe all promises.
15. Require no daughter to work before she can read well.
16. Teach children to fear the rod.

The man on a business trip received a letter from his wife containing a sketch of their car's instrument panel. Attached was a note: "This is exactly the way the dashboard looks. Do we need a quart of oil?"

A lady was entertaining her friend's small son. "Are you sure you can cut your meat?" she asked, after watching his struggles.

"Oh, yes," he replied, without looking up from his plate. "We often have it as tough as this at home."

BABIES: ANGELS WHOSE WINGS GROW SHORTER AS THEIR LEGS GROW LONGER.

ALL HELL CANNOT TEAR A BOY OR GIRL AWAY FROM A PRAYING MOTHER.

—*Billy Sunday*

Deceptive Packaging

Through its laws, our country declares it a crime to lie about the contents in a box of cereal. These laws demand that the outside of the package tell the truth about what is on the inside.

Deceptive packaging is illegal. "Truth in advertising" regulations are another way to protect the public. A good example of this is the warning on a pack of cigarettes: Smoking causes lung cancer, heart disease, emphysema, and may complicate pregnancy."

Unfortunately, there are no such laws about people. We require no one to tell what really lies behind the packaging—the clothes, facial expressions, mannerisms, speech patterns or affected behavior. No one is forced to tell you what he or she is really feeling, thinking or planning to do.

Our deceptive packaging—the way we appear to others—is an accepted, even an expected, part of our way of life. We have become experts in this type of trickery. Before we are going to get the help we need, we need to confess this sin of hypocrisy. Only then can we go on the path of discovering and knowing our real selves.

—*Peter Lord*

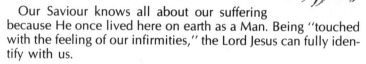

"I Guess She'll Need a Lot of Love"

"For we have not an high priest which cannot be touched with the feeling of our infirmities."—Heb. 4:15.

Our Saviour knows all about our suffering because He once lived here on earth as a Man. Being "touched with the feeling of our infirmities," the Lord Jesus can fully identify with us.

Someone put up a sign:

PUPPIES FOR SALE

Among those who came to inquire was a young boy. "Please, Mister," he said, "I'd like to buy one if they don't cost too much."

"Well, son, they're $25."

The boy looked crushed, "I've only got $2.05. Could I see them anyway?"

"Of course. Maybe we can work something out."

The lad's eyes danced at the sight of those five little balls of fur. "I heard that one has a bad leg," he said.

"Yes, I'm afraid she's crippled for life."

"Well, that's the puppy I want. Could I pay for her a little at a time?"

The man responded, "But she'll always have a limp."

Smiling bravely, the boy pulled up one pant leg, revealing a brace. "I don't walk good either." Then looking at the puppy sympathetically, he continued: "I guess she'll need a lot of love and help. I sure did. It's not so easy being crippled."

"Here, take her," said the man. "I know you'll give her a good home. And just forget the money."

The boy's own experience had given him feeling for the puppy.

That is an accurate illustration of our Saviour's sympathetic understanding. Having suffered Himself, He has a compassion far beyond human measure.

Jesus is touched by your distress and grief. Trust yourself to His care. His arms of love will enfold you and carry you through every trial.

No one understands like Jesus.
Every woe He sees and feels;
Tenderly He whispers comfort,
And the broken heart He heals.

—*Peterson*

A Children's Heaven

Heaven is greatly made up of little children—sweet buds that have never blown, or which death has plucked from a mother's bosom to lay on his cold breast, just when they were expanding flower-like from the sheath and opening their engaging beauties in the budding time and spring of life. "Of such is the kingdom of heaven." Indeed it may be that God does with His heavenly garden as we do with our own gardens. He may chiefly stock it from nurseries and select for transplanting what is yet in its young and tender age—flowers before they have bloomed, and trees ere they begin to bear.

—*Guthrie*

IT'S A HAPPY HOME WHERE THE ONLY SCRAPS ARE THOSE BRUSHED OFF THE DINING TABLE.

Why does a rooster crow early in the morning? Because he can't get in a word after the hens get up.

Sign on the door of a marriage license bureau:

OUT TO LUNCH—THINK IT OVER

I'm Getting Ready to Move

Father Time is telling me every day
That the house I live in is wearing away;
The building is old, and for the days that remain
To seek to repair it would be quite in vain,
    So I'm getting ready to move.

In this house of mine I have seen many joys,
Have watched from its windows the girls and the boys
Grow to womanhood and manhood so fine.
To leave this old house will not make me repine,
    So I'm getting ready to move.

But a wonderful King has sent me the news
That He's building a place from which I may choose
A house most beautiful that is not built with hands;
'Tis far, far away on the bright golden strands,
    So I'm getting ready to move.

Now the news has gone forth that quickly someday
As a flash in the sky of the lightning's ray
This King will return and take His subjects away;
And He bids me joyfully watch for the day.
    I'm bound to be ready to move.

—Author Unknown

Men Will Sleep; Women Will Watch

In our Civil War, men cast the cannon, fashioned the musketry, cried to the hosts, "Forward, march!" Men hurled their battalions on the sharp edges of the enemy, crying, "Charge! Charge!" But women scraped the lint, ministered to the wounds, watched by the dying couch, wept at the solitary burial, attended by herself and four men with a spade.

We greeted the generals home with brass bands, triumphal arches and wild huzzas. But the story is too good to be written anywhere, save in the chronicles of Heaven, of Mrs. Brady, who came down among the sick in the swamps of the Chickahominy; of Annie Ross, in the cooper-shop hospital; of Margaret Breckinridge, who came to men who had been for weeks with their wounds undressed—some of them frozen to the ground, and when she turned them over, those who had an arm left, waved it and filled the air with their "Hurrah!"; of Mrs. Hodge, who came from Chicago with blankets and pillows, until the men shouted, "Three cheers for the Christian Commission!"

God bless the women sitting down to take the last message: "Tell my wife not to fret about me, but to meet me in Heaven; tell her to train up the boys whom we have loved so well; tell her we shall meet again in the good land; tell her to bear my loss like the Christian wife of a Christian soldier." Of Mrs. Shelton, into whose face the convalescent soldier looked and said, "Your grapes and cologne cured me."

So it was also through the war with Spain—women heroic on the field, braving death and wounds to reach the fallen, watching by their fever cots in the West Indian hospitals or on the troopships or in our smitten home camps.

Men did their work with shot, shell, carbine and howitzer; women did their work with socks, slippers, bandages, warm drinks, coffee, Scripture texts, gentle strokings of the hot temples and stories of that land where they never have any pain.

Men knelt down over the wounded and said, "On which side did you fight?" Women knelt down over wounded and said, "Where are you hurt? What nice thing can I make for you to eat? What makes you cry?"

Tonight, while we men are sound asleep in our beds, there will be a light in yonder loft; there will be groaning down the dark alley; there will be cries of distress in that cellar.

Men will sleep, and women will watch.

—*T. DeWitt Talmage*

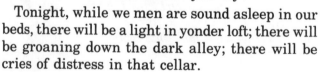

MUST WE BE BOUND BY TRADITION?

What Makes Us Beautiful?

It would be sheer hypocrisy, because we may not have personal charms ourselves, to despise or affect to despise beauty in others. When God gives it, He gives it as a blessing and as a means of usefulness.

David and his army were coming down from the mountains to destroy Nabal and his flocks and vineyards. The beautiful Abigail, the wife of Nabal, went out to arrest him when he came down from the mountains. She succeeded.

Coming to the foot of the hill, she knelt. David, with his army of sworn men, came down over the cliffs. When he saw her kneeling at the foot of the hill, he cried, "Halt! Halt!"

That one beautiful woman kneeling at the foot of the cliff had arrested all those armed troops. A dewdrop dashed back Niagara. The Bible sets before us the portraits of Sarah, Rebecca, Abishag and Job's daughter and says, "They were fair to look upon."

By outdoor exercise and by skillful arrangement of apparel, let women make themselves attractive. The sloven has only one mission: to excite our loathing and disgust.

But, alas, for those who depend upon personal charms for their happiness! Beauty is such a subtle thing. It does not seem to depend upon facial proportions, the sparkle of the eye or the flush of the cheek. You sometimes find it among irregular features. It is the soul shining through the face that makes one beautiful.

—*T. DeWitt Talmage*

The six-year-old daughter of a clergyman was sick and was put to bed early. As her mother was about to leave, she called her back. "Mommy, I want to see Daddy."

"No, dear; Daddy is busy and must not be disturbed."

"But, Mommy," the child persisted, "I want to see my daddy."

Mother again replied, "No, your daddy must not be disturbed."

But the little one came back with even more determination: "Mommy, I am a sick woman, and I want to see my minister."

*   *   *

Life is so short that someone has remarked: "The wood of the cradle all but scratches the marble of the grave."

"finis"

No matter what else you are doing—
  From cradle days through to the end—
You're writing your life's secret-story.
  Each day sees another page penned,
Each month ends a thirty-page chapter,
  Each year means the end of a part,
And never an act is misstated,
  Nor ever a wish from the heart.

Each day when you wake the book opens
  Revealing a page clean and white:
What thoughts and what words and what actions
  Will cover its surface by night?
God leaves that to you—you're the writer,
  And never one word shall grow dim
Till someday you write the word "Finis"
  And give back your life book to Him.

                  —Author unknown

Don't Be Another Potiphar's Wife

A woman—possibly a very beautiful lady—once tempted a youth. He was the Joseph of our Old Testament. Joseph did not commit the great sin. When Potiphar's wife took hold of Joseph to coerce him, he lost his coat—but not his character! The young man stood as firmly morally as if he had been an unmoveable mountain.

Of course no one knows what might have resulted had Joseph sinned. All the good he did in his 110-year life, much of which was spent as prime minister of Egypt, would have been rewritten with the record of so many years of sin, spent perhaps as a bad character, a good-for-nothing.

Somewhere recently I read these words: "Boys will be boys, yes, and they have a habit of becoming men."

Joseph made his first step in the right way. "The steps of a good man are ordered by the Lord"—and so are his stops!

Women, let us be careful how we dress, act, behave toward men. Don't be another Potiphar's wife!

••••

One man said, "It's terrible to grow old alone. My wife hasn't had a birthday in ten years."

A SMILE CAN ADD A GREAT DEAL TO ONE'S FACE VALUE.

THE REALLY HAPPY PERSON IS ONE WHO CAN ENJOY THE SCENERY WHEN ON A DETOUR.

When a frazzled mother sent her little boy to bed, she heard him grumbling to himself, "Every time she gets tired, it's me that has to take a nap."

Dr. Kelly Pays in Full

Dr. Howard Kelly was a renowned physician and surgeon, and, with-al, a devout, practicing Christian.

During the summer holidays when in medical school, Dr. Kelly sold books to help with expenses. Becoming thirsty, he stopped one day at a farmhouse for a glass of water. A girl came to the door. When he asked for a glass of water, she sweetly said, "I will give you a glass of milk if you wish!" He drank the cool, refreshing milk heartily.

The years passed. Dr. Kelly graduated from medical school and became the chief surgeon in the Johns Hopkins Hospital.

One day a seriously ill patient was admitted to the great hospital. She was given special care and placed in a private room with a private nurse. The skilled chief surgeon spared no effort to make the patient well.

After undergoing surgery, she convalesced rapidly.

One day she was told by the head nurse, "Tomorrow you will go home!" Her joy was somewhat less-ened by the thought of the large bill she must owe the hospital and surgeon. When she asked for it, the nurse brought the itemized bill.

With a heavy heart, the pa-tient began to read the different items from the top downward. She sighed. But as her eyes lowered, she saw the following notation at the bottom of the large bill:

Paid in full with one glass of milk!

It was signed: Howard A. Kelly, M.D.

Americans are getting strong-er. Twenty years ago it took two people to carry $25 worth of groceries. Today, a child can handle them well.

Which One?

One of us, dear—
  But one—
Will sit by the bed with marvel-
  ous fear
And clasp the hand
Growing cold as it feels for the
  spirit land—
  Darling, which one?

One of us, dear—
  But one—
Will stand by the other's coffin
  pier
And look and weep,
While those marble lips strange
  silence keep—
  Darling, which one?

One of us, dear—
  But one—
By an open grave will drop a
  tear
And homeward go,
The anguish of an unshared
  grief to know—
  Darling, which one?

One of us, darling, it must be;
  It may be you will slip from me,
Or perhaps my life may first
  be done;
I'm glad we do not know
  Which one.

—From *Home Duties*,
published by Moody Press

A young couple were deciding on a name for their new offspring.

"I've decided on a name for the baby," said the young mother. "I shall call her Euphrosyne."

Her husband didn't care for the selection; but being a tactful fellow, he was far too wise to voice his objection.

"Splendid," he said cheerfully. "The first girl I ever loved was called Euphrosyne, and the name will revive pleasant memories."

There was a brief period of silence; then, "We'll call her Elizabeth, after your mother," said the young wife firmly.

Freedom's Perfect Light

Not more light I ask, O Lord,
  But eyes to see what is;
Not sweeter songs, but ears to hear
  The present melodies.

Not more strength, but how to use
  The power that I possess;
Not more of love, but skill to turn
  A frown to a caress.

Not more of joy, but how to feel
  The loving presence here,
To give to others all I have
  Of courage and of cheer.

Not other gifts, dear Lord, I ask
  But only sight to see
How best those precious gifts to use
  Thou hast bestowed on me.

Give me all fears to dominate,
  All purest joys to know.
To be the friend I wish to be,
  To speak the truth I know.

To love the pure, to seek the good,
  To help with all my might
All souls to dwell in harmony,
  In freedom's perfect light.
          —Florence Holbrook

A love this big, this high

"I love you more than you love me,"
  My little grandson said.
"I love you most!" I challenged him,
  Then tucked him into bed,
And then he'd measure with his arms
  A love "this big, this high.
You cannot love me more than this,
  It's bigger than the sky."
This act became a ritual,
  And every single night
We had to play this bedtime game
  Before I dimmed the light,
And then I got to wondering,
  What love do I portray?
Do I play games like this with God
  When I kneel down to pray?
O Lord, forbid that I mouth words.
  Let tongue and lips proclaim
The height of love, the depth of love;
  Don't let me play a game.
So often weariness would tempt
  A token prayer at night,
But at such time possess my tongue
  And pray the prayer that's right.
As moon and stars reflect the rays
  Of sun-glow, Lord, so I
Absorb Your love, then give it back—
  "A love this big, this high."
          —Mary Mason

Adam and Eve had an ideal marriage: he didn't have to hear about all the men she could have married; she didn't have to hear about the ways his mother cooked it.

She Feathered His Nest!

The young husband wrote home from his new job: "Made foreman—feather in my cap."

A few weeks later he wrote again: "Made manager—another feather in my cap."

After some weeks, he wrote again: "Fired—send money for train fare."

His wife unfeelingly telegraphed back: "Use feathers and fly home."

All husbands are alike, but they have different faces so you can tell them apart.

Fanny Crosby's Determination

We can learn a lot from reading biographies!

S. Trevena Jackson has written such a book entitled *Fanny Crosby's Story*. As we all know, Fanny Crosby was a famous hymn writer, and today we still sing her hymns.

But Fanny's life was not without difficulties. Through illness she became blind when but a baby, but she didn't let her handicap spoil her fruitfulness for the Lord.

When she was in the sunset years of her life, she said:

> During these ninety years I have been careful of cultivating a sunny disposition, for I have found in my experience so many who when they grow old become bitter and difficult to get along with. I made up my mind, years ago, that I would never become a disagreeable old woman, and that wherever I went I would take sunshine. I belong to the Sunshine Society. It is my purpose in old age to grow ripe and rich and heavenly. I must be loved rather than feared.

Isn't that terrific!

Fanny didn't become a sweet, loving lady overnight. She worked at it. In fact, she was determined that her life would always give forth the sweet savor of Jesus Christ.

There were probably days when Fanny was tempted "just for today" to let herself go, to insist upon her rights, or to give in to some disappointment. But she knew this was a battle you can't leave even for a day, and she didn't.

In a sense deeper than the meaning Zophar had when he said these words, we can say of such people as Fanny Crosby, "And thine age shall be clearer than the noonday; thou shalt shine forth, thou shalt be as the morning" (Job 11:17).

Where Did the Woodshed Go?

There is one thing I miss in our modern new homes: it's the old kitchen stove and the *woodbox* behind it that had to be filled every morning. An ever greater loss in our modern homes, however, is the old-fashioned WOODSHED! Its use was not only to be a storehouse for beech and maple stove wood; it was also a "schoolroom" where often a valuable lesson was driven home which would not soon be forgotten.

I still believe in the "woodshed" as the place to train disobedient and recalcitrant children—especially in the light of our modern pedagogy of "self expression" which frequently condones the folly of letting a child give vent to all its emotions.

The Bible way is still best! We have experimented long enough with the wishy-washy, namby-pamby, pantywaist philosophy that we must never spank our children lest we hinder their "expression patterns" and cause "damaging frustrations and inhibitions."

As the old saying goes: "The proof of the pudding is in the eating," and the mounting number of delinquents and teenage sadists is its own commentary on the effectiveness of this new twist in child training. If Johnny is Mama's "little angel," why then does he act so much "like the Devil"?

We hear so much about "revival" today, but see little of it. What is needed more than anything else is an old-fashioned "WOODSHED REVIVAL"! Unless we as parents learn to practice BIBLE child training, things will never get better. We need a revival of well-administered "spankings" in a place where you can't break any bones. If you disagree with me, you don't believe what God says in Proverbs 13:24; 19:18; 23:13; and 29:17.

Let's get back to God's Word and the tried-and-true principles of the woodshed!

THOT: Realizing that Christian citizens usually develop from well-disciplined children, my father often proved he was a very patriotic man: he applied the "stripes" to me and I saw "stars"!

—By Richard DeHaan

Children sometimes have questions about the Holy Family that can't be answered by the Scriptures. A 7-year-old told his mother, "I know who the Virgin Mary was...but who was the King James Virgin?"

Miss Daisy's Sandwich Shop opened in East Chattanooga around the first of the year. It is now closed and on the window is this notice: OPENED BY MISTAKE.

Menu

"Why didn't you stop when I blew my whistle?" demanded the cop.

"I'm a little deaf," the lady driver explained apologetically.

"Well, don't worry," the officer reassured her. "You'll get your hearing tomorrow."

Woe to the house where the HEN crows louder than the ROOSTER.

TO KEEP A SMALL BOY OUT OF THE COOKIE JAR, LOCK IT AND HIDE THE KEY UNDER A CAKE OF SOAP.

"My husband just refuses to put up those storm windows for me!"

Think back! Perhaps you approached it wrong. Nagging never works, but a chocolate pie sometimes does. Suggest that while he puts up the windows you will bake his favorite pie.

A tongue three inches long can ruin a man six feet tall.

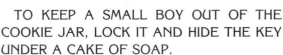

In order to maintain a balanced perspective on life, the one who has a dog to adore her should also have a cat to ignore her.

"Forgive Us Our Ulcers!"

In one of his prayers in the U. S. Senate, Peter Marshall prayed, "O Lord, forgive us our ulcers, the badges of our anxieties and insecurities!"

To allay anxious fears and corroding cares, many resort to tranquilizers, which are now the largest selling prescription drugs in the United States.

Quiet trust in the provident care of God is the best remedy for corroding care and anxious, disquieting fears: "Trust in the Lord with all thine heart . . . and depart from evil" (Prov. 3:5,7).

Marriage resembles a pair of shears, so joined that they cannot be separated; often moving in opposite directions, yet always punishing anyone who comes between them.

"Religion Runs in My Family"

H. A. Ironside sat in a railway coach reading his Bible. A woman, sitting across the aisle from him, said, "I am glad to see that there is at least one religious person on this train beside myself."

In reply, Dr. Ironside said, "That's interesting. Tell me more."

She said, "Two of my uncles are ministers and their father before them was a minister. So you see, religion runs in my family."

Dr. Ironside said, "Let's assume that your kinsmen are born-again believers through faith in Christ. You don't want to go to Heaven hanging on their coattails, do you? Salvation is a personal matter. One must individually accept Christ as one's only hope of eternal life and a home in Heaven.

"Isn't it interesting that the Saviour said to a devoutly *religious* man, 'Except a man be born again, he cannot see the kingdom of God'" (John 3:3)?

A puzzled look came on the face of the woman as she replied, "You don't seem to understand that religion runs in our family, and I am a very religious person."

As the woman arrived at her destination and left the train, Dr. Ironside mused, *How tragic! Religious but lost!*

To a Departed Mother

My Good Mother:

Now, as I stand here, you do not see any hand outstretched towards me, and yet there are hands on both my shoulders. They are hands of parental benediction. It is quite a good many years ago now since we folded those hands as they began their last sleep on the banks of the Raritan, in the village cemetery; but those hands are stretched out towards me today, and they are just as warm and they are just as gentle as when I sat on her knee at five years of age.

And I shall never shake off those hands. I do not want to. They have helped me so much a thousand times already, and I do not expect to have a trouble or a trial between this and my grave where those hands will not help me.

It was not a very splendid home, as the world calls it; but we had a family Bible there, well worn by tender perusal; and there was a family altar there, where we knelt morning and night; and there was a holy Lord's Day there; and stretched in a straight line or hung in loops or festoons, there was a scarlet line in the window.

Oh, the tender, precious, blessed memory of a Christian home!

Is that the impression you are making upon your children? When you are dead—and it will not be long before you are—when you are dead, will your child say: "If there ever was a good Christian father, mine was one. If there ever was a good Christian mother, mine was one"?

—T. DeWitt Talmage

No person was ever honored for what he/she received. Honor is the reward for what he/she gave.

In Which House Do You Live?

"I got two A's," the small boy cried.
His voice was filled with glee.
His father bluntly asked,
 "Why didn't you get three?"

"Mom, I've got the dishes done,"
 The girl called from the door.
Her mother very calmly said,
 "Did you sweep the kitchen floor?"

"I've mowed the grass," the tall boy
 said,
 "And put the mower away."
The father, looking at the rug,
 "Didn't you clean off the clay?"

The children in the house next door
 Seem happy and content.
The same things happened over there,
 But this is how it went:

"I got two A's," the small boy cried.
His voice was filled with glee.
His father proudly said, "That's great;
 I'm glad you belong to me."

"Mom, I've got the dishes done,"
 The girl called from the door.
Her mother smiled and softly said,
 "Each day I love you more."

"I've mowed the grass," the tall boy
 said,
 "And put the mower away."
His father answered with much joy,
 "Son, you have made my day!"

Children deserve a little praise
 For tasks they're asked to do;
If they're to lead a happy life,
 So much depends on you.

—Badger Legionnaire

The Last Hug

The wedding was about to begin. The groom was nervous. The bride was radiant. The guests were in their places. I was trying to calm the anxiety-stricken groomsmen.

Then the father of the bride caught my attention. Serene. Pensive. Almost tearful. "I wonder when the last time was that I picked her up and held her," he said. "I mean the *very last time.* I don't remember. Was she six, seven or maybe nine? I don't remember. I only know that, if I would have realized that it was the last time to hold my little girl, I would have held her longer, tighter and with more feeling."

"*The Last Time!*" Those are serious words. The last football game for the quarterback. The last workday for the retiree. The last kiss for the widow. The last time.

What if you were to invest your energy into every day as if it were your last day? How would it be different from the routine? Think of the automatic change this would make in most of our relationships with parents, children, spouse, friends.

Are there feelings in your heart that are destined to stay locked inside? The body in the coffin does not hear the words of the loved one standing beside it.

Whoever the writer of Hebrews was, he certainly understood this principle.

"*To day if ye will hear his voice, Harden not your hearts*" (3:7,8).

"*. . . exhort one another daily, while it is called To day*" (3:13).

Today there may be opportunities which may never come again. Doors may be open today which tomorrow may be shut. There will be a last hug for all of us.

. . .A last church service.

. . .A last singing of a favorite hymn.

. . .A last kiss.

. . .A last goodbye.

. . .A last hug.

—Terry Bell

A hundred years ago today
   A wilderness was here;
A man with powder in his gun
   Went forth to hunt a deer.

But now the times have
   changed somewhat
Along a different plan:
A dear with powder on her
   nose
   Goes forth to hunt a man.

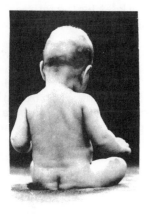

Instructions

I searched,
but there definitely was not
a packet of instructions
attached to my children
when they arrived.
And none has since
landed in the mailbox.
Lord, show me how
to be a good parent!
Teach me to
correct without crushing,
help without hanging on,
listen without laughing at,
surround without smothering,
and love without limit—
the way You love me!

              —Susan Lenzkes

First Ten Years Most Important

No years are so important for impression as the first ten. Then and there is the impression made for virtue or vice, for truth or falsity, for bravery or cowardice, for religion or skepticism.

Suddenly start out from behind a door and frighten the child, and you shatter his nervous system for a lifetime.

During the first ten years you can tell him enough spook stories to make him a coward until he dies.

Act before him as though Friday were an unlucky day and it were baleful to have thirteen at the table or see the moon over the left shoulder, and he will never recover from the idiotic superstitions.

You may give that girl before she is ten years old a fondness for dress that will make her a mere "dummy frame" or fashion plate for forty years. "As is the mother, so is her daughter."

Before one decade has passed, you can decide whether that boy shall be a Shylock or a George Peabody. Boys and girls are generally echoes of fathers and mothers. What an incoherent thing for a mother out of temper to punish a child for getting mad, or for a father who smokes to shut his boy up in a dark closet because he has found him with an old stump of a cigar in his mouth, or for that mother to rebuke her daughter for staring at herself too much in the mirror when the mother has her own mirrors so arranged as to repeat her form from all sides!

The great English poet's loose moral character was decided before he left the nursery. His schoolmaster in the schoolroom overheard this conversation: "Byron, your mother is a fool." He answered, "I know it."

You can hear all through the heroic life of Senator Sam Houston

the words of his mother when she, in the War of 1812, put a musket in his hand and said, "There, my son, take this and never disgrace it, for remember I had rather all my sons should fill one honorable grave than that one of them should turn his back on an enemy. Go and remember, too, that while the door of my cottage is open to all brave men, it is always shut against cowards."

Agrippina—the mother of Nero, a murderess—you are not surprised that her son was a murderer.

Give that child an overdose of catechism, make him recite verses of the Bible as a punishment, make Sunday a bore, and he will become a stout antagonist of Christianity. Impress him with the kindness, the geniality, the loveliness of religion; and he will be its advocate and exemplar for all time and eternity.

On one occasion while I was traveling in the West on the Louisville and Nashville Railroad, the preceding train had gone down through a broken bridge, twelve cars falling a hundred feet, then consumed. I saw that only one span of the bridge was down and all others were standing.

Plan a good bridge of morals for your sons and daughters; but have the first span of ten years defective, and through that they will crash down, though all the rest keep standing.

              —T. DeWitt Talmage

These days, if you see a housewife on her hands and knees, she's probably just lost a contact lens.

Once Every Seven Days It's Sunday Morning!

The chance of things going haywire on a Sunday morning are at least seven times greater than on any other morning of the week. Dead car batteries, hot water that is cold, milk that is sour, wet underwear, clogged toilets, stuck zippers, stained suits, cologne mistaken for mouthwash, lost Bibles, curling irons that hiss, nylons that run, sick puppies, power failure, touchy tempers, grumpy attitudes and daylight saving time. Thieves break in on Saturday nights just to steal one of a nicely matched pair of socks.

What is really happening? First, God is not honored. Attitudes for proper worship are formed in advance. Isaiah spoke of those who worshiped the Lord with their lips while their hearts were far from God (Isa. 29:13). It is next to impossible to worship God with the latest family feud still on your mind.

Second, God's Spirit is hindered. Enthusiastic song leaders grow discouraged trying to lead people who are still steaming over cross words fired 15 minutes ago. So what can be done to arrive for church on time with a minimum of frustration? Have the kids sleep in the car? Camp out in the church parking lot? Here are some ideas that may help.

Guard Saturday night functions. Late Saturday nights are the prelude to chaotic Sunday mornings. Plan to get to bed early. "Early to bed, early to rise, makes Sundays a pleasant surprise."

Plan ahead. It was not raining when Noah built the ark. Set out clothes, shoes, socks, diaper bags, strollers and Bibles ahead of time. If sufficient hot water is a problem,

schedule some family members for a Saturday night bath.

Dad, do you think you could help Mom get the kids ready while she prepares breakfast? This is particularly important when the children are small. She will love you for it. Set a departure time that does not require split-second timing and race-car driving. Plan to arrive 5-10 minutes early. Spend those early moments in prayer and reading your Bible. Ask God to speak to you. He will!

Expect the unexpected. Satan will do his utmost to hinder your worship of God. I should add, if you find yourself running late on a Sunday, do not stay away. Just quietly slip in, smile at the usher, and hold up your watch and shake it. He will understand. We have all been there. See you in church Sunday.

—Copied

Someday

*Someday—I'm going down the street
And sit and chat with one whose feet
Have had to pause and rest awhile
Before they travel that last mile:
Well—someday.*

*Someday—a cake or pie I'll bake
And with a cheery smile I'll take
It to a home where there is need:
Just folks, of quite a different creed:
Well—someday!*

*Someday—a letter I will send
To that distant, lonely friend:
I'll tell her every little thing
That will joy and comfort bring:
Well—someday.*

*Someday—a quiet place I'll seek
Where I can hear my Father speak,
Where I can listen undisturbed
To His precious guiding Word:
Someday.*

*Someday—I'll surely take the time
To tell some soul of love divine,
Of salvation full and free,
Meant for them as well as me:
Someday.*

*Someday—I said it long ago.
The days slip by, and well I know
"Someday" will never come until
Today bends to my Father's will.
Why not today?*

—Copied

S	M	T	W	T	F	S
						1
2	3	4	5	6	7	8
9	10	11	12	13	14	15
16	17	18	19	20	21	22
23	24	25	26	27	28	29
30	31					

A woman hurried across the street to see her neighbor. "It's a principle of mine never to say anything about a person unless it is something good." She paused for breath, then added, "And girl, is this good!"

He Sets No Example

A stout woman in Topeka was told by her doctor, "You have too much around the hips, and the weight has retreated to your rear giving you lordosis and abetting your posture. You'll have to reduce."

She looked at him, then at his protruding stomach. He was as much out front as she was pointing rearward. "Seems to me, Doctor," she retorted, "I'd rather pull it than push it."

Give Up?

Give up because the cross is heavy,
  Sink down in weakness 'neath its load?
Give up and say you can't endure it,
  Too rough, too toilsome is the road?

Ah, no; rejoice you have a cross,
  A cross which none but you may bear;
Why, you are rich, when by that cross
  You earn your right a crown to wear.

Give up while there is still in Heaven
  A God who notes the sparrow's fall?
Give up when He so longs to help you,
  But only wants to hear you call?

He clothes the lilies, feeds the birds;
  Would He to you, then, pay less heed?
Look up to Him with prayerful heart—
  He will supply your every need.

—*Grace B. Renfrow*

Omissions

It isn't the thing you do;
  It's the thing you leave undone
Which gives you the bitter heartache
  At the setting of the sun.

The tender word unspoken,
  The letter you did not write,
The flowers you might have sent,
  Are your haunting ghosts tonight;

The stone you might have lifted
  Out of your brother's way,
The bit of heartsome counsel
  You were hurried too much to say.

The loving touch of the hand,
  The gentle and winsome tone
That you had no time or thought for
  With troubles enough of your own;

These little acts of kindness
  So easily out of mind,
These chances to be angels
  Which even mortals find;

For life is all too short
  And sorrow is all too great
To suffer our slow compassion
  That tarries until too late.

And it's not the thing you do;
  It's the thing you leave undone
Which gives you the bitter heartache
  At the setting of the sun.

—*Adelaide Procter*

Clearly, having authority over a wife is not an ego trip. You are to deny yourself, set an example, be the first to repent, the first to apologize—the visual aid, as it were, of understanding and tact and tenderness and consideration.

—*Ethel Barrett*

"*I'm the head of the house?*"

By a Little Girl

A little girl wrote this in a composition: "People are composed of girls and boys, and men and women. Boys are no good at all until they are grown-up and get married. Men who don't get married are no good either. Boys are an awful bother. They want everything they see except soap. My mom is a woman and my Dad is a man. A woman is a grown-up girl with children. My Dad is such a nice man that I think he must have been a girl when he was a boy."

This composition reminded me of a saintly and elderly missionary who spoke at a chapel service at college. She quoted Psalm 84:11, "No good thing will he withhold from them that walk uprightly." And then she said, "I've endeavored to live a godly life ever since I became a Christian many years ago. God has allowed me to remain a spinster all these years, so I can only assume that man is a 'no good thing.'" The Word of God says, "There is none righteous, no, not one; there is none that doeth good, no, not one" (Rom. 3:9-11).

—From *Selah.*

Children touring a retirement home were asked by a resident if they had any questions. "Yes," one girl said. "How old are you?"

"I'm 98," she replied proudly.

Clearly impressed, the child's eyes grew wide with wonder. "Did you start at one?"

A little boy was told by his mother one night to put the milk bottles out on the porch so that they would be ready for the milkman in the morning. The boy took the bottles, opened the door, and looked out into the pitch blackness. Turning, he hesitated, and said, "It's too dark to go out without a father." He spoke more wisely than he knew.

*   *   *   *   *

Skepticism

A little boy, after attending Sunday school, was asked by his mother what he learned. His reply:

"We heard about a man named Moses. He went behind the lines and rescued the Israelites. Then he came to the Red Sea and called his engineers and they built a pontoon bridge. After they got across, he saw the enemy tanks approaching, so he got on his walkie-talkie and called headquarters, and they sent the dive bombers and blew up the bridge. Then the Israelites rode on."

"Now, son, it wasn't like that at all, was it?"

"Well, not exactly. But, if I told you how the teacher said it really happened, you wouldn't have believed it either!"

A Christian physician died some time ago, and his widow, though sadly bereaved, was victorious in her sorrow. She kept up over his surgery door the little card he used when he was called out on business—

GONE FOR A LITTLE WHILE: WILL BE BACK AGAIN SOON

Yes, believers who have died are gone for a little while. They are to be back soon with Him, for He says, 'We shall be caught up together in the clouds to meet the Lord in the air.'

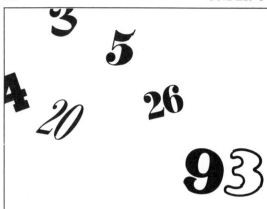

Quoting an Old Proverb...

There is an old proverb which says, "Four things are more numerous than we think: our years, our debts, our enemies and our faults."

The years certainly rush by. Despite the creaking of "this old house," on the inside I still feel like a teenager. I forget sometimes that I'm middle-aged, and that I must seem over the hill to my youth group. I forget because, to me, middle age is always 10 years older than I happen to be at the time.

There is one good thing about our numerous years. As Montaigne put it, "I speak truth not so much as I would, but as much as I dare, and I dare a little more as I grow older."

Our debts add up every bit as fast as our years. I dare you to put pencil and paper to what you really owe. It will frighten you. We tend to rationalize the things we buy on credit and to underestimate just how much in hock we are to this old world.

If you want to write something that will live forever, sign a mortgage. It will probably outlive us all. But money is not everything, even if it does seem to keep us in touch with our children.

Here's a surefire way to double your money—fold it in half and put it in your pocket. If there are any other ways, I don't know about them. I can't help but think how much a good shot of contentment would save us each month in interest charges alone.

Then there's the matter of our enemies. What? You didn't think you had any? If you think it's hard to make enemies, just try picking up the wrong golf ball sometime.

I sometimes forget that not everybody likes me; indeed, that some people hate me. And I shudder to think I actually have enemies in spite of the fact that I consider most folks to be my friends. Still, it's no disgrace to have enemies, just as long as you have God on your side.

And finally there are—more numerous than we think—our faults.

Have you heard what one earthquake said to another earthquake? "It's not my fault!" Is that where we learned to pass the buck?

Alas, my list of strengths will fit on the back of a postage stamp, while my weaknesses more closely resemble an unabridged dictionary. Seeing as how we judge ourselves by our intentions and others by their actions, it's not surprising that we are often unaware of our numerous faults.

Robert Frost once wrote, "People who read me seem to be divided into four groups: 25% like me for the right reasons; 25% like me for the wrong reasons; 25% hate me for the wrong reasons; 25% hate me for the right reasons. It's that last 25% that worries me."

Well, that's the 25% that should worry all of us. None of us are as good as some folks think we are or as bad as others think we are. And it can be a bit disconcerting when someone comes along who has us pretty much figured out.

I believe there is no better test of a person's character than his behavior when he's wrong. It's so hard to say, "I'm sorry. I was wrong." But we never stand any taller than when we stoop to apologize, whether to God or to our neighbor.

An old proverb needn't discourage us.

Yes, our years are more numerous than we think; but when we consider the alternative, we should be grateful for every one of them.

Yes, we are in debt, but this world is not our home. We're just passing through.

Yes, we have enemies. But better to have enemies than to be a friend of the world and an enemy of God.

Yes, we have lots of faults. But they needn't overcome us. Let them put your character to the test every time you stop, take a deep breath, and say, "I'm sorry. I was wrong."

—By Maggie Chandler, whose articles I enjoy so much from *Baptist Trumpet*

A WORD TO THE WISE

If God is not in your typewriter as well as your hymnbook, there is something wrong with your religion. If your God does not enter your kitchen, there is something wrong with your kitchen. If you can't take God into your recreation, there is something wrong with the way you play. If God for you does not smile, there is something wrong with your idea of God.

We all believe in the God of the heroic. What we need most these days is the God of the humdrum, the commonplace, the everyday.

—*Peter Marshall*

Only Lent to Us for a Time

A beautiful story is told of a devout Christian home in which were twin boys who were greatly beloved.

In the absence of the father, both boys suddenly died. When the father returned, not knowing of the sorrow in his home, the mother met him at the door and said, "I have had a strange visitor since you went away."

"Who was it?" asked the father.

"Five years ago," his wife answered, "a Friend lent me two precious jewels. Yesterday He came and asked me to return them to Him. What shall I do?"

"Are they His?" asked the father, not dreaming of her meaning.

"Yes, they belong to Him and were only lent to me."

"If they are His, He must have them again, if He desires."

Leading her husband to the boys' room, the wife drew down the sheet, uncovering the lovely forms, white as marble. "These are my jewels," said the mother. "Five years ago God lent them to me, and yesterday He came and asked for them again. What shall we do?"

With a great sob, the father said, bowing his head, "The will of the Lord be done."

That is the way to find God's comfort. He has a right to take from us what He will, for our joys and treasures belong to Him and are only lent to us for a time. It was in love that He gave them to us; it is in love that He takes them away.

—*J. R. Miller*

"It was Noah's heart God smelled!"

A man was reading to his little boy from chapter 8 of Genesis about the offering Noah made to God after he had been released from the ark. The reading said that, as the smoke ascended from the altar, "the Lord smelled a sweet savour."

Turning to the little lad the father said, "Doesn't it seem strange to think that God could smell a SWEET savor from that burning meat? To us the smell of burning meat is very unpleasant."

The boy answered at once, "Well, it wasn't the meat God smelled, Daddy; it was Noah's HEART God smelled!"

The little fellow was right. The Bible tells us that God is quick to sense the fragrance of beautiful deeds that come forth from a heart given over to the Lord Jesus. Paul says, "We are unto God a sweet savour of Christ" (II Cor. 2:15).

God cannot be pleased with the odor of sin that comes from a heart when Satan is being given his way. "The blood of Jesus Christ, God's Son, cleanseth us from all sin" (I John 1:7).

"Use Your Eyes as if Tomorrow You Would Go Blind."

I who am blind can only give one hint to you who can see. Use your eyes as if tomorrow you would go blind. Do the same with all your senses. Hear the song of a bird as if tomorrow you would go deaf. Touch everything as if tomorrow you would never be able to touch anything again. Smell flowers, taste every bit of food as if tomorrow you would never smell or taste again.

—*Helen Keller*

Going Up!

A tourist visiting New York took his little boy up to the top of the Empire State Building by elevator.

As they went higher and higher the boy watched the floor numbers flashing—25, 30, 35, 40— it seemed they would never stop. Finally, not able to contain himself any longer, he said, "Dad, does God know we're coming?"

Yes, God knows we're coming. When the church is raptured, we will rise much higher than the tallest skyscraper. We shall rise to meet our Lord in the clouds. He knows we're coming, and He will come halfway to greet us.

TOO GOOD TO BE TRUE

By DAVID CRAIG

Have you ever had something happen that was so good that you could not believe it was true? How about so good you *knew* it was not true?

Yvonne recently made a bank transaction at one of those twenty-four-hour, automated teller machines. She noticed that the balance showed about $3,500 more than we really had. That's when we knew it was too good to be true.

In a later conversation with a real live person, Yvonne was told that the indicated figure was indeed our balance. When Yvonne insisted that it was not our balance, she was told that maybe her husband had made a deposit (Ha!). "Well, maybe someone was just being nice," the teller suggested (Ha! Ha!). I know some nice people, but nobody that nice.

Finally, a supervisor was called. They searched out the deposit slip and discovered that the money really did belong in someone else's account. I wonder who was the more surprised, we or the people who would have been $3,500 short?

As long as people have anything to do with the world, there will always be mistakes made. Some are more interesting than others, but we can count on the fact that there will always be some.

God, on the other hand, never makes mistakes. He never incorrectly debits or credits an account. He never charges my sin to someone else, not does He ever miss a sin I commit. He never credits someone else's good deeds to me, and He has also promised that the smallest deposit, even a cup of water given to a child, will not go unrewarded.

If, however, as a Christian, I would check my balance, I would find a strange thing—an apparently enormous mistake. In the place of my overwhelming debt is an infinitely larger balance. When I inquire, I find that no mistake has been made. God has made a deposit—the blood of His own Son—which has placed all of His assets at my disposal.

The Bible calls this grace. It's too good to be true.

But it is!

No Time to Play

My precious boy with the golden hair
Came up one day beside my chair
And fell upon his bended knee
And said, "O Mommy, please play with me!"
I said, "Not now, go on and play;
I've got so much to do today."
He smiled through tears in eyes so blue
When I said, "We'll play when I get through."
But the chores lasted all through the day,
And I never did find time to play.
When supper was over and dishes done,
I was much too tired for my little son.
I tucked him in and kissed his cheek
And watched my angel fall asleep.
As I tossed and turned upon my bed,
Those words kept ringing in my head,
"Not now, son, go on and play;
I've got so much to do today."
I fell asleep and, in a minute's span,
My little boy is a full-grown man.
No toys are there to clutter the floor;
No dirty fingerprints on the door;
No snacks to fix; no tears to dry;
The rooms just echo my lonely sigh.
And now I've got the time to play;
But my precious boy is gone away.
I awoke myself with a pitiful scream
And realized it was just a dream;
For across the room in his little bed
Lay my curly-haired boy, the sleepy-head.
My work will wait 'til another day
For now I must find some time to play.

—Dianna Neal in
Pulpit Helps

TEACH HIM EARLY

Ere a child has reached age seven,
Teach to him the way to Heaven;
Better still, the work will thrive,
If he learns before he's five.

—Spurgeon

"If I should die 'fore I wake...."

Little Donny was kneeling at Grandmother's knee. "If I should die 'fore I wake—I pray—"

"Go on, Donny," prompted Grandma.

"Wait a minute," said Donny, getting to his feet and hurrying away downstairs. Soon he was back. Dropping to his knees, he took up the prayer where he had left off. When he was carefully tucked into bed, Grandma lovingly rebuked the interruption in his evening prayer.

"But I thought of what I was saying, Grandma. That's why I had to stop. You see, I had upset Ted's menagerie. I stood all his wooden soldiers on their heads, just to see how he'd tear around in the morning. But if I should die 'fore I wake, I didn't want him to find 'em that way; so I had to go down and fix 'em right. There's a lot of things that seem funny if you're goin' to keep on livin'—but you don't want 'em that way if you should die 'fore you wake!"

"That was right, dear," commended Grandma, with a tender quaver.

Pray—stop praying—then pray honestly!

Home, Home at last!
Here's to you, my friends!
    May you live a hundred years
Just to help us
    Through this vale of tears.
And may I live a hundred years
    Short just one day,
Because I do not want to be here
    After all my friends have gone away.

—Anon.

An ecology-conscious teenage boy was talking with his father. "I can't stand all this dirt, pollution and trash!" he shouted.

The man looked at his son for a moment, then coolly replied, "Okay, let's get out of your room and talk somewhere else."

*   *   *

IT MATTERS NOT

It matters not if I've been hurt;
* It matters not at all*
That sometimes from my weary eyes
* The scalding teardrops fall.*

What matters most—is if I've erred
* And not confessed the sin,*
And through my lack some needy soul
* Has failed to follow Him.*

It matters not if cherished friends,
* On whom I lean in vain,*
Have wounded me by word and deed
* And left me with my pain.*

What matters is—can I forgive
* Again and yet again?*
It's not, "Have they been true?" but,
* "Lord, have I been true to them?"*

'Twill matter not, when evening comes,
* How rough the road I've trod,*
If only I have walked with Him
* And led some soul to God!*

—Selected

"I'd like to have your mansion when you are called Home!"

Ian McClaren tells about visiting an old Scotch lady who was very sad, unusually sad. She wiped her eyes; and when the minister asked her what was the matter, she confessed, "I am so miserable and unhappy."

"Why?"

"Because I have done so little for Jesus. When I was just a wee girl the Lord spoke to my heart, and I did so very much want to live for Him."

"Well, haven't you?" asked the minister.

"Yes, I have lived for Him, but I have done so little."

"What have you done?"

"I have washed dishes, cooked three meals a day, taken care of the children, mopped the floor and mended clothes. That is all I have done all my life, and I wanted to do something for Jesus."

The preacher, sitting back in the armchair, looked at her and smiled. "Where are your boys?" he inquired.

"Oh, my boys! You know where Mark is. You ordained him yourself before he went to China. There he is preaching for the Lord. Why are you asking?"

"Where is Luke?" questioned the minister.

"Luke? He went from your own church; didn't you send him out? I had a letter from him the other day." And then she became so happy and excited as she continued: "A revival has broken out on the mission station, and he said they were having a wonderful time in the service of the Lord."

"Where is Matthew?"

"He is with his brother in China. And isn't it fine that the two boys can be working together? I am so happy about that. And John came to see me the other night—he is my baby, only nineteen, but he is a great boy—and said, 'Mother, I have been praying and tonight in my room the Lord spoke to my heart, and what do you suppose the Lord told me? I have to go to my brother in Africa. But don't cry, Mother; the Lord told me I was to stay here and look after you until you go home to Glory'"

The minister looked at her: "And you say your life has been wasted in mopping floors, darning socks, washing dishes and doing trivial tasks. I'd like to have your mansion when you're called home."

—*Gems of Truth*

TV—
Master or Servant?

A TV set is only a machine—glass, metal wires, and little gadgets—until you place it in your house.... In some houses, TV becomes a babysitter for babies of all ages. In other houses, TV is a narcotic, an escape from reality. Or it may be a thief, stealing time, thoughts, friendships, creativity and opportunities for much-needed recreation and companionship. In too few houses, TV is a servant, providing information, insight, commentary on life, news, laughter, music and worthwhile entertainment.

What TV becomes depends on you, the user. If you accept it as a tool, use it sparingly, wisely, and purposefully, it can become a servant. If you accept it as a friend, watch and listen continuously, it will become your master.

❖◆❖◆❖◆❖◆❖◆❖◆❖◆❖

After Work

Lord, when Thou seest that my
*   work is done,*
Let me not linger on,
With failing power,
Adown the weary hours—
A workless worker in a world
*   of work.*
But, with a word,
Just bid me home,
And I will come
Right gladly—
Yes, right gladly
Will I come.

—John Oxenham

The Exasperated Cop!

By Viola Walden

I love people. I love the crazy things they do. The better stories writers write about people are the true stories.

I remember so well reading this one. I hope you, too, after reading it, will remember it as long as I have.

The little lady was 5-foot-3, 120 pounds, and in her sixties. She drove a '73 Impala, and on this occasion her daughter rode with her. And here was the daughter's story.

A car pulled up on their rear bumper on the interstate, started around them, and suddenly they saw a blue light flashing on the car.

"Let's stop," said the mother, "and see what the boy wants." She slowed and pulled off the road.

The patrolman walked up beside the car. "Lady," he said, "do you know what the speed limit is?"

In her most motherly voice, the little lady answered, "No, child, I surely don't. Why don't you try that service station over there. They could probably tell you."

"Lady, it's 55 miles an hour," he said.

"Oh," she said, smiling, "did it just come to you?"

"No, lady; I knew it all the time. You were doing 65." He didn't waver. Not at that point. "My job," he said, "is to try to keep the highway safe, Ma'am, and to save lives."

"How perfectly sweet of you!"

That's when he began to waver. In fact, he looked as if he wanted to do something else! "May I see your driver's license?"

She dug in a huge purse for a few minutes, glancing sweetly and apologetically at him now and then. Once she said, "My, how trim you are! I'll bet all the girls at Weight Watchers would like to meet you."

He gave up. "Lady, please drive carefully. And have a nice day."

He tipped his hat and stepped back, checked the traffic, and motioned for her to drive on.

She had stopped just before a large mud hole; and, when she drove away, her daughter looked back and saw the nice patrolman standing there with muddy water running down his pants legs.

"I would swear," the daughter said, "that he had his pistol cocked and aimed at his temple!"

Her mother was pleased. "Wasn't he a nice boy?" she said, and pushed the Impala back up to 65 miles an hour!

TOO MANY MODERN YOUNGSTERS WERE SPOCKED WHEN THEY SHOULD HAVE BEEN SPANKED.

—*Paul Harvey*

What would you take for your Bible if you knew you could not obtain another?

The Meanest Mother in the World

the truth, the whole truth, and nothing but the truth, even if it killed us—and it nearly did.

By the time we were teenagers, she was much wiser; and our lives became even more unbearable. None of this tooting the horn of a car in front of the house for us to come running. She embarrassed us to no end by making our dates and friends come to the door to get us.

I forgot to mention: while our friends were dating at the "mature" age of 12 and 13, my old-fashioned mother refused to let us date until the age of 15 and 18—15, that is, if you dated only to go to school functions, and that was twice a year.

My mother was a complete failure as a mother! None of us has ever been arrested or beaten his mate! Each of my brothers served his time in the service of his country.

And whom do you think we have to blame for the terrible way we turned out? You are right—our mean mother!

Look at all the things we missed—we never got to march in a protest parade nor take part in a riot; burn draft cards or a million things that our friends did. She forced us to grow into God-fearing, educated, honest adults.

Using this as a background, I am trying to raise my three children. I stand a little taller and I am filled with pride when my children call me "mean." Because, you see, I thank God, He gave me the "meanest mother in the whole world"!

—Orien Fifer

My mother insisted upon knowing where we kids were at all times. You'd think we were on a chain gang. She had to know who our friends were and what we were doing. She insisted if we said we'd be gone an hour, that we be gone not one hour and one minute.

I am ashamed to admit it, but she actually struck us; not once, but each time we did as we pleased. Can you imagine someone actually hitting a child just because he disobeyed? Now you can begin to see how mean she really was.

The worst is yet to come! We had to be in bed by nine each night, and up early the next morning. We couldn't sleep till noon like our friends. So, while they slept, my mother actually had the nerve to break the child-labor law. She made us work. We had to wash dishes, make beds, learn to cook, and do all sorts of cruel things.

I believe she laid awake at night thinking up mean things to do to us. She always insisted upon our telling

Four Things to Keep

Almost everyone wants to keep something which he prizes very much. Here are four "keeps" which are jewels from a treasure chest:
Keep the commands of the Lord.
Keep thyself in the love of God.
Keep thy lips from speaking guile.
Keep thy feet from the way of evil.

—Selected

PSALM 17
(verse 11)

I'm glad I cannot shape my way;
I'd rather trust Thy skill.
I'm glad the ordering is not mine;
I'd rather have Thy will.
I do not know the future,
And I would not if I might;
For faith to me is better far
Than faulty human sight.

—Anon.

What Would You Name This Baby?

The Betty Sues of yesteryear are the Tiffany Nicoles of today! And currently a young gent of 12 months is more likely to be addressed as Matthieu Jason than Mark Robert.

The days of plain and simple names that didn't need spelling or repeating to be understood—John, Paul, Jim and Joe of before—have given way to a myriad of what some would call "romantic" names with eccentric spellings, historical connections and biblical roots.

"Mothers just want to be different nowadays," says Mrs. Carol Richardson in the medical records department at Baptist Hospital in Nashville.

Different, indeed. A look through the birth records for the past three months at the hospital turned up these tongue-twisters: Calesha Auntranese, Kayonna Doshan, Ambet Karenea, Tameka Clyennetta Alene, Adrienne Proteus, Lanaris Unika and Tamare Donvale.

Of course not all of today's names are this complicated, but compared to the names of the mothers on the records—most often Donna, Karen, Pamela, Mary, Judy, Linda, Connie, Ellen, Betty, Sharon and Diane—today's names definitely have a different sound.

According to Mrs. Richardson the most common girls' names today are Michelle, Jennifer, Dawn, Kimberly, Christy, Lynn, Melanie, Danielle and Nicole. Boys are most commonly named Jason, Christopher, Michael, Shawn, Sean, Brandon, Thomas and Scott. Twenty years ago those names would more likely have been: Robert, William, John, James, Charles and Richard.

The proliferation of biblical names is also apparent from the records. First or middle names in many cases were Benjamin, Timothy, Gabriel, Joshua, Isaac, Jeremy, Daniel and Matthew.

Also, Mrs. Richardson pointed out that many mothers are spelling relatively common names in odd ways: Matthieu, Renae, M'lisa, Shari, Robyn, Aimee, Keri, Jae and Aly.

In addition to getting more complicated, names are getting longer, she added. Many more infants are being harnessed with three names, and the use of "Jr." is declining. "Mothers want their little boys to have distinctive names, ones other than their fathers'," she said. The practice of using the same initials for the child's name as the parent's is increasing in popularity, however, she said (e.g., John Thomas for the father, Jason Timothy for the son).

Surprisingly, Nashville's Music City babies rarely are named after country music stars. But television and the movies do have an effect on baby names, she said. These silver screen names are turning up more and more: Dustin, Ryan, Sean, Vanessa, Marcus, Chad, Fonda, Candace and Everett.

Also, popular songs have had an effect on names.

Among blacks, who tend to use more complicated names than whites, according to Mrs. Richardson, Danielle is the rage. It also appears as Danyelle, Donyale and Daniele.

Although Mrs. Richardson claims that most mothers of twins are no longer choosing "twin" names, some seem simply to be picking more elaborate "twin" names: Christi Lynn and Misti Layne, or Lanaris Unika and Landrace Shauntrell, or Nikita Yolanda and LaQuita Monique.

According to an article in the Lansing (Michigan) *State Journal*, on a study done by two hospital administrators there, the new names may be "simply part of the cultural revolution taking place in America. Americans have become alienated from their ethnic heritage and have lost track of their past," said one at the hospital. "Because of this, they are seeking to establish their own traditions. Parents today are seeking new and distinctive names for their children and, in addition, creating names which reflect cultural change."

Who's Watching the Kids?

It has been stressed repeatedly that parental involvement is a key ingredient in a successful education plan. It is another truism that it is also vitally important for parents to pay attention to their children at home.

One study found that parents today spend 40 percent less time with their children than did parents in 1965. Sociologist John Robinson of the University of Maryland reports that parents in 1965 were spending about 30 hours per week with their children. He said the parent-child sharing time had dropped to 17 hours a week by 1985.

Today there are many one-parent homes, with the single parent having to be away much of the time earning a living. Where there are two-parent homes, often both the father and mother hold down full-time jobs.

Much of the nurturing of children has been turned over to sitters or to the government.

William Galston and Elaine Ciulla Kamarck of the Progressive Policy Institute had some cogent remarks on this subject: "Government cannot, under any set of conditions, provide the kind of nurturance that children, particularly young children, need. Given all the money in the world, government programs will not be able to instill self-esteem, good study habits, advanced language skills, or sound moral values in children as effectively as can strong families."

Parents need to remember to make as much time available as possible for that most precious commodity—their children.

—Chattanooga, *News Free Press*

"You Shaped This Soul of Mine"

You painted no Madonnas
On chapel walls in Rome,
But with a touch diviner
You lived one in your home.

You wrote no lofty poems
That critics counted art,
But with a nobler vision
You lived them in your heart.

You carved no shapeless marble
To some high-souled design,
But with a finer sculpture
You shaped this soul of mine.

You built no great cathedrals
That centuries applaud,
But with a grace exquisite
Your life cathedraled God.

Had I the gift of Raphael,
Or Michelangelo,
Oh, what a rare Madonna
My mother's life would show!

—Thomas W. Fessenden

What is the difference between a home and a house? Anybody can build a house; we need something more for the creation of a home. A house is an accumulation of brick and stone, with an assorted collection of manufactured goods; a home is the abiding place of ardent affection, of fervent hope, of genial trust.

Many a homeless man lives in a richly furnished house. Many a modest house in the crowded street is an illuminated and beautiful home. The sumptuously furnished house may be only an exquisitely sculptured tomb; the scantily furnished house may be the very hearthstone of the eternal God.

The Bible does not say very much about homes; but it says a great deal about the things that make them. It speaks about life and love and joy and peace and rest! If we get a house and put these into it, we shall have secured a home.

—*John Henry Jowett*

I Am a Mother's Prayer

I want to introduce you to a mother's prayer, one of the mightiest influences that God ever released through human channels; and yet you may not be able to see our guest, not hear the actual voice. I shall read the biography of a mother's prayer.

I am a mother's prayer: I am sometimes clothed in beautiful language that has been stitched together with the needles of love in the quiet chambers of the heart, and sometimes I am arrayed only in the halting deep soil of human emotion. I am a frequent watcher of the night. I have often seen the dawn break over the hills and flood the valleys with light, and the dew of the gardens has been shaken from my eyes as I waited and cried at the gates of God.

I am a mother's prayer: There is no language I cannot speak; and no barrier of race or color causes my feet to stumble. I am born before the child is born; and ere the day of deliverance comes, I have often stood at the altars of the Lord with the gift of an unborn life in my hands, blending my joyful and tearful voice with the prayers and tears of the father. I have rushed ahead of the nurse through the corridors of the hospital praying that the babe would be perfect, and I have sat dumb and mute in the presence of delight over a tiny bit of humanity, so overwhelmed I have been able to do nothing but strike my fingers on the harps of gratitude and say, "Well, thank the Lord!"

I am a mother's prayer: I have watched over the cradle; I have sustained a whole household while we waited for a doctor to come. I have mixed medicine and held up a thermometer when the fever read: 104°. I have sighed with relief over the sweat in the little one's curls because the crisis was past. I have stood by a graveside and picked a few flowers to take home like old memories, and cast my arms around the promises of God just to hang on and wait until I could feel underneath me the everlasting arms.

I am a mother's prayer: I have walked and knelt in every room of the house; I have fondled the old Book, sat quietly at the kitchen table and been hurled around the world to follow a boy who went to war. I have sought through hospitals and army camps and battlefields. I have dogged the steps of sons and daughters in college and university, in the big city looking for a job. I have been in strange places, for I have even gone down into honky-tonks and dens of sin, into nightclubs and saloons and back alleys and along dark streets. I have ridden in automobiles and planes and ships seeking and sheltering and guiding and reminding and tugging and pulling toward home and Heaven.

I am a mother's prayer: I have filled pantries with provision when the earthly provider was gone. I have sung songs in the night when there was nothing to sing about but the faithfulness of God. I have been pressed so close to the promises of the Word that the imprint of their truth is fragrant about me. I have lingered on the lips of the dying like a trembling melody echoed from Heaven.

I am a mother's prayer: I am not unanswered, although Mother may be gone, although the home may be dissolved into dust, although the little marker in the graveyard grows dim. I am still here: and as long as God is God, and truth is truth, and the promises of God are 'yea and amen,' I will continue to woo and win and strive and plead with boys and girls whose mothers are in Glory, but whose ambassador I have been appointed by the King Emmanuel. I am a mother's prayer....

(From a tract published by the Osterhus Publishing House)

WASH YOUR OWN WINDOWS AND SEE HOW CLEAN YOUR NEIGHBOR'S ARE!

Blessed is the Christian homemaker who walketh not constantly to and from club meetings, nor standeth in the department store running up her charge account, nor sitteth idly chatting on the telephone.

Her delight is in building a Christian home; she buildeth with a believing husband—or despite an unbelieving one—and toward this end she worketh by day and dreameth by night.

She shall reveal loving wisdom in its season of necessity; her patience shall not wither because of the demands of her family; and her housework shall give her joy.

The homemaker without God cannot reveal loving wisdom, but she is as unstable as a piece of lint caught in a draft.

Therefore she shall be unprepared for calamity or even minor difficulty; however, her complaint shall fold up in the presence of the Christian homemaker.

The Lord hath fellowship with the Christian homemaker and guideth her in preparing her family to dwell in His eternal home.

—Alice Kay Rogers

Real Hindrances to the Cause of Christ

A prominent Christian confidentially told a friend that "Rev. P. is not the man for this congregation. We'll never get anywhere until we get another man."

This word got back to Rev. and Mrs. P. just after they had decided to set aside some days for prayer, first by themselves, then with trusted Christian members, seeking God's blessing on the congregation.

Feeling self-conscious and discouraged, Rev. P. gave up his prayer project and accepted the next call that came his way.

Mrs. S. meant never to mention except in private intercession the personal problem that Mrs. F. had confided in her. But when another good friend became confidential one afternoon, the secret slipped out easily. After awhile the news was backfence gossip available to all, and Mrs. F.'s testimony among her friends was never influential again.

R., growing up in a Christian home, heard the faults and failings of church members, pastor and Christian workers freely discussed day after day. When he reached his twenties, his cynical atti-

tude toward all Christians and Christianity itself was a deep grief to his parents.

After she made her way slowly down the crowded church aisle, Mrs. H.'s thoughts were much occupied with the sermon she had just heard. Maybe there was something better to life than that it just would come out all right in the end. Maybe she should talk things over with the pastor as he had so cordially invited. Just ahead of her were two Christian women.

Said one, "Rev. N. is a wonderful preacher."

Said the other, "Yes, and he knows it, too. Talk about conceit—you can't touch him with a ten-foot pole. Why, he made me feel like a worm when I went to ask about the choir concert bulletins."

Mrs. H. passed the "unapproachable Rev. N." with a hurried handshake and went home.

N., a college student, felt called to work under the home mission executive and felt more sure than ever that he had found God's place for him. Mr. R. remarked to his secretary, "I can't agree with all of N.'s ideas, but he is a wonderful young man and has a clear-cut testimony. I'm sure he will be a valuable worker."

Said the secretary to a friend, "I guess N. has some ideas that Mr. R. just can't see."

Said the friend to another, "Mr. R. thought N. had some screwy ideas."

Said this one to N., "I guess you and Mr. R. didn't hit it off so well, eh?"

And so it developed that N., feeling it would be impossible to do his best work under

a two-faced official, never turned in his application for the home mission position at all.

At the family dinner table, Rev. C. spoke disparagingly of the methods of the visiting evangelist. Hearing this, his own daughter, who had been touched through the evangelist's ministry, hardened her heart to the Lord.

A disagreement arose at the church business meeting. The next day one Christian called another and told about the "heated discussion." Next, it became "a quarrel," then "a real row." The remark was passed on to the hard-shelled lawyer who had always maintained, "I'll be converted when the Christians can get along with each other." He chuckled and began to draw up papers for another shady legal deal.

Have such instances happened in your home and church? Will they happen again? This is a serious matter, for it brings real hindrances to the cause of Christ.

The only cure for careless talk is a love that so grips the heart that it controls the tongue. Love finds its delight in approving that which is good. Love hastens to pray for and help a failing brother and does not hasten to condemn. Love finds a cover for a multitude of sins glimpsed in others, guards them as a family secret, and bears them only to God in intercession. Love wins and helps, encourages and cheers.

"Beloved, let us love one another: for love is of God."

—Mrs. Orloue E. Gisselquist
Condensed from *Evangelize*

There are many powerful words in every language spoken by men. Among those words are some that are universal. They are spelled and pronounced differently by various national tongues, but each language has its own word for that emotion, feeling or fact.

Everywhere you go, whatever people say when they mean our word for love, it has a universal meaning. Happiness, joy, sorrow, fear, doubt, hate, greed and a whole lexicon of words convey the same meaning and draw similar responses from people in all nations.

Among those words, few, if any, are as powerful and as moving as the word LOVE. The Bible treats with care that word almost as much as it does with any.

We are exhorted by love to serve one another, to walk in love as Christ walked in love, and we are told that God loveth a cheerful giver.

In truth, love does not become love until we have given of ourselves to someone or something else. The spirit that takes but gives not is not a spirit of love but a spirit of greed and selfishness. The spirit that takes and holds but does not give and share is not a spirit of purity but a spirit of ego and snubbery.

One evening, just before she was to make her first entrance in the stage musical SOUTH PACIFIC, Mary Martin was handed a note, handwritten by Oscar Hammerstein, the composer of the lyrics for SOUTH PACIFIC. At that moment Martin knew Hammerstein lay dying, but still he had taken time to write and send her the following note:

A song is no song 'til you sing it;
A bell is no bell 'til you ring it;

Love in your heart isn't put there to stay;
Love isn't love 'til you give it away.

She quickly read the note, made her entrance, and gave an outstanding performance.

Some of her dearest friends felt a new kind of power in the role she played, heard a new strength in her notes, and felt the tug of some unusual spirit.

Rushing back to ask why tonight had been such an especially good performance, blinking back the tears, Mary Martin answered, *"Tonight I gave my love away."*

Every person realizes that a special kind of both inner and physical strength surges to the surface in various kinds of emergency.

To save the life of his child, many a father performs impossible feats. To protect an infant from harm, many women have become momentary towers of strength. A father who had never learned to swim rescues his five-year-old son out of twelve feet of water. He couldn't swim, but he swam!

Love can and does do tremendous things when its power is used—especially when used for the welfare and comfort of others.

Jesus said in concise words: "A new commandment I give unto you, That ye love one another."

—*Viola Walden*

"Take Him?"—"Took"!

The Texas oil man was getting married and was nervous about it. He told the minister that the fee would be in proportion to the brevity of the service and that, if he used a long service, he wouldn't receive a cent.

When the wedding day came, the couple stood before the minister in the bride's home. The minister said to the man, "Take her?"—to the woman, "Take him?"—then closed the ceremony by pronouncing, "Took"—a whole ceremony in five words.

P. S. He got a $500.00 fee—or to be brief—$100 a word.

▲▲

Mrs. Massimilla has written this very lovely poem for the retarded child.

Heaven's Very Special Child

A meeting was held quite far from Earth!
It's time again for another birth.
Said the angels to the Lord above,
"This Special Child will need much love.
His progress may be very slow,
Accomplishment he may not show.
And he'll require extra care
From the folks he meets down there.
He may not run or laugh or play;
His thoughts may seem quite far away.
In many ways he won't adapt
And he'll be known as handicapped.
So let's be careful where he's sent.
We want his life to be content.
Please, Lord, find the parents who
Will do a special job for You.
They will not realize right away
The leading role they're asked to play.
But with this child sent from above
Comes stronger faith and richer love.
And soon they'll know the privilege given
In caring for their gift from Heaven.
Their precious charge so meek and mild
Is Heaven's Very Special Child."

—*Edna Massimilla*

Let Me See Your Hands

What kind of hands do you have? Are they long and slender? Or are they short and plump? Are they rough and red? Or are they smooth and soft? Maybe they are strong and steady, or maybe they are weak and shaky. I don't know which of these things are true of you; but if you are a mother, I think I can safely say your hands are *full!*

When your husband was courting you, his first show of affection probably was to hold your hand. It was your hands, more than anything else, that gave your baby assurance of your love and protection.

My mother knows whether or not her pie crust will be good by the feel of the dough in her hands. And what woman would buy a piece of material that she had not first run her hand carefully over?

The Bible has a lot to say about hands. In fact, long before the FBI knew it, God told us in Job 37:7 that a man could be traced through his fingerprints. And as far as a woman's hands—if you'll check the verses concerning the "virtuous woman" in Proverbs 31, you'll find the words *"her hands"* used seven times. They tell us that she worked willingly with her hands, planting a vineyard, making cloth, caring for the poor and her household in general.

If God feels that the feet of a preacher are beautiful because they are used to spread the news of the Gospel, then surely He must think busy, helping hands the loveliest part of a woman. Remember the little song the children sing: "Oh, be careful little hands what you do. Oh, be careful little hands what you do. There's a Father up above looking down in tender love, so be careful little hands what you do."

Say, what kind of hands do you have???

—Mrs. Richard Sandlin

A group of women were talking together. One lady said, "Our congregation is sometimes down to thirty and forty on Sunday night."

Another said, "That's nothing; sometimes our group is down to six or seven."

An old maid added her bit: "It's so bad in our church on Sunday night that, when the minister says, 'Dearly beloved,' it makes me blush."

■■■■■■■■■■■■■■■■■■■■■■■■■

CHILDREN, LIKE CANOES, BEHAVE BETTER IF PADDLED FROM THE REAR.

❧❧❧

We're Going Home!

We're going Home! We're going Home!
  No more o'er barren wastes to roam:
And if the way seem long we've trod,
  We're going Home to Heaven and God.

What if the way be ofttimes rough?
  We're going Home—that is enough!
How sweet the welcome that awaits
  Our entry at Heaven's pearly gates.

What hallowed bliss within its walls!
  What peaceful rest within its halls!
No sense of sin, no sound of strife—
  Just radiant, joyful, endless life.

What fellowship we then shall share!
  How wonderful the frames we'll wear
In that dear realm—Heaven's Homing-place,
  And all through Christ's redeeming grace.

—F. Danson Smith

A Horrible Crime

"Abortion is the killing of human life—biologically, medically and scientifically. It is factual that life begins at fertilization," affirmed Steven Hotze, M.D., founder of Texas Doctors for Life, Inc.

"Over ninety-nine percent of all abortions have nothing to do with rape, incest or threat to the mother's life. At 18 to 25 days after conception, the heart begins to beat. At 45 days, brain waves can be detected. By 6 to 7 weeks, the fetus will respond to touch sensations. Even at this early stage, there is no reason to think that the unborn baby does not feel pain as his/her body is dismembered, poisoned, or otherwise destroyed by the various brutal techniques concealed under the bland euphemism 'termination of pregnancy'!"

What Are They Worth?

Nobody knows what a boy is worth;
  A boy at his work or play,
A boy who whistles around the place,
  Or laughs in an artless way.

Nobody knows what a boy is worth;
  A boy with his face aglow,
For hid in his heart there are secrets deep
  Not even the wisest know.

Nobody knows what a girl is worth;
  With her carefree laugh and her sparkling
    smile,
With eyes like pools of dancing mirth,
  To lighten the burdens of many a mile.

Nobody knows what a girl is worth;
  A girl with her dolls and dreams,
For hidden away in the depths of her soul
  The jewel of character gleams.

Nobody knows what a girl is worth;
  Nobody knows what the future holds,
When the flowers of womanhood blossom
    forth
  In a life of holiness lived for God.

Yes, Someone knows what a boy is worth,
  A boy with his barefoot feet;
Yes, Someone knows what a girl is worth,
  A girl with her smiles so sweet.

Yes, the Master knows and has given us
    them
  To love, to train, to win, and to keep;
Each one is a gem in a diadem,
  A trophy of grace to lay at His feet.

—J. F. Leist

MOTHER'S KISS

My mother allus kissed away
  My troubles an' my pain.
No matter how bad hurt I wus,
  Ur distressed wus my brain,
She'd take me in her lap an' then
  She'd ask me, "What is this
That ails my boy?" An' make me well
  By givin' me a kiss.

One time I had my finger mashed
  Until the nail comed off;
Another time I sprained my wrist
  By fallin' from the loft;
An' lots uv times my heart was broke
  Beyond all hopes of bliss,
But Mother allus made me well
  By givin' me a kiss.

But now there isn't any cure,
  For Mother's gone away,
An' won't come back no more, because
  She's gone to Heaven, they say—
I feel a lump rise in my throat
  That hurts me, an' I miss
Her—still she don't come back
  To cure me with a kiss.

—Author Unknown

Never mind the man;
pity the poor cow
having to listen to
that dreadful music!

The Choir of Heaven

A Christian woman, the wife of a minister of the Gospel, was dying in the parsonage, near the old church, where on Saturday night the choir used to assemble and rehearse for the following Sunday. She said, "How strangely sweet the choir rehearses tonight; they have been rehearsing there for an hour."

"No," said someone about her, "the choir is not rehearsing tonight."

"Yes," she said, "I know they are. I hear them sing; how very sweetly they sing!"

Now it was not a choir of earth that she heard but the choir of Heaven. I think that Jesus sometimes sets ajar the door of Heaven to let a passage of that rapture greet our ears. The minstrels of Heaven strike such a tremendous strain that the walls of jasper cannot hold it.

The first great concert I ever attended was in New York, when Julien, in the "Crystal Palace," stood before hundreds of singers and players upon instruments. It was the first one of the kind at which I was present, and I shall never forget it. I saw that one man stand and with the hand and foot wield that great harmony, beating the time. It was to me overwhelming.

But, oh, the grander scene when they shall come from the East and from the West, and from the North and from the South—"a great multitude that no man can number"—into the temple of the skies, host beyond host, rank beyond rank, gallery above gallery; and Jesus shall stand before that great host to conduct the harmony with His wounded hands and His wounded feet! Like the voice of many waters, like the voice of mighty thunderings, they shall cry, 'Worthy is the Lamb that was slain to receive blessings, and riches, and honour, and glory, and power, world without end. Amen and Amen!'

Oh, if my ear shall hear no other sweet sounds, may I hear that! If I join no other glad assemblage, may I join that.

I was reading of the battle of Agincourt, in which Henry V figured; and it is said after the battle was won, gloriously won, the king, wanting to acknowledge the divine interposition, ordered the chaplain to read the Psalm of David. When he came to the word, 'Not unto us, O Lord, but unto Thy name be the praise,' the king and all the cavalry dismounted; and all the great host, officers and men, threw themselves on their faces.

Oh, at the story of the Saviour's love and deliverance, shall we not prostrate ourselves before Him now, hosts of earth and hosts of Heaven, falling upon our faces and crying, 'Not unto us, not unto us, but unto Thy name be the glory!'

—*T. DeWitt Talmage*

"For Bitter or for Worse?"

"Family life among the Egyptians was easier than it is today," wrote a little girl in her history composition. "They were all facing the same way."

It is well to get it straight right off that no marriage is simple, whether you're facing the same way or not. You are going to find out later anyhow, so you may as well know it sooner: you have some needs that are *not* going to be met. And there will be some things upon which you will *never* totally agree.

Now you can go on scratching the itch of your disillusionment, or you can stop and contemplate what God has to say about the duties and relationship of husbands and wives. What He says, in effect, is not "Are you in love?" but rather, "*Wilt thou love?*"

—*Ethel Barrett.*

"Such a little way together"

"Why didn't you tell her she was taking more than her share of the room and encroaching on your rights?" someone asked a young girl who was merrily describing a woman who had taken a seat beside her in a crowded railway car and crammed into the small space a birdcage, a basket of apples, and bundles numerous and varied.

"It wasn't worthwhile to trouble about it; we had such a little way to go together," was the reply.

What a motto that would be for a Christian's life journey! So many little annoyances are not worth noticing; so many small unkindnesses, even, may be passed by silently, because we have only "such a little way to go together."

Parents or "Sparents"

A little girl, who was disciplined by her mom, was overheard as she prayed, "Please, Lord, don't give her any more children, for she doesn't know how to treat the ones she's got now."

We may smile at this, but the Bible contains numerous examples of the tragic results of undisciplined homes.

Adonijah, David's rebellious son, sought to take his father's throne. Reason—"And his father had not displeased him at any time in saying, Why hast thou done so?" (I Kings 1:6). Judgment fell on the house of Eli due to his failure to give strong parental direction. "...his sons made themselves vile, and he restrained them not" (I Sam. 3:13).

Proper discipline, whether instruction or punishment, is an attitude of love (Heb. 12:6, 10, 11).

Many of America's homes are suffering from a lack of discipline. Some feel that to refuse a child's request or to punish misconduct shows a lack of love. However, scriptural discipline and true love go hand in hand.

How is your home?

"Sparents" are those who "spare the rod"
  When offspring need attention.
They find their troubles multiplied
  In ways too sad to mention!

—Rich Lieghley

My Choicest Piece of Jewelry

In my jewelry box, blue velvet-lined, is a necklace unlike those you'll find in any smart shop or jewelry store. And it's the one I most adore.

Not wrought of silver nor fashioned of gold, no diamonds or rhinestones like those that are sold, this piece of jewelry that I most enjoy was made with love by a five-year-old boy. It has no pearls, either real or phony, but four different colors of dyed macaroni.

—Selected

Sing Unto the Lord

By Viola Walden

There is never a day so dreary,
  There is never a night so long,
But the soul that is trusting Jesus
  Will somewhere find a song.

Wonderful, wonderful Jesus,
  In the heart He implanteth a song;
A song of deliverance, of courage, of strength,
  In the heart He implanteth a song.

Is there a song in your heart today?

"Not today!" somebody says. "I'm too tired to sing today. I'm too tired to think, even. It is really discouraging to be so weary."

"Don't expect me to sing today! The night has been long and the darkness oppressive. Grief has taken the place of song in my heart; disappointment chokes back the music."

"I'm too busy even to think about a song—don't expect me to have a song in my heart when things are this hectic!"

What about it—is there a song in your heart? Or is there misery, grief, loneliness, frustration, disappointment, discouragement? Is there a day too weary for song, or is Annie B. Russell right in the words just quoted?

For the Christian, there is never a day so dreary, a night so long, that there isn't a song *somewhere,* if we only find it. For a Christian, in whose heart Christ has planted a song, ought never to be without the melody of His love and His care ringing in the arches of the soul.

If a Christian is defeated, sad, songless, it is because he doesn't have his antenna tuned in the right direction! He is listening to the rumbling of the world, not to the clear, sweet message God is sending, "I will never leave thee nor forsake thee"—surely the most beautiful music in the world!

Why do we let worldly static and selfish interference distort the song of faith and hope God sends us? Why do we look at small things, unimportant things, instead of into His face?

This song of His—you can't hear it if you're talking. You can't hear Him if you're listening to someone else. And you can't hear Him if you're deafened by a noisy ego making plans out loud.

The song He gave may be in your heart, but you won't hear it unless you listen!

I like that little verse Mary Helen Anderson wrote...and I think all of us could place it in a prominent spot on memory's wall:

> We mutter and sputter,
>   We fume and we spurt;
> We mumble and grumble,
>   Our feelings are hurt;
> We can't understand things,
>   Our vision grows dim,
> When all that we need is
>   A moment with Him!

If you've been letting your song get a little bit faint...the melody weak and the words drowned out, it would be good to take a few minutes to make a better contact with the Maker of Songs. Let *Him* give you the right song, even if it's in a minor key for that grief you're bearing, that worry that won't go away. Let Him handle the frustrations and disappointments and show you how bright tomorrow is. Whether the song soars in beauty or throbs in darkness, let it be His song you carry in your heart, planted deep and firm to sustain you.

God gives songs of joy. But there are other kinds of songs, too; and sometimes we need songs of consolation, of comfort.

He is the one who "giveth songs in the night." The psalmist said, "Thou art my hiding place; thou shalt preserve me from trouble; thou shalt compass me about with songs of deliverance."

We are to have a song in our hearts when He saves us, but there is more. We are to have that song in our *mouth* so that others can hear and be blessed, too! "He hath put a new song in my mouth, even praise unto our God: many shall see it, and fear, and shall trust in the Lord," says Psalm 40:3. If the song in our hearts bursts forth from our lips, others will trust in the Lord, too! A melody is catching and none more infectious than a heart song of praise to God!

Do we really obey His command to sing forth a new song, a song of salvation? Let's try to keep the song flowing in our hearts—and then to let it flow out to others, as He has commanded!

"Sing unto the Lord a new song, and his praise from the end of the earth" (Isa. 42:10). Let's be *singing* Christians!

xxxxxxxxxxxxxxxxxxxxxxxxxxxxxxxxxxxxxx

You Are Very Special to God

Did you know you're very special to God? It's a fact. He made you to be just what you are because He wants you that way, to play a unique role in the work of His kingdom.

And you can play that role better than anyone else. I was reminded of this the other day by something James H. McConkey wrote:

> Every life is a fresh thought from God to the world. Every jewel gleams with its own radiance. Every flower distills its own fragrance. Every Christian has his own particular bit of Christ's radiance and Christ's fragrance which God would pass through him to others.

You are unique. In all the world there is no other person just like you. The God of infinite variety never makes two leaves or two lives alike. Every star, every snowflake is different, and every human being, too. That's why the Lord needs *YOU.*

Has it ever occurred to you that the Lord needs you? Perhaps you've always thought it was the other way around: that you need the Lord. Of course, that's true, too. You do need the Lord; we all do. We need Him every hour. Oh, how much we need Him! For we are nothing without Him. We need to acknowledge our weakness and our dependence on Him continually.

Queen Elizabeth I said, *"They are most deceived that trust the most in themselves."* Our trust must be in the Lord, not in ourselves. We need to measure our smallness against His greatness and be clothed with humility. Do you have this clothing? Or are you scantily clad in this respect?

Modesty is becoming to the Christian, but our humility should not be such that we lose sight of our importance to God.

Phillips Brooks wrote:

> There is not one life which the Lifegiver ever loses out of His sight; not one which sins so that He casts it away; not one which is not so near to Him that whatever touches it touches Him with sorrow or with joy.

In God's eyes you are very precious. He made you for His delight, and He is expecting something from you that He will get from no one else.

Thomas Carlyle wrote:

> The older I grow—and I now stand

on the brink of eternity—the more comes back to me that sentence in the Catechism I learned when a child, and the fuller and deeper its meaning becomes: "What is the chief end of man? To glorify God and enjoy Him forever."

You were made to enjoy Him—in this life and the next—and to be enjoyed by Him. He longs for your love and fellowship. He desires your loyalty and service.

You are unique, and you have a unique opportunity to glorify your Creator.

McConkey said:

> Just a hair's breadth of shift in the focus of the telescope, and some man sees a vision of beauty which before had been all confused and blurred. So, too, just that grain of individual and personal variation in your life from every other person's, and someone sees Jesus Christ with a clearness and beauty he would discern nowhere else.
>
> In you there is just a bit of change in the angle of the jewel—and, lo, some man sees the light! In you there is just a trifle of variation in the mingling of the spices— and behold, someone becomes conscious of the fragrance of Christ.

—Robert C. Cunningham

Don't Wait 'Til Too Late!

A "Dear Abby" Letter From a Grieving Son

Dear Abby: Yesterday was the saddest day of my life. I buried my mother. And now many thoughts come to mind that make me even sadder.

I recall the many times I meant to call her and ask if there was anything she needed, but I seldom got around to it.

I recall the day I ran into Mom in the bakery. Her winter coat looked so shabby and worn, and I thought, *I've got to take Mom downtown and buy her a new coat.* But I never found the time. I was too busy.

On her last birthday I sent her an azalea plant, but I forgot to enclose a card. I had wanted to get over to see her; but there was a football game that day, so I never made it.

The last time I saw Mom was at my cousin's wedding. She looked so old and tired. I told myself, *I must send Mom to Florida to visit her brother and get a little sun;* but I just never got around to buying the tickets.

If only I could turn the clock back I'd buy Mom that coat and spend every birthday with her and take her anyplace she wanted to go. But it's too late now and I am heartsick.

Please print this letter. Maybe if I had seen one like it, I would have done things differently.

—Grieving Son.

(Clipped from *Washington Star*)

The Case of the Banished Bridegroom

The wedding was over. The confetti has been thrown. The cake has been cut; the presents, opened. Tom and his bride were alone at last. As the car pulled away from the curb, the bride moved over to the far end of the seat, as far away from her new husband as she could. "Tom, take me home!"

"HOME, Kathy? We haven't started our honeymoon yet. Our new home won't be ready for three weeks!"

"I don't want to go to that house you're building. At least not yet— not for a long time. Take me back to my flat."

Tom looked at his bride in amazement, but there could be no doubt about it. She was serious. His amazement grew as she continued. "Tom, I'm glad we're married. We belong to each other, and I can use your name as mine. But, please, I want to go back to my old apartment. Now that we're married, I'll try to see you once a week. But as far as living with you is concerned, nothing doing! I'm going back to my old occupation, my old friends, my old pastimes.

"Oh, yes, I do love you! I've accepted you as my husband, haven't I? I belong to you forever; but I refuse to let you interfere with my life. I'm going to live to please myself. Of course, if I'm sick or if I need any money I'll call for you at once because, after all, I have accepted you as my husband. In the meantime, thank you for loving me. Thank you for asking me to be yours. Thank you for being my husband, but HANDS OFF MY LIFE."

Now such an arrangement would not be a marriage but a mockery. To accept a person as husband or wife is an act of committal.

That is exactly what it means to be a Christian.

There are many who call themselves "Christians" whose attitude to Christ is exactly the same as Kathy's to her groom. They say in effect, if not in so many words: "Lord, I have accepted You as my Saviour. Thank You for saving me. Now leave me alone. I'm going back to my old friends, to my old pleasures, to my old way of life. I'll expect You to help me if I need it since You are my Saviour. But as far as living for You is concerned, nothing doing! Of course, when I die I want to come and share the home You are preparing. But I hope that will not be for a long, long time."

Am I really Christ's if I act like that? Have I truly accepted Him? Have I sincerely given my heart to Him?

"*I beseech you . . . that ye present your bodies . . . unto God.*"—Rom. 12:1.

—From *The Orthodox Baptist*

Cat Chat

Four women were having coffee. Said one, "My husband bought me some diamond bracelets. Then my skin broke out. The doctor said I was allergic to diamonds. So we had to return them."

A second lady said her husband had bought her a fur coat that had to be returned. The doctor said she was allergic to furs.

Another fainted. When she was revived, she explained, "I'm allergic to hot air."

Whatever you write on the heart
   of a child
     No water can wash away.
The sand may be shifted when
   billows are wild,
     And the efforts of time may decay.

Some stories may perish,
     Some songs be forgot;
But this graven record—
     Time changes it not.

Whatever you write on the heart
   of a child,
     A story of gladness or care
That Heaven has blessed or earth
   has defiled,
     Will linger unchangeably there.

TO MY EVER-PRESENT TEMPTATION

I have tried to love you lightly
But without success;
To love you very little
And never to excess.
I have sought to love you wisely,
   But this I cannot do;
   For all my vows are shattered
   Each time I look at you.

            —Author Unknown

"Thank You, Lord . . ."

Even though I clutch my blanket and growl when the alarm rings each morning,
   Thank You, Lord, that I can hear.
   There are those who are deaf.

Even though I keep my eyes tightly closed against the morning light as long as possible,
   Thank You, Lord, that I can see.
   There are many who are blind.

Even though I huddle in my bed and put off the physical effort of rising,
   Thank You, Lord, that I have the strength to rise.
   There are many who are bedfast.

Even though the first hour of the day is hectic, when socks are lost, toast is burned, tempers are short,
   Thank You, Lord, for my family.
   There are many who are lonely.

Even though our breakfast table never looks like the pictures in the ladies' magazines and the menu is at times unbalanced,
   Thank You, Lord, for the food we have.
   There are many who are hungry.

Even though the routine of my job is often monotonous,
   Thank You, Lord, for the opportunity to work.
   There are many who have no work.

Even though I grumble and bemoan my fate from day to day and wish my modest circumstances were not quite so modest,
   Thank You, Lord, for the gift of life.

            —Author Unknown

"*If Folks Could Have Their Funerals When They Are Alive. . .*"

"If folks could have their funerals when they are alive and well, struggling along, what a help it would be!" sighed Aunt Jerusha, folding her Paisley shawl with great care.

"Now, there is poor Mrs. Brown," she added, as she pinned her green veil to her Sunday bonnet. "How encouraged she would have been if she could have heard what the minister said today! I wouldn't wonder if she'd have got well.

"And Deacon Brown a-wiping his eyes, and all of them taking on so! Poor soul! She never dreamed they thought so much of her!

"Mrs. Brown was discouraged. You see, her husband—Deacon Brown—he'd got a way of blaming everything onto her. I don't suppose the deacon meant it—'twas just his way—but it's awful wearing. When the things wore out, or broke, he acted just as if Mrs. Brown did it herself on purpose. And they all caught it, like measles or the whooping cough.

"And the minister a-telling how the deacon brought his young wife here when it was nothing but a wilderness; and how patiently she bore hardships, and what a good wife she'd been! Now the minister wouldn't have known anything about that if the deacon hadn't told him.

"Dear, dear! If he'd only told Mrs. Brown herself what he thought, I believe he might have saved the funeral.

"And when the minister said how the children would miss their mother, as though they couldn't stand it, poor things! Well, I guess it is true enough; Mrs. Brown was always doing for some of them. When they were singing about 'sweet rest in Heaven,' I couldn't help thinking that there was something Mrs. Brown would have to get used to, for she never had none of it here.

"She'd have been awful pleased with the flowers. They were pretty, and no mistake. You see the deacon wa'n't never willing for her to have a flower bed. He said ' 'twas far prettier sight to see good cabbage a-growin' '; but Mrs. Brown always kind of hankered after sweet-smelling things, like sweet peas and such.

"What did you say, Levi? Most time for supper? Well, so it is! I must have got to meditating. I've been thinking, Levi, you needn't tell the minister about me. If the pancakes and the pies are good, you just say so as we go along. It ain't best to keep everything laid up for funerals."

DON'T LOOK OVER THE FENCE

A fence is intended to keep one in and at the same time to keep others out. Cattle like to look over the fence, and things seem to taste better just over the line than inside the enclosure. Boys think that stolen watermelons are better than others. This is according to a very wise man's conclusion when he says, "Stolen waters are sweet, and bread eaten in secret is pleasant."

This is where temptation becomes sin—in letting down just one top rail and glancing over; in listening to the first thought which brings one near the border edge of yielding. This was where Eve, David, and many others since their day went down in defeat.

On the other hand, thank God, Joseph and others came through untarnished. Joseph's secret of victory was, "He got him out!" Many a man has stayed five minutes too long.

Satan is too wise to suggest open and disgraceful things. No! No! But what is the harm in just one secret glance? Oh, how subtle! Remember, this first little glance has resulted in strong men becoming stone blind and like a mad animal breaking down the entire fence, in view of a present gratification.

Say, Friend, are you afraid, yea, deathly afraid of getting too near the line and glancing over? This is your only safety! Crush as you would a viper the first suggestion to bitterness, jealousy and unchastity. Do not glance the second time in the wrong direction.

—E. E. Shelhammer

During a house visit, while the woman patient chattered on, the doctor interrupted her and said, "Now, Mrs. Smith, put this thermometer beneath your tongue and keep your mouth closed for two minutes."

When the doctor finally removed the thermometer, the woman's husband, who had been an interested observer, took the doctor to the side and whispered: "Say, what will you take for that gadget?"

• *As to matters of dress, I would recommend one never to be first in the fashion nor the last out of it.*

—John Wesley

I went out to find a **friend**,
But could not find one there;
I went out to be a **friend**,
And **friends** were everywhere!

After the Wedding

Recently a sweet little Texas grandmother was in our town for the wedding of one of her grandsons. She sat in on the bridal showers, participated in the prenuptial festivities, and watched the excited bride and groom anticipate the Big Day. She had experienced over fifty years of married life before her husband died, and watched all of the activities of her grandson and his fiancée with a rather philosophical detachment. She had experienced the struggles, the joys, the heartaches and the fun of married life; she had been through the changes we go through as a family and had a perspective which was valuable.

She said, "If there is one thing I would tell a young couple, it would be this. . . ." I waited for some immensely profound statement, full of the wisdom of her experience, and she replied with her eyes twinkling, ". . . after the wedding, there's a marriage."

—*Carole C. Carlson*

"Better Start Now!"

A young girl said to her mother just after a white-haired visitor left her home, "If I could be such an old lady as that—beautiful, serene, sweet and lovable—I shouldn't mind growing old."

The discerning and keen-witted mother replied, "Well, if you want to be that kind of an old lady, you'd better begin making her right now. She does not impress me as a work that was done in a hurry. It has taken a long time to make her what she is. If you're going to paint that sort of portrait of yourself to leave the world, you had better be mixing your colors now."

What If?

For 58 hours we, as a nation, gathered in a Midland, Texas, backyard. We anxiously hovered above the small opening of an abandoned well shaft. Wedged 29 feet below was 18-month-old Jessica McClure.

During those hours, we fearfully followed the heroic struggle of the men who sought to save her. We prayed for this toddler, for her young parents, for the determined rescuers. The life of Jessica McClure mattered.

Until that time, few folks had heard of Jessica. However, while in that terrible prison, she became everyone's child. Her cries tore at us; her brave singing of Winnie the Pooh compelled us to care.

Hours became days. Could a little tyke like Jessica survive such a long entrapment? No food. No water. No one to hold her. So utterly helpless, could she last?

Please, rescuers, hurry! There are yet so many songs for a little girl to sing.

Happily, Jessica was at last lifted from the shaft. We cheered! We wept! We rejoiced! The life of this dear person had been saved.

What if Jessica had fallen down that same shaft six months earlier?

Would we have been concerned over her rescue then? Of course. We are a people who love our children. Without a doubt, we would have called, *"Please, rescuers, hurry! There are yet so many songs for a little girl to sing."*

What if it were more than a year earlier that Jessica's plight occurred—too young to respond to calls above her, too young to sing "Winnie the Pooh"? Would her recovery have mattered? Absolutely. We love our babies. Our united voices would surely have urged, *"Please, rescuers, hurry! There are yet so many songs for a little girl to sing."*

But what if, what if we pushed back time further—not six months, or one year, but two years? What if the very same little girl lay, not in the cold hold of an abandoned shaft, but in the warmth of her mother's womb? What if her future depended, not on the skills of dedicated rescuers, but on the hands of those who prematurely empty the womb? Would we have cared then for the life of Jessica McClure?

Please, rescuers, hurry! There are yet so many songs for a little girl to sing.

—Nina M. Bergman

SHIFT CENTER OF LIFE FROM SELF TO OTHERS. A quaint old lady set this truth in homely phrase: "I have learned that if I am going to be happy in this world, I have to commit suicide every day and attend my own funeral."

She was precisely correct, "for whosoever will save his life shall lose it: and whosoever will lose his life for my sake shall find it."

○○○○○○○○○○○○○○○

When a boy or girl truly accepts the Saviour, God does not change a young head or a young heart into an old one.

A little child of six prayed one night: "Dear Lord, please make me the kind of boy You were when You were six."

Madame Guyon was shut up in a dungeon, but with radiant spirit she wrote:

Strong are the walls around me that hold me all the day;
But they who thus have bound me cannot keep God away;
My very dungeon walls are dear, because the God I love is here.
They know, who thus oppress me, 'tis hard to be alone;
But know not One can bless me who comes through bars and stone.
He makes my dungeon's darkness bright and fills my bosom with delight.

"THE LIGHT OF THE WORLD" by W. Holman Hunt, presented to St. Paul's Cathedral in London by the late Rt. Hon. Charles Booth, is a replica of the original painting in Keble College, Oxford.

"Why Don't They Open the Door, Daddy?"

Reuben and Esther Jones were as devoted to each other, their home, and only child who had brought much happiness into their lives, as man and wife could be.

They had not much sympathy with religious folks or churches. Sundays were "rest days" with the newspaper as their "guide, philosopher and friend."

They had, however, allowed the district visitor to call, which she did monthly; and the day of which I write she had brought the *New Sheet Almanac*, the central picture being a reproduction of Holman Hunt's famous painting, *"Christ, the Light of the World."* Mother and son looked at it with wonder as it was placed in a prominent position on the wall.

When Father came in to dinner, his attention was called to it by the boy. "Look, Daddy! Who is it, Daddy? Who is it?"

Reuben looked at the picture, but gave no answer, although he knew whom the picture represented.

But the little fellow was not to be denied, and again came the question, "Who is it, Daddy? Tell me, Daddy."

At last he blurted out, "A Man, of course!"

"What Man, Daddy? What is His name?"

Compelled by the earnestness of the child, he said, "Christ!"

"But what is He doing, Daddy?"

"Can't you see He is knocking at a door!" said the father.

"How long will He knock, Daddy?"

"I don't know," came the reply.

Still the boy asked, "What is He knocking for?"

"Because He wants to go inside," said his father.

"Why don't they open the door, Daddy?"

This question was repeatedly asked, and it proved to be too pointed; for Reuben Jones turned away, saying, "I don't know, my child."

Very little was said that dinner hour, except the boy's repeated statement, "I'd open the door. Wouldn't you, Daddy?"

Dinner over, the father hurried away, saying to his wife, "I cannot stand any more of his questions."

That evening Reuben Jones and his wife talked chiefly about their son, the picture, and the child's questions. "Oh!" said the wife, "he's been on it ever since. His last words going to bed were 'I wish they had let the Man in.'"

"It is very strange," said the husband, "I have thought of little else since dinner. I cannot get it out of my mind—'Why don't they open the door? Why don't they open the door?' Esther, I believe the same hand has been knocking at my door for some time, but the knocking has been louder today. But still the door is closed."

"Why don't they open the door?" he said. "Ah, that is the question.

"I am sure, Esther, God is knocking by the hand of our own child. It's time we began to be more serious about things."

"Well," said the wife, "if you are going to be religious I shall come, too."

That very week a mission was being held in the Town Hall. Reuben's workshop mates had held up this effort to scorn, asking, "Who's going to get saved?" But notwithstanding this spirit of derision, Reuben and Esther attended three of the meetings until on the closing night the preacher asked, "Who will open the door and let the Stranger in?" It brought back to husband and wife the question of their own child, "Why don't they open the door?"

The preacher cried, "Behold, now is the accepted time! Behold, now is the day of salvation!"

That was enough; husband and wife decided that He who had been a Stranger should henceforth be trusted as Saviour and Friend.

For more than ten years He has been to them "The Light of the World." That *Sheet Almanac* became a treasure, for they never tired of recounting the way they had been led to Christ.

Do you know where Christ is in your life? Is He inside, or outside? He said, "Behold, I stand at the door, and knock: if any man hear my voice, and open the door, I will come in to him, and will sup with him, and he with me." Have you opened the door?

—*Rev. J. L. Thomas*

Modern technology since World War II has brought our nation a high standard of living, never before realized in the history of the world. Americans enjoy a life style previously enjoyed only by royalty. With a twist of a knob, genie-like machines wash and dry our clothes and dishes, provide instant heat, instant meals, instant entertainment and instant transportation, but technology has two faces. We sacrifice, for our easier gadget-filled lives, the satisfaction of sincere human relationships.

Today we know most of our neighbors only as the shadowy figures encased inside of automobiles driving down the street. Neighborhood children are strangers who disappear into their houses after school to watch TV and spend summers traveling or at camp. Due to the postwar mobility of people, these neighbors change frequently and leave little of their identity behind.

Life was harder in the prewar years, with few labor-saving devices, but perhaps we remember those years with fondness because people interacted with, and had faith in, people rather than machines. People knew their neighbors and could depend upon them in times of need. Children, known by name, could be seen playing sandlot baseball on corner lots or following the ice wagon on hot days. Families sat on their front porches on summer evenings, exchanging conversation with passing neighbors on their way to the drugstore for ice cream before listening to Fibber McGee and Molly on the radio.

Of all the conveniences that modern technology has provided the American family, I believe the clothes drier is most responsible for neighbors not knowing one another. In the prewar years, Monday was washday in my neighborhood. Housewives strung clotheslines across their yards while chattering and gossiping with the neighbors. Preschool children would wander from yard to yard as their mothers called to each other over their wet wash and scolded children for running between the sheets. The air smelled of Fels Naptha soap as the clothes danced and billowed in the breeze.

As the clotheslines provided social communication between neighbors, they also provided a sort of neighborhood newspaper. Neighbors knew how to read the clotheslines and knew what social action to take from the news they read there. For example, lines of fluttering white squares and tiny blue blankets broadcast to all that the Wagners had a new son. (Many times now we are unaware of a new baby in the neighborhood as cars replace baby carriages for outings, and diapers are either machine dried or disposable.)

No one would have to organize a shower for Mrs. Wagner. Neighbors would stop by frequently with handmade gifts, casseroles or an offer of aid. Watching Mr. Wagner awkwardly hanging the wash for a few weeks after the baby's birth provoked humorous, yet tender, smiles from the neighbor ladies.

Clotheslines carried another kind of news, like when Mary Lou's tiny dresses disappeared from the Mitchells' line. Mary Lou had died of leukemia. People today feel embarrassed and self-conscious about approaching a neighbor they hardly know to offer condolences upon a death in the family. The

(More next page)

(Clothesline Gazette cont.)

The Importance of the Home

deceased is removed to a formal funeral home, and too quickly the neighborhood forgets. Mary Lou was known and missed by her neighbors. They cried with her family and consoled each other. Her clothes missing from the line were a constant reminder of her absence.

Clotheslines announced a new bride in the neighborhood by the newness of her linen.

An overabundance of nightclothes and bed linen meant someone was ill. The neighbor ladies would stop by and welcome the bride with their favorite chocolate cake recipes and prepare soup or little gifts for the sick.

Pink undershirts and grey towels hung crookedly over the clothesline told everyone that Mr. Browne's wife was off visiting her mother in St. Louis again. Women would send over dinner for Mr. Browne along with washing instructions.

When more and more patches appeared on the weekly wash of Mrs. Frey, the neighbors knew her husband was having no luck finding a job. Mrs. Frey didn't feel ashamed to accept the outgrown clothes of her neighbors' children or the casseroles the good people sent. People helped people in time of need. Mrs. Frey would help her neighbors in the same way when hard times hit them.

Modern technology has made it possible for us to pick up our daily paper and read about people thousands of miles away in some remote corner of the world. Strangely, we feel we know those people better than the family living down the street. Regardless of how advanced communication has become, no newspaper has brought people together more than the old *Clothesline Gazette*. The backyard newspaper involved neighbors in neighborhood problems, joys and sorrows. Within the last twenty-five years, the *Clothesline Gazette* has folded as neighbors learned to depend on machines rather than people.

—D. A. Woodliff

In days gone by when most families had woodsheds and chicken coops, a mother tried to persuade her boy to go up to bed. Finally she said: "See! the little chickens went to sleep a long time ago."

Her little son answered: "I know, Mother. I have been watching them, and you know what? The mother hen always goes up first."

Children usually follow in the footsteps of their parents. That's why the home is so important. Jesus appreciated the values of the home. At Bethany He enjoyed staying at the home of Mary, Martha and Lazarus. At Emmaus He gladly accepted the invitation of the two disciples who constrained Him saying, "Abide with us; for it is toward evening, and the day is far spent."

Jesus comes to you and to me and pleads, "Behold, I stand at the door and knock: if any man hear my voice, and open the door, I will come in to him, and will sup with him, and he with me."

—Paul Splett

TALK IS CHEAP, BUT YOU CAN'T BUY IT BACK.

"Are All the Children In?"

I think ofttimes as the night draws nigh
  Of an old house on the hill,
Of a yard all wide and blossom-starred
  Where the children played at will.
And when the night at last came down,
  Hushing the merry din,
Mother would look around and ask,
  "Are all the children in?"

'Tis many and many a year since then,
  And the old house on the hill
No longer echoes to childish feet,
  And the yard is still, so still.
But I see it all as the shadows creep;
  And though many the years have been,
Even now I can hear my mother ask,
  "Are all the children in?"

I wonder if, when the shadows fall
  On the last short, earthly day;
When we say goodby to the world outside,
  All tired with our childish play;
When we step out into that Other Land
  Where Mother so long has been,
Will we hear her ask, as we did of old,
  "Are all the children in?"

And I wonder, too, what the Lord will say
  To us older children of His;
Have we cared for the lambs?
  Have we showed them the fold?
A privilege joyful it is.
  And I wonder, too, what our answers
    will be
When His loving questions begin:
  "Have you heeded My voice?"
  "Have you told of My love?"
  "Have you brought the children in?"

—*Author Unknown*

Both Are Needed

A lecturer recently said that he received his moral training at the knee of a devout mother and across the knee of a determined father. Both knees are needed.

—*Selected*

Madame Guyon, a refined, cultured and exceedingly beautiful woman, for Christ's sake was exposed to the indignities and tortures of the French prisons for ten years—1695-1705. Why? Because she loved the Lord Jesus Christ and was determined to serve Him.

While in prison she wrote that exquisite poem so filled with thought:

A little bird I am
Shut from the fields of air;
Yet in my cage I sit and sing
To Him who placed me there;
Well pleased a prisoner to be,
Because, my God, it pleases Thee.

Naught have I else to do;
I sing the whole day long;
And He whom most I love to please
Doth listen to my song;
He caught and bound my wandering wing,
But still He bends to hear me sing.

My cage confines me round;
Abroad I cannot fly.
But though my wing is closely bound,
My heart's at liberty;
My prison walls cannot control
The flight, the freedom of the soul.

Oh, it is good to soar
These bolts and bars above,
To Him whose purpose I adore,
Whose Providence I love;
And in Thy mighty will to find
The joy, the freedom of the mind.

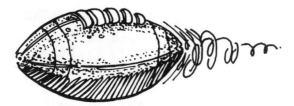

For when the One Great Scorer comes
To write against your name,
He writes—not that you won or lost—
But how you played the game.

—*Grantland Rice*

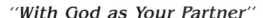

"With God as Your Partner"

*It takes a Groom, it takes a Bride,
Two People standing side by side . . .*

*It takes a Ring and Vows that say
This is Our Happy Wedding Day . . .*

*But marriage vows are sanctified
And loving hearts are unified*

*When standing with the bride and groom,
Unseen by others in the room,*

*The "Spirit of the Lord" is there
To bless this happy bridal pair . . .*

*For "God is Love," and married life
Is richer for both man and wife*

*When God becomes a partner, too,
In everything they plan and do . . .*

*And every home is specially blest
When God is made a "Daily Guest,"*

*For married folks who pray together
Are happy folks who stay together . . .*

*For when God's love becomes a part
Of body, mind, and soul and heart,*

*Their love becomes a wondrous blending
That's both Eternal and Unending,*

*And God looks down and says, "Well done". . .
For now you Two are truly One.*

As Loud as Saturn Rocket

In front of the bandstand at a Gainesville club for teenagers, a University of Florida researcher team found the noise measured 120 decibels—as loud as the Saturn 5 moon rocket measured from the press site at Cape Kennedy.

Dr. Kenneth C. Pollock said his associates at the audiology laboratory were forty feet outside the club before the sound dropped below ninety decibels, which the American Medical Association says is the threshold above which damage is caused.

By the time they are twenty-five years old, the youngsters will have the problems of the aged as sounds of consonants become hard to hear.

How Old and Wise and Venerable You Look!

I asked my wife if she knew any woman who was unaware of the arrival of those first gray hairs. "Are not the beauty parlors, the tints, the rinses, the dyes eloquent testimony to women's awareness of gray hair?" she replied.

Even men try to cover gray with washes of black and brown. Why should the pot call the pan black?

I admit I have more than one gray hair . . . many more. Five years ago my hair was brown. The gray ones came so quickly I was hardly aware of their arrival. My wife was the first to see them. There were just two of them then, to be sure, but there they were—the first signal of declining years, the first warning of reduced strength. They were so thinly interspersed that I tried to forget them. Time, however, was with them and not with me.

Today the brown and gray fight for first place.

Anthropologists take a great interest in our hair. They determine the ethnic or racial group by examining *one* hair. I am no anthropologist; but I enjoy its colors of yellow, red, brown and black—you know, the natural colors. Natural hair is attractive. I am fascinated by the straight, the wavy, the curly, the fuzzy, the woolly and the popcorn. The styles . . . well, they keep the women rushing to the beauty parlor and the men guessing.

The *Encyclopedia Britannica* states that hair is more than a decoration. It is an insulation against cold. And, as confession is good for the soul, I will be honest: I am losing my insulation!

To the Chinese, gray hair is a sign not only of age but also of dignity and wisdom. To them it is more complimentary to say, *"How old and wise and venerable you look!"*

—*Dick Hillis*

An "X" for a Kiss!

Our custom of putting X's at the ends of letters and notes to symbolize kisses grew out of medieval legal practices. In order to indicate good faith and honesty in those days, the sign of St. Andrew—a cross—was placed after the signature on all important documents.

Thereafter, contracts and agreements were not considered binding until each signer added St. Andrew's cross after his name. Then he was required to kiss the document to further guarantee faithful performance of his obligations. The cross was drawn hurriedly, and often it was tilted and looked much like the letter "X."

Over the centuries the origin of the ceremony was forgotten. But people still associated the "X" with the kiss instead of the pledge of good faith, and the custom has continued into modern times.

—Marvin Vanoni

Every day remember that you have a God to glorify, a Saviour to imitate, virtue to acquire, eternity to meditate upon, temptation to resist, the world to guard against, and perhaps death to meet.

A PRAYER FOR MOTORISTS:

Teach us to drive through life without skidding into other people's business. Preserve our brake lining, that we may stop before we go too far. Help us to hear the knocks in our own motors and close our ears to the clashing of other people's gears. Keep alcohol in our radiators and out of our stomachs. Absolve us from the mania of trying to pass the other automobile on a narrow road. Open our eyes to the traffic signs, and keep our feet on the brakes.

A kindergarten tot describing *Whistler's Mother:* "It shows a nice old lady waiting for the repairman to bring back her T.V. set."

Too Many Headless Homes Today

"*. . . As for me and my house, we will serve the Lord.*"—Josh. 24:15.

One thing is certain: Joshua was the head of his house. There is no account of his calling the family together to ask their approval or if the children had other ideas.

Jacob did the same thing at Bethel. Dinah had sinned after making her debut among the daughters of the land. The family had been disgraced, but Jacob obeyed the call of God to return to Bethel. He said to his household, "Put away the strange gods that are among you, and be clean, and change your garments: And let us arise, and go up to Bethel" (Gen. 35:2,3). He had come to Shechem to get rich, and he had paid the price; but at least his family followed him when he changed his course.

Stand in many a pulpit on Sunday morning and call for a return to Bethel; Jacob will resent it because it may mean a change of business. Mrs. Jacob will object, for she has social plans for the children. And Dinah will complain, for she will not renounce the world.

One basic trouble is that Jacob and Joshua are no longer heads of the houses. Bishops and deacons are to rule their households well (I Tim. 3:4,12). There is no double standard. What is good for the bishops and deacons is good for all Christians.

There are too many headless homes today. The husband is not the human head, and the Lord is not the divine head; and the family goes in all directions. We need new revivals at Shechem such as Jacob and Joshua began long ago.

EARTH IS OUR INN: HEAVEN IS OUR HOME. We may well

put up with discomfort in this world, for we shall soon be away from it; it is only for a few days that we accept its hospitality. Archbishop Leighton often said that, if he were to choose a place to die in, he would choose an inn; for it looked like a pilgrim going home, to whom this world was all as an inn, and who was weary of the noise and confusion in it.

He had his desire, for he died at the Bell Inn, in Warwick Lane.

—Spurgeon

Why pray when you can worry?

(The Scripture According to Catabias)

"Where's my food?"

"Worry without ceasing."—Catabias 1:1.

You never read any Scripture like the verse above. Mainly because it is not even Scripture. And please don't go rummaging around in your Bible looking for the Book of Catabias.

But I'm sure that, if our cat could write and felt inspired to put some good cat principles on paper, the above admonition would get top billing. For our cat is an inveterate worrier. His name, incidentally, is Catabias. (This is an ancient [?] adjective meaning slightly askew, out of whack or cockeyed—and our cat is all of that.)

When Catabias is not sleeping, he's worrying. I can't understand it. This crazy cat gets fed just like clockwork. But he spends most of his waking hours meowing, stewing and generally fretting about his next meal.

I've almost fractured a leg uncounted times immediately after opening the cupboard or refrigerator. It's like a trigger. Catabias can hear the sound from the most distant part of the house and be running between your feet tripping you up before you can close the door. And the sound of the can opener being operated practically sends him into hysterics.

This fur-covered stomach should know better by now, but he has the absolute conviction that anytime anyone reaches for food it is meant for his consumption.

Catabias has other endearing qualities. He once hated to leave the house, but now goes out at night. The problem is that he gets on the garage roof and begins running his claws down our bedroom window screen around 4:30 a.m. This is a sound guaranteed to shatter your pleasant dreams and bring you roaring out of bed with an ill-repressed desire to declaw that cat with a pair of hedge clippers.

But what really bugs me is that this ungrateful feline, after all the cans of cat food we've opened, after getting hundreds of meals right on time, still doesn't trust us. He gets all kinds of TLC; I've often restrained the impulse to kick him clear to Bangor, Maine, but he still (can you believe it?) doesn't trust us to come up with his next meal.

Somehow this cat reminds me of me. You may reply that, well, that's fine, but he doesn't remind you of you. But hang on a minute.

Have you ever started worrying about your next problem almost the instant the Lord has solved the last one? Jesus said, "Let not your heart be troubled . . ." (John 14:1). We often act as if He said, "Let not your fretting cease; neither quit your worrying for a minute."

Jesus had no sooner fed four thousand men, besides women and children, with seven loaves and a few fish than his disciples were, a few hours later, worrying about how much bread they had on hand.

Like Catabias, our stock of trust is often in short supply. God has been supplying one meal after another for most of us for more years than we care to count. Problems that had us upset a week, a month and a year ago, are gone, probably forgotten. God has taken care of them.

Yet, like Catabias fearing for his next meal, we act as if the Lord has a poor track record. "Why pray when you can worry?" seems to be the motto of some Christians.

"Trust and obey, for there's no other way . . .," says the hymn. And this is the answer. God loves me infinitely more than I love our cat; yet we're still providing him with regular meals, warm shelter and a certain amount of affection.

And we, despite our lack of trust, are of infinitely greater value than that cat (or sparrow, cf. Matt. 10:29-31). How much more then can I, and all of us, trust God to supply our every need (Phil. 4:19)?

Tired of worrying? Lacking in personal peace? Put God's Word into practice; don't just pay lip service to it in theory. Read it, meditate upon it, believe it and live by it.

"Be careful for nothing; but in every thing by prayer and supplication with thanksgiving let your requests be made known unto God. And the peace of God, which passeth all understanding, shall keep your hearts and minds through Christ Jesus."—Phil. 4:6,7.

Do it; it works!

Better stop preaching. It's time to go open another can of cat food.

—George Keck (from *Evangelical Beacon*)

How Staying Home Makes Cents

I began thinking about going back to work the day my youngest child entered school. Most of my friends were working, and I felt guilty about having so much free time at home. *But more importantly,* I asked, *shouldn't I be contributing financially to our family?*

So I settled into a half-time job at a nearby preschool. I thoroughly enjoyed it. But it seemed the mornings I worked were always when one of the children woke up with a runny nose or a fever. I would have to find a substitute teacher, leave my child at home alone or send her to school sick.

Even if one of the children wasn't sick, I found I could no longer attend school activities during the day. There was no time to bake cookies for the PTA meetings or sew robes for the youth choir. I was continually having to refuse tasks I had previously enjoyed.

My husband listened to my tales of woe as long as he could, then suggested I quit my job.

"I'll bet with a little ingenuity you could save more money at home than you're now earning," he challenged me. Never one to turn down a challenge, I handed in my resignation at the end of the school year.

That summer, I came across Proverbs 31:10-31, a survey of the tasks a truly fine wife performs. The writer states that she weaves and sews and purchases food for her family. "She looketh well to the ways of her household, and eateth not the bread of idleness" (vs. 27).

This quieted my guilt about staying home. I could be fulfilled working where my heart was.

I soon found I was able to save a considerable amount of money on groceries. No longer needing to use prepared items, I could buy less expensive cuts of meat to marinate or cook slowly. I had time to study the sales and could go to several grocery stores instead of rushing through a single one each week. I could plan carefully and buy in quantity. All this took extra time, but time was what I had.

I had time to sew again. Children's clothing takes such small amounts of fabric that I would often use only remnants. I was amazed at the little tops and skirts I could make for the summer months that cost only pennies. I noticed how clothing and food prices varied greatly from store to store, so I took the time to shop around and gained a reputation for bargain hunting.

In the summer I picked fruit from local orchards and made enough jam to last the year. I planted a garden and canned my own tomatoes. Turning on the stereo and working at the kitchen sink, I scrubbed, chopped and filled containers with produce I had either picked or grown myself. When I was finished, I would proudly look at the colorful jars neatly lined in a row.

I was able to make most of my Christmas and holiday gifts. With so many of my friends back at work, handcrafted or baked items became more valued and appreciated. I even made our own family Christmas cards.

I had time to shop at garage sales. I had time to bake birthday cakes, weed the garden, wash the car and clean the house—things I had been paying to have done when I was employed.

When the final tally came in and I took into account the taxes I'd paid the year before, the babysitters I'd had to hire and the extra clothes my job had required, I was actually saving a considerable amount of money by staying home! To that add the benefits of choosing my own daily tasks, having no boss to report to and being available at all times for my children or for lunch with my husband. I could nap in the afternoon after a sleepless night, take unlimited sick leave and sport a suntan from working in the yard.

Twelve years have now passed. I look back with pleasure on the thirty costumes I made for a talent show, the countless number of formals I made for my daughters and the Mason jars I repeatedly filled. I have been able to sneak in visits to convalescent homes, do volunteer work and begin free-lance writing.

When I turn the pages of our family albums, I have to smile at the picture of my three children with chocolate frosting all over their faces from the time we decorated cookies together. My form of Social Security is not measured in dollars and cents, but, as the woman of Proverbs 31, in deeds.

Yes, I realize my choice is not for every woman. But I'm proud to call myself a housewife—especially since I proved that it does make cents.

—June Kolf
(Reprinted from *Pulpit Helps*)

"Why Ain't It?"

I guess we all feel like the young boy who stopped in front of an abstract painting in an exhibition of local talent in Arizona.

"What's that?" he asked his mother.

"It's supposed to be a cowhand and his horse," she explained.

"Well," asked the boy, "why ain't it?"

Wrong Church— Right Pew!

A woman who "enjoyed her religion" visited a very staid and formal church. "Amen!" she said, as the preacher brought out a point with which she agreed.

"Madam," said the usher standing nearby, "please try to restrain yourself. We don't allow that in this church."

In a few moments she was so carried away by the sermon that she shouted, "Amen! Praise the Lord! Hallelujah!"

The usher rushed to her side: "Madam! You must quiet down immediately or leave!"

"I didn't mean to disturb the service. . .but I am just so happy since I found the Lord," she explained.

"You may have found the Lord," retorted the usher severely, "but I am quite sure you didn't find Him here!"

He's Gone Now, and I Helped to Damn Him

I used to take my son to church, and then I'd
     drive away,
"I've more important things to do," is what
     I used to say.
I lived a normal, honest life but never
     entered in
The sanctuary with the lad, to learn the fear
     of sin.
Of course, for children it was best; I gladly had
     him go
And thought the church would teach him some
     lessons he should know.
But he grew up and quit it all, nor did he ask
     of me,
And soon was out in deepest sin, as vile as vile
     could be.

*We took him to the church today. I entered with
     the rest,
To hear the robed choir stand and sing of
     mansions of the blest.
My face was wet with scalding tears as I remem-
     bered then,
Had I but gone with him before, the man he
     might have been.
Yes, I went to the church today, as long I should
     have done,
And wept, because I knew I'd helped to damn
     my only son.*

—Geo. E. Blanchard

LUCKY PEOPLE!

The bathtub was invented in 1850, although Bell didn't invent the telephone until 1875. This doesn't mean much until we stop to think how lucky the people of that day were. They could have sat in the tub for 25 years without the phone ringing!

A SWELLED HEAD MAY MAKE YOUR HALO TOO TIGHT.

The Fireside Hearth

Where is the fireside hearth,
The glowing ember,
The flowing spring,
The quiet mirth
Of yesteryear,
Where kindred souls gather
To muse and to grow
In the afterglow of sunset,
In the gloaming?

Where is the security of home,
Where Father takes the Book
And inspires discipline and trust,
While children learn
To remember their Creator
In the days of their youth?

No more do the shades of night
     steal quietly over the hills
And welcome the weary to rest.
They come with a flash,
They come with a roar,
Milling in on a thousand wheels;
And men come out of their homes
Like lions
To the business of night.

—Laurence A. Davis

His Choice Better Than Mine

I would have chosen a sunlit path,
  All strewn with roses fair,
With never a cloud to darken my way,
  Nor a shade of anxious care.
But He chose for me a better way—
  Not sunshine or roses sweet,
But clouds o'erhead, and thorns below
  That cut and hurt my feet.
I have deep joys of another kind,
  My Rose of Sharon is He;
And as for sunshine—His lovely face
  Is perfect sunshine to me.

I would have chosen my life to be
  Active, tireless and strong;
A constant, ceaseless working for Him,
  Amid the needy throng.
But He chose for me a better lot—
  A life of frequent pain,
Of strength withheld when needed most,
  And loss instead of gain.
He gave me work of another kind,
  Far, far above my thought,
The work of interceding with Him,
  For souls that He had bought.

'Tis far, far better to let Him choose
  The way that we should take,
If only we leave our life with Him
  He will guide without a mistake.
We, in our blindness, would never
    choose
  A pathway dark and rough,
And so we would never find in Him,
  "The God who is enough."
In disappointment, trouble and pain
  We turn to the changeless One,
And prove how faithful, loving and wise
  Is God's beloved Son.

            —Catherine A. Miller
            of Africa Inland Mission

Tomorrow's Bridge

Tomorrow's bridge, as I look ahead,
  Is a rickety thing to view;
Its piers are crumbled, its rails are down,
  Its floor would let me through.

The chasm it spans is dark and deep,
  And the waters foam and fret;
I have crossed that bridge a thousand times,
  Though I never have reached it yet.

It has crashed beneath me to let me through,
  Although it's miles away;
But strange, the bridges I have crossed
  Have all been safe today.

Perhaps I shall find when I reach the one
  That lies in the distant blue,
Some hand may have mended its rickety floor,
  And its piers may be strong and new;

And I can pass over, lighthearted and free
  As a bird on the buoyant air.
Forgive me, God, for my fearful heart,
  My anxious and foolish care.

            —Grace Noll Crowell

*****

The schoolboy's essay on cats read:

"Cats that's made for little boys and girls to maul and tease is called Maltese cats. Some cats is known by their queer purrs—these are called Pursian cats. Cats with bad tempers is called Angorrie cats. Cats with deep feelin's is called Feline cats."

You Utter Some 30,000 Words a Day

A famous publisher declares, "If you are an articulate person, you utter some 30,000 words each day."

If these words were put in print, they would amount to a fair-sized book a day. These books would, in a lifetime, fill a good-sized college library.

All these books are from the same author. All reflect the life and thoughts of the author, in his own words. And not a book can be taken down from the shelves or withdrawn from circulation.

The thought is a bit frightening. It emphasizes the fearful responsibility that goes with the gift of speech, and also the glorious privilege that is inherent in 'speech seasoned with grace' (Col. 4:6).

Man probably has no greater power for good or for evil than the power of speech. Job had the testimony of his friend that his "words" had kept men on their feet—had kept men from falling (Job 4:4). What a rebuke to those whose words have thrown men off their feet—causing ill will, suspicion, alienation, broken hearts!

Probably most of us talk too much. And we seldom realize this until it is too late. Perhaps this was what the psalmist felt when he exclaimed, "Set a watch, O Lord, before my mouth; keep the door of my lips" (Ps. 141:3).

An elderly black woman, much beloved in her community, was asked for her formula for making and keeping friends. "Well," she replied, "I stop and taste my words before I let them pass my teeth."

"Out of the abundance of the heart the mouth speaketh" (Matt. 12:34). Therefore we read, "Keep thy heart with all diligence; for out of it are the issues of life" (Prov. 4:23). And "Every idle word that men shall speak, they shall give account thereof in the day of judgment" (Matt. 12:36).

Men in court have turned pale upon the introduction of recordings of their own speech. And souls will tremble in the judgment, upon finding that every utterance from the first wail of infancy till the tongue was silenced by death, has been noted by the Great Recorder.

Sweeter to our Lord than the melody of music and more important than the oratory of statesmen or the proclamations of kings are the conversations of His children talking together about the things of the Heavenly Father. All is written in His "book of remembrance" (Mal. 3:16). "They spake . . . and the Lord hearkened." Others also "spake," and the Lord hearkened. And into the record went every whispered conspiracy, every word of slander, every falsehood, every cutting remark, every obscene utterance, every foul blasphemy.

What a noble attribute is the gift of speech! And what finer tribute to the Giver than to present to the library of Heaven, each day, one clean volume—30,000 words—dedicated to His honor!

(From *Tents Toward the Sunrise*, by Chas. W. Koller)

MENTAL BLOCK

I followed her for several blocks,
But was afraid to pass,
Because first she'd slow to a creep
And then step on the gas.
With each block my patience ebbed,
And finally in disgust,
I pulled around, about to pass
And leave her in the dust.

Then sure enough, it happened
When our cars were neck to neck;
She took a left without a glance
And caused an awful wreck!
My car was smashed, my face was cut,
My nerves were all ajar;

And when the dust had cleared away,
I walked up to her car.

I asked her why she'd chosen to turn
Without a single sign,
Or why she didn't look around
To see who was behind.
With innocent smile, she turned to me
And this excuse did give:
"You should have known that I'd turn here,
For this is where I live!"

—Carolyn Jacobs Johnson in *GRIT*

How Much Does a Prayer Weigh?

How much does a prayer weigh? There is a story of a man who tried to weigh one. He owned a little grocery store. It was a week before Christmas, shortly after World War I.

A tired-looking woman came into the store and asked for enough food to make a Christmas dinner for the children. The grocer asked her how much she could spend.

"My husband did not come back; he was killed in the War. And I have nothing to offer but a little prayer," she answered.

The storekeeper was not very sentimental or religious, so he said, half mockingly, "Write it on paper, and I'll weigh it."

To his surprise, the woman took a piece of paper from the pocket of her dress and handed it to the man, saying, "I wrote it during the night while watching over my sick baby."

The grocer took the piece of paper before he could recover from his surprise; and, because other customers were watching and had heard his remarks, he placed the unread prayer on the weight side of his old-fashioned scales. Then he began to pile food on the other side; but to his amazement, the scale would not go down. In his embarrassment, he continued to put food on the scale, but still the scale refused to go down.

He became angry and flustered and finally said, "Well, that's all the scale will hold. Here's a bag; you will have to put it in yourself. I'm busy."

With trembling hands the woman filled the bag, and through moist eyes expressed her gratitude and departed.

Now that the store was empty of customers, the grocer examined the scales. Yes, they were broken, and they had become broken just in time for God to answer the prayer of the woman.

But as the years passed, the grocer often wondered about the incident. Why did the woman come at just the right time? Why had she already written the prayer in such a way as to confuse the grocer so that he did not examine the scales?

The grocer is an old man now, but the weight of the paper still lingers with him. He never saw the woman again, nor had he seen her before that date. Yet he remembered her more than any of his customers.

And he treasures the slip of paper upon which the woman's prayer had been written—simple words, but from a heart of faith, "Please, Lord, give us this day our daily bread."

—Selected

She Did What She Couldn't

John Henry Jowett once told of a little graveyard beside a church in a small village where the memory of a devoted soul, who had spent herself freely and untiringly in the service of that small community, is enshrined in this brief and touching epitaph:

SHE HAS DONE WHAT
SHE COULDN'T.

Children in Choirs

All of life is set to music. We have but to listen to hear the singing water of the brook, the tinkling melody of the waterfall, the murmur of the summer breeze, the whistling of the winter wind. We have but to look to see the rhythmic vibrations of the leaves, the graceful movements of the flowers or the aesthetic swaying of the evergreens.

Human life grows rhythms. Every normal child has an inherent ability to appreciate music, if not to produce it. Music is made up

principally of melody, harmony and rhythm. It is the accompaniment of life. Therefore, every child should have the blessed privilege of musical education as a means of

Personal Expression

This is of psychological impor-tance. The child is entitled to the utmost in mental, spiritual and cultural advantages. When his hunger for music has been suppressed, through neglect or otherwise, he has been robbed of an essential mode of expression that will dwarf his whole life and personality.

Appreciation for the Best

The child should have musical training in order that he may know and appreciate good music. The sensitive fibers of many a child's nature have been outraged and coarsened through continued contact with trashy, jangling sounds, hackneyed, syncopated songs, jive "hot" music, and with the morbid crooning so frequently heard on TV and radio, as well as occasionally from recital sources.

Social Adjustment

The child who is taught to sing with others in a choir or to properly play a musical instrument in an orchestra, not only finds expression for his innermost feelings, but he is learning to become a properly adjusted member of the great human family through cooperation with others in the rendition of worthwhile music.

A minister parked his car in a no-parking zone in a large city and attached the following message to his windshield: "I have circled this block 10 times. I have an appointment to keep. *Forgive our trespasses.*"

When he returned to his car he found this reply attached to his own note along with a ticket: "I've circled this block for 10 years. If I don't give you a ticket I lose my job. *Lead us not into temptation.*"

YOU CAN'T WALK OUT THEN

A woman was listening to a sermon about the coming judgment. She was so mad that she got up and started to leave. The preacher interrupted his message and said to her, "Lady, you can walk out on my sermon, but you will never be able to walk out on the judgment day when you meet the Judge personally."

Early Impressions on Children

As I stood in a house in one of the Long Island villages I saw a beautiful tree and I said to the owner, "That is a very fine tree; but what a curious crook there is in it."

"Yes," said he; "I planted that tree, and when it was a year old, I went to New York and worked as a mechanic for a year or two; and when I came back I found they had allowed something to stand against the tree, and so it has always had that crook."

And so I think it is with the influence upon children. If you allow anything to stand in the way of moral influence against a child on this side or that side, to the latest day of his life on earth and through all eternity, he will show the pressure.

No wonder Lord Byron was bad. Do you know his mother said to him, when she saw him one day limping across the floor with his unsound foot, "Get out of my way, you lame brat!" What chance for a boy like that!

—*Talmage*

A minister concluded a powerful sermon on the Ten Commandments. As the people filed out, a glum-faced Susie Quagmire was overheard to remark: "Well, anyway, I have never made a graven image."

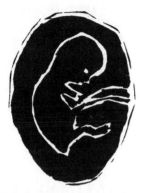

Ballad of the Unborn

My shining feet will never run
On early morning lawn;
My feet were crushed before they had
A chance to greet the dawn.

My fingers now will never stretch
To touch the winning tape;
My race was done before I learned
The smallest steps to take.

My growing height will never be
Recorded on the wall;
My growth was stopped when I was still
Unseen, and very small.

My lips and tongue will never taste
The good fruits of the earth;
For I myself was judged to be
A fruit of little worth.

My eyes will never scan the sky
For my high-flying kite;
For when still blind, destroyed were they
In the black womb of night.

I'll never stand upon a hill,
Spring's winds in my hair;
Aborted winds of thought closed in
On motherhood's despair.

I'll never walk the shores of life
Or know the tides of time;
For I was coming but unloved,
And that my only crime.

Nameless am I, a grain of sand,
One of the countless dead,
But the deed that made me ashen grey
Floats on seas of red.

—Fay Clayton

What Do You Say to an Undertaker?

At a luncheon meeting the other day I happened to sit next to one of our local undertakers. Usually my contact with him is very brief, for we each have a job to do during funerals, and there isn't much time for conversation. But this time the waitress was slow, and I found myself with plenty of time to talk. Then it hit me. *What do you say to an undertaker?*

I was just about to start off with the standard conversation starters, like, "How's business going?" or, "Are they keeping you busy?" when something told me that didn't sound quite right for an undertaker. Remembering the current economic slump, which makes a good topic for talk these days, I started to say, "I hope business picks up soon, don't you?" when the implications of that wish for his business stopped me cold.

Not long before this, his establishment had run an ad in the paper that didn't exactly send me rushing out, check in hand, to invest. It offered a free burial vault, worth $150, to anyone who dies this year. Surely I could at least congratulate him on offering such a good deal, but somehow I found it difficult to work up the necessary enthusiasm to discuss it. I thought about inquiring from him whether he had any kind of a layaway plan, but somehow the word "layaway" seemed in bad taste, so I thought better of it.

For once in my life, this preacher was tongue-tied. I longed for the waitress to come so we could at least complain about the food together. I was caught in a grip of a genuine communication gap!

And then the realization came to me that he was having the same problem. He was not exactly bubbling over with sparkling conversation either. I suppose he was thinking, *What do you say to a preacher?*

Perhaps he thought of saying, as one cartoon put it, "Is the world sinful enough to suit you?" Or maybe he thought about asking, "What did you do over the weekend?" when the obvious answer made the question seem ridiculous.

So we sat there, two grown men with tongues tied, searching for ways to bridge the chasm created by the two different worlds we live in.

That's pretty much the problem all over the world today. There is a gap between black and white, young and old, rich and poor, labor and management, long hair and short hair, parent and child—and most of the time we could bridge it if we learned a little more about the other's problems. We're too wrapped up in our own world to know much about the other fellow's. There is wisdom in the oft-quoted Indian prayer, "Great Spirit, grant that I may not criticize my neighbor until I have walked a mile in his moccasins."

One thing is pretty certain: any witnessing we attempt to do for Christ will be a hundred times more effective when we begin to share one another's lives. We must be like Ezekiel and 'sit where they sit' (Ezek. 3:15).

—Rev. Wendell E. Kent

Songs You Used to Sing:

Silver Threads Among the Gold

Darling, I am growing old,
Silver threads among the gold.
Shine upon my brow today—
Life is fading fast away;
But, my darling, you will be, will be
Always young and fair to me;
Yes, my darling, you will be
Always young and fair to me.

Chorus:

Darling, I am growing, growing old.
Silver threads among the gold
Shine upon my brow today—
Life is fading fast away.

When your hair is silver white,
And your cheeks no longer bright,
With the roses of the May,
I will kiss your lips and say:
Oh, my darling, mine alone, alone,
You have never older grown—
Yes, my darling, mine alone,
You have never older grown.

Love can nevermore grow old—
Locks may lose their brown and
*   gold;*
Cheeks may fade and hollow grow,
But the hearts that love will know,
Never, never winter's frost and chill;
Summer warmth is in them still—
Never winter's frost and chill,
Summer warmth is in them still.

Love is always young and fair.
What to us is silver hair,
Faded cheeks or steps grown slow
To the heart that beats below?

Love's Old Sweet Song

Once in the dear dead days beyond
*   recall,*
When on the world the mist began
*   to fall,*
Out of the dreams that rose in
*   happy throng,*
Low in our hearts love sang an old
*   sweet song;*
And in the dusk where fell the
*   firelight gleam,*
Softly it wove itself into our dream.

Even today we hear Love's song
*   of yore,*
Deep in our hearts it dwells forever-
*   more;*
Footsteps may falter, weary grow the
*   way;*
Still we can hear it at the close of
*   day;*
So till the end, when life's dim
*   shadows fall,*
Love will be found the sweetest song
*   of all.*

Just a song at twilight, when the
*   lights are low,*
And the flick'ring shadows softly
*   come and go,*
Tho' the heart be weary, sad the day
*   and long,*
Still to us at twilight comes Love's
*   old song,*
Comes Love's old, sweet song.

—G. Clifton Bingham (Eng. 1882)

"Thou God Seest Me!"

When Bishop Ditchfield was a little boy, he visited an aged woman, a devout Christian. On the wall in her room hung the framed text, "Thou God seest me."

The aged saint said, "Read the text."

He read it aloud.

"My lad," said the aged woman, "when you are older, people will tell you that God is always watching you to see you when you do wrong, so that He might punish you. I do not want you to think of this text in this way. I want you to take the framed text home with you. Whenever you see it, I want you to know that God loves you so much that He cannot take His eyes off you!"

Then—Face to Face

"Now we see through a glass, darkly; but then face to face: now I know in part; but then shall I know even as also I am known."— I Cor. 13:12.

"They shall see his face...."—Rev. 22:4.

Then—face to face! No hindered, holden vision;
*   No twilight reading in that full-orbed day;*
No erring judgment; no wrong, rash decision;
*   Then shall uncertainty have fully passed away.*

Then—face to face! No mystery then o'er sorrow,
*   Things so appalling that we oft are numb:*
No mystery then! oh, clear and gladsome morrow—
*   What rest, what bliss, when Thou at last shall come!*

Then—face to face! Clear then the tragic trials,
*   Now oft the lot of those intense for Him:*
Saints who here drink the full of bitter vials,
*   Then, then shall know what here, at best, is dim.*

Then—face to face! Here—oft the baffling story;
*   To finite minds all cannot here be shown;*
But—when doth burst the Everlasting Glory,
*   Then we shall know as we e'en now are known.*

Peculiar Mother

To the accompaniment of loud, angry and profane words, two chickens came flying over the fence that divided our yard from the neighbor's garden. The chickens were flying but not under their own power; their necks had been thoroughly wrung.

We children had been playing hide-and-seek. Now we froze in wide-eyed horror and listened in wordless awe to the colorful language of our neighbor, Mr. _____, as he viewed the damage mother's prize White Rocks had wrought to a row of his tender young lettuce.

Recovering from our stunned silence, we wasted no time racing into the kitchen to inform Mother of this most shocking occurrence.

Four excited, angry children, talking all at once, described the situation most dramatically and adequately and waited to see what Mother would do. Would she rush out and shout angrily across the fence to Mr. _____ as Mrs. Pickett, on the other side of his house, often did? Or would she cry and call Papa, and let him deliver the retaliation that was surely due our hot-tempered neighbor?

Mother did neither, sad faced (for these were expensive, purebred stock); but calmly she viewed the still flapping chickens. "Bring the axe," she instructed my brother, "and heat the big kettle of water," she told big sister.

Soon the delicious aroma of stewing chicken permeated the house. No loss without some small gain was the general feeling as our young appetites began to look forward to suppertime. Would it be chicken and dumplings or chicken pot pie, I wondered.

It was to be chicken pie, I soon discovered; two of them, in fact. I watched as Mother cut her own special leaf design into the crusts, fitted them carefully over the casseroles of savory chicken and set them into the oven to brown golden and flaky.

I watched as she put a lemon cake together with a creamy filling and frosted the whole with fluffy white icing and coconut. *M-m-m! Almost like a birthday or a Sunday school picnic,* thought I, as I licked the bowl.

When the chicken pies were done, Mother told the older girls to set the table, as she had to run over to Mr. _____'s for a moment.

"To Mr. _____'s! What on earth for?" was the incredulous question we all cried simultaneously.

"To take him one of the chicken pies and a piece of cake and to tell him I am sorry my chickens damaged his lettuce," replied Mother matter-of-factly.

"But, Mother!" I cried indignantly. "That mean old man! He called all of us and all of our chickens such terrible names! Why, he said . . . ."

"Hush, dear. Never mind what he said. Mr. _____

is a lonely, unhappy old man, and he is not a Christian. We should be sorry for him and be very kind to him, for he is our neighbor and our responsibility. Our chickens did destroy some of his lettuce, and the least we can do is show him we are sorry and try to repay the damage."

Anxiously I watched from behind a snowball bush. What would happen to Mother? A man capable of wringing chickens' necks in anger might do just about anything. I picked up a large stick. Just holding it gave me a sense of security. I knew the others were watching from the dining room window. Trembling, we waited.

But there was nothing timid in Mother's manner as she went swiftly, shoulders erect, to Mr. _____'s front door, bearing the napkin-covered tray. I can still see her white apron strings blowing and feel the knot of fear in my throat as she knocked on the door and presented her peace offering to the terrible-tempered Mr. _____.

Poor Mr. _____. He whose vocabulary never lacked epithets with which to express his anger now had not a word at his command! Even an outraged child could feel a tinge of pity for him as he stood there in the doorway, embarrassed, ashamed and wordless in the face of Mother's sincere and kindly overture.

Remembering Mother as she lived and as she died, I realize that she never stepped out of character; she was always and only herself in any circumstance or situation. Her belief in God and the unshakable quality of His Word was profoundly simple. If Jesus said, "Love your enemies, bless them that curse you, do good to them that hate you, and pray for them which despitefully use you"—then He meant just that, and a follower of His must obey the injunction quite literally.

I have often laughingly said that Mother lived by the "Three G's." "Living the Christian life takes a certain amount of gumption," she often said, "and all the grit you can scrape up; and then, when God adds His wonderful grace, anybody can get along just fine."

Come to think of it, I guess Mother was a peculiar woman. I would like to be more like her!

—Selected

How God Fed the Children!

"God always does above all we can ask or think," said Miss Clara. "He delights in giving us good things."

I am going to tell you a true story of how God sent us food. My father was a minister, and often people failed to pay promptly, so sometimes we saw hard times. Once when I was a little girl, Father had to go to the Conference, and he didn't even have one cent to leave Mother to buy food with while he was gone. He told Mother he would not go without leaving us money. She told him he must go, that God would take care of us.

We had some potatoes, a few cans of fruit, a little dried corn, and salt and sugar in the house; but the flour bin was empty. Mother did not believe in going in debt, and we bought only what we could pay for.

We still had one loaf of bread when Father left. When that was gone there was no flour to make any more. Mother smiled and told us that God knew we needed flour, and for us not to worry. She had us all kneel with her while she asked our Heavenly Father to send us a sack of flour.

She arose and made the rising for the bread just as if the flour bin were full. Then she said, "Now, children, I've done all I can; God will do the rest."

We all went to bed strong in faith that God would answer our prayers. I almost expected to wake up in the morning and find a sack of flour in the kitchen. When my brother came downstairs, the first thing he asked was, "Has God sent the flour yet?"

Mother lifted the lid from the bread bowl and let us see how light and foamy the rising was. All it needed was the flour.

We ate our scant breakfast of potatoes and salt, then Mother knelt by the empty flour bin and praised God because He had said His children would never need to beg for bread.

Mother and I washed the dishes, and Mother started to sing the old song: "O for a faith that will not shrink." My little brother, who was looking out of the window, said, "Somebody is tying a horse and buggy to our fence." A woman came up the path empty-handed.

She talked about the weather and kept twisting her scarf. Finally she said, "I want to tell you a strange thing that happened to me this morning. As I was getting breakfast, I heard a voice say, 'Take Brother Hayden some flour.' I knew no one was in the kitchen but me, and I was scared. Then I heard it again, 'Go take Brother Hayden some flour.' I suppose I'm a fool, but do you need any flour?"

By this time Mother was crying and exclaiming, "Praise the Lord!" She told the woman of her prayers for flour, showing her the empty flour bin and the crock of yeast rising. The woman began to cry and, going to her buggy, gave my brother a sack of flour, handed me a part of a smoked ham, gave the younger brother and sister a jug of milk and a bucket of butter.

"I just thought if the Almighty was telling me to take you the flour, like as not you needed the butter, too, so I brought some things along," she said.

Mother kissed her and said, "You look like an angel to us!" Then we held a real thanksgiving prayer meeting. And then the dear woman gave her heart to Jesus right at our house.

Before Father came home from the Conference, people came from all parts of his parish and paid Mother both in food and money a great deal more than they owed.

—*Selected*

The POISON of Self Pity

Get angry with yourself, pat yourself on the back, commend yourself, praise, blame, love or hate yourself—do anything but don't pity yourself.

Self-pity has a certain septic satisfaction, like picking at a sore, and there is an undeniable "luxury of self-dispraise," but it's as dangerous as getting drunk. It's habit-forming. It grows on one. Quit it.

Pity is a glorious and credible attribute—when it flows out toward another. Then it is like the mountain brook, sparkling, chattering, leaping the laughter of the woods, the refreshment of bird and beast, carrying health and joy to all who drink of its cool flood or even gaze upon its happy play.

But pity, when it turns upon self, is like a stagnant pool, covered with hateful scum and concealing ugly, slimy things in its foul ooze.

One who is sorry for himself is already half-beaten.

The self-pitying are abused. Nobody treats them right. People talk about them. Others are promoted over them. They get no proper thanks. They are unappreciated. Alas! Also alack, and woe is me! Let us all go into the garden and eat worms.

The self-pitiers invite every variety of spiritual microbe to come in and breed. They are the clouds, mud and slush of mankind. They are rarely efficient. No man that hasn't enough egotism to admire himself a bit ever amounted to much.

Bad as egotism is, it is infinitely better than self-contempt.

The self-pitiers are hard to love, trying to live with and impossible to please. They cannot enjoy riches nor appreciate poverty.

When they are well they think they are sick, and when they are sick they think they are worse. They are gloom-spreaders and heart depressants.

Self-pity is the most exquisite form of selfishness, the camouflage of impotence, the acme of disagreeableness. Self-pity requires no brains, no capacity, no worth. It is sheer and utter no-accountness.

If you pity yourself, you are hypnotized by yourself. Come out of it!

No self-pitying troops ever won a battle; no self-pitying clerk ever rose to be general manager; no self-pitying merchant ever made his business thrive; no self-pitying woman ever retained her husband's love; no self-pitying human being was ever a help to another human being.

Self-pity is the collapse of all the faculties; it is cowardly surrender in the face of the enemy.

Don't complain! Keep your chin up! The courageous soul, in no matter what condition, is a point of cheer, a lamp of brightness, a tonic draught to his fellow men.

In every city there ought to be a public spanker for all self-pitiers.

—*Dr. Frank Crane*

★★★★★★★★★★★★★★★★★★★★★★★★★★★★★★★★★★★★★

The House That Never Was

In London, England, there is a strange house.

It looks like any other house on the block. But wait! Nobody ever comes out of No. 23 Leinster Gardens. There is neither a doorbell not a letterbox. From the windows no one at all peers out. And nary a soul ever sits on one of the balconies.

Yes, No. 23 is a sham. It's a dummy house whose door and windows are merely painted on a cement wall. Behind this deceiving oddball facade there is nothing except a network of girders, some train tracks and the entrance to a tunnel. Every so often a fresh coat of paint is applied to the facing wall to keep it looking exactly like the neighboring buildings.

"The House That Never Was" was put up by London's Metropolitan Railway (the so-called Underground), whose officials decided it would be the best way to hide the entrance to the subway tunnel and fill the gap in the row of houses so as not to spoil the harmonious look of the street (Nino Lo Bello in *The Calgary Herald*, September 27, 1975).

But No. 23 is not the only sham house in the world! There are other houses that deceive the onlooker. There are homes that outwardly have all the signs of being Christian: church attendance, abstinence from liquor and cigarettes, etc., but inwardly these homes lack all the distinctive marks of the truly Christian home. Love, joy, peace, harmony are nonexistent. Parents argue and fight; children are physically abused; and the principles of the Bible are not honored.

What about your home? Is it supposed to be Christian, but actually it is a sham? Is it a whited sepulcher—beautiful from the outside, but inside full of dead men's bones?

God wants to change your home through His grace and His power.

—*The Prairie Overcomer*

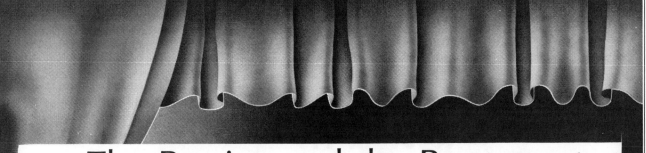

The Passing and the Permanent

"Weeping may endure for a night, but joy cometh in the morning" (Ps. 30:5). This is a verse of sharp contrasts. "Weeping" versus "joy," "night" versus "morning," the uncertain "may" and the positive "cometh."

Every day is made up of twenty-four hours. In the summer, the days are long and the nights are short; in the winter, the days are short and the nights are long; but ever since God called the light day and the darkness night, they have faithfully followed their appointed assignment.

There is no ready answer to the question all of us have sought an answer for: why is it that some of God's children have so much darkness while others are basking in perennial light? I can only assure them on the authority of God's Word that "joy cometh in the morning."

Some suffering patients have said, "Wish to God it was morning," while others have said, "Wish to God it was night." To all and to you "weeping may endure for a night, but joy cometh in the morning."

God doesn't have to shake His watch to see if His timepiece is moving. It is, and accurately so. Some nights are so dark that you can't see your own hand, but never fear, His hand is there.

During the German blitz on the British Isle—I believe it was Coventry—after the stukas had left, the citizenry began to search among the ruins for the dead, the dying and the missing. There was an old grandmother they could not account for. Then someone found her soundly asleep in her little bedroom.

"Grandma," one exclaimed, "how could you sleep with all the commotion going on?"

The reply was both instant and firm, "It says in the Bible, 'He that keepeth Israel will neither slumber nor sleep,' so I figured there was no need for both of us to stay awake."

There is always a morning for God's people. "There's a great day coming by and by." Don't ever envy a rich, ungodly person—he may be in his daylight now, but he is going toward an endless night. God's people may be in the night now, but they are going onward to a glorious morning, an eternal A.M. followed by no P.M.

Most of us have sung, "Work for the night is coming," but I like the one better that was written by Dr. Fitzwater of Moody Bible Institute, "Work for the day is coming." It is deeply regretted that that wonderful song didn't have wider acceptance, for it expressed so effectively this blessed truth that "weeping may endure for a night, but joy cometh in the morning."

Dr. Paul Rood once told of their having company one evening. His little son Paul, Jr., didn't want to go to bed for fear he would miss something; and, of course, he would. He sent his boy upstairs twice before he "stayed put."

The following morning when little Paul came down for breakfast, he said to his father, "Daddy, I want to go to Heaven." Naturally his father was pleased, but he added, "Why do you want to go to Heaven just now?" Though spoken long ago, his answer has long thrilled me—"Because there won't be any night there."

—*Pastor Eric W. Johnson*

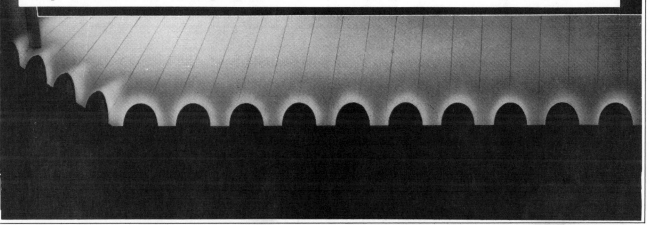

> ## It's nice to be important, But it's more important to be nice.

PRAYER OF A DEAF CHRISTIAN

Do angels sing in Heaven, Lord?
Will I hear music there?
Or must I in a corner stand,
While others join in prayer?

Will I wonder what they are saying,
Lord,
Like I often do down here?
Must I sit still and be patient, Lord,
While the bells ring loud and clear?

Can I read Your lips in Heaven, Lord,
Or will I be brushed aside?
Will I hide my hands in my pockets,
Lord,
Because of wounded pride?

Will the saints all stand to praise
Thee, Lord,
While I in silence wait?
Will there be someone in Heaven,
Lord,
To lead me through the gate?

And God, who loves the humble, bent
To soothe the anxious fear.
"My child, has no one told you that
There is no silence here!

"Hold out your hands, My little one,
For all in Heaven to see.
We've seen them pray so many times;
Each prayer reached up to Me.

"See all the angels waiting now;
The gates are open wide.
Your crown of life is waiting, child,
And I shall be your Guide.

"I have a song to give you, and
You will sing loud and clear.
Your new song will fill the sky,
The sweetest song up here!"

—Margaret Morgan in *Tabernacle Times*

What's the World Coming To?

(It may come to the following fictitious story if the Lord doesn't come soon!)

Dear Mom,

Can you believe it's 2023 already? I'm still writing '22 on everything. Seems like yesterday I was sitting in first grade celebrating the century change.

I know we haven't chatted since Christmas. Sorry. Anyway, I have some difficult news, and I really didn't want to call and talk face to face.

Ted's had a promotion, and I should be up for a hefty raise this year if I keep putting in those crazy hours. You know how hard I work. Yes, we're still really struggling with all the bills.

Joey's been OK at kindergarten although he still complains about going. But then he wasn't happy about day care either, so what can we do?

He's become a real problem, Mom. He's a good kid, but quite honestly, he's an unfair burden at this time in our lives. Ted and I have talked this through and finally made a choice. Plenty of other families have made it and are so much better off.

Our pastor is supportive and says hard decisions sometimes are necessary. The family is a system, and the demands of one member shouldn't be allowed to ruin the whole. He told us to be prayerful, consider all the factors, and do what is right to make the family work. He says the decision is ours, and was kind enough to refer us to children's clinic right here in town, so at least I know that part is easy.

I'm not an uncaring mother. I do feel sorry for the little guy. I think he heard Ted and me talking about "it" the other night. I turned around and saw him standing on the bottom step in his pj's with the little bear you gave him under his arm and his eyes sort of wetting up.

Mom, the way he looked at me just broke my heart. But I honestly believe this is the best for all of us. It's not fair to force him to live with a family that can't give him the time and attention he deserves. And please don't give me the kind of grief Grandma gave you over your abortions. It's the same, you know.

We've told him he's just going in for a vaccination. Anyway they say the whole termination procedure is painless.

I guess it's just as well you haven't seen that much of him.

Love to Dad,

Jane

What I Say to a Dying Child

By DR. C. EVERETT KOOP
Surgeon-in-Chief, Children's Hospital, Philadelphia
(Was U. S. Surgeon General)

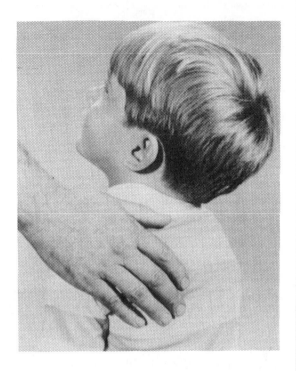

One must be himself in dealing with a dying child and not assume an unusual attitude. Children are perceptive and readily detect a phony.

If a youngster says to me, "Dr. Koop, am I going to die?" I always say the same thing: "Of course you are going to die someday. So am I. What makes you ask that question now?" The youngster will usually tell me what is in his mind. I have had youngsters say such things as this: "You know I am going to die, and I know I am going to die. But let's not tell my mother because she couldn't take it."

If a five-year-old asks if he is going to die, I never flat-footedly say, "Yes, you are going to die." On the other hand, if a sensitive ten-year-old asked something like that of me, I would hedge the answer until I knew more about his thinking. With adolescent children I am very frank. If they say, "Do you think I am going to die from my tumor?" I might very well say, "Yes, I think you are." Then I back it up with my confidence in the hope of eternal life that exists for those who place their trust in Christ.

When a child complains to me about getting better and the slow progress he thinks he is making, I frequently will tell him that before he gets any better he is going to have to feel a lot worse.

Children view Heaven positively. They think of dying as the opportunity to see a grandmother or an uncle whom they believe to be in Heaven. I have talked with many youngsters who were looking forward to Heaven with much creative imagination and without fear. Even adults who do not fear death itself fear the process of dying. Children do not seem to be concerned with that at all.

Even dying children can be disciplinary problems. I recall one child, threatened with punishment, who said to her mother, "You wouldn't hit a kid with cancer, would you?" Another, asking for an almost impossible favor, said, "You wouldn't deprive a dying child of her last wish, would you?" That youngster then talked of going to Heaven where she would be with Jesus and would never have any more pain.

Children have an uncanny way of reducing the unexplainable to their own terms. Witness the child explaining how God creates people: "He draws us first, then cuts us out."

Or the child describing what a halo is: "They have this circle over their heads, and they always try to walk careful so they stay right underneath it. It lights up."

Or take the child who, when asked what one must do before obtaining forgiveness for sin, replied, "Sin."

Or take the child who heard the story of the Prodigal Son for the first time: "In the midst of all the celebration for the prodigal," said the teacher, "there was one for whom the feast brought no happiness, only bitterness. Can you tell me who this was?" "The fatted calf?" suggested a sad little voice.

A child, when asked what the story of the Good Samaritan taught him, answered: "That when I'm in trouble, someone should help me."

One boy, when asked why there are no longer burnt offerings to God, suggested, "Air pollution."

Letters to God:

Dear God: If You made the sun, the moon and stars, You must have had a lot of equipment.—*Paul.*

Dear God: There were no clouds Saturday, so I think I saw Your feet. Did I really?—*Kenny.*

Dear God: Where does yesterday go? Do You have it?—*Stanley.*

I know there is a God because I go to His house and see all His cars parked there.—*George.*

Dear God: Is it okay to talk to You even when I don't want anything?—Love, *Eric.*

"Out of the mouth of babes."

One Way to Get Attention

A minister habitually told his congregation that if they needed a pastoral visit to drop a note in the offering plate.

One evening after services he discovered a note that said, "I am one of your loneliest members and heaviest contributors. May I have a visit tomorrow evening?" (It was signed by his wife.)

SIXTEEN ANGELS AND SAM

By LINDA WILSON

As a 5-year-old pupil at our local Jack and Jill Kindergarten, our daughter Kim announced how lucky we were that she was going to school. The reason, she said, was that her father and I could learn from her and be smarter people.

And learn we did! That was the year Grandma Roork remarked God was making kids smarter than He used to—and we were inclined to agree with her.

Kim is now in the 5th grade, and we are thankful for her words of childish wisdom. Her father and I are smarter now than we were six years ago!

Like all children, she has her own ideas about everything. One bit of theology came as a shock, but we didn't argue with it.

After saying her prayers one night she announced she was not afraid. I readily assured her she was right; there was nothing in the darkness of the night to fear. However, I wasn't prepared for her reasons:

First, she had 16 angels watching over her; and second, Sam was guarding her.

Now the second I agreed with. Sam is our next door neighbor's German shepherd. He is the watchdog of our home and his. In fact, very little goes on that Sam is not aware of. Every morning when the shades are pulled in the girls' room, Sam is at the fence waiting for us to say good morning. Sam guards everyone on our street.

But where did she get 16 angels? I don't know. Perhaps God sees she needs that many.

One evening at our city park, as she and Angela were swinging, some older boys pulled a knife on them. Instead of running to us, Kim decided to explain to the boys that they wouldn't go to Heaven if they weren't saved. And if they didn't go to Heaven with Jesus, they would be left to go through the Great Tribulation.

The incident ended with the boy dropping the knife, putting his fingers in his ears, and saying he didn't want to hear about that.

As I pondered what might have taken place, fear gripped my heart. The girls could have been seriously injured, perhaps knifed to death, only a few feet from us. But "16 angels" were on duty, and the prophecy teaching a little girl had sat through for five services was put to good use. Maybe her theology was a bit off, but the message was there.

I recalled how amazed we were that she should be so interested in the revival we had two months before. I also vividly remembered our evangelist saying, "Bring your children and let them hear this teaching." Once again God's Word bore fruit.

I wonder at times about the boy with the knife. Perhaps there's fear in his heart in the darkness of the night as he recalls something about being left behind when Jesus comes.

Linda Wilson is the wife of D. Terry Wilson, pastor of Evangel Temple in Big Spring, Texas.

While talking with a friend, she got a telephone call bringing some disturbing news. Instead of panic, her response was, "Well, here we GROW again!"

She was right. We can go through painful trials, or we can grow through them.

*   *   *

SOMEONE HAS SAID, "KIDS ARE NOT A SHORT-TERM LOAN; THEY ARE A LONG-TERM INVESTMENT!"

Smart Kid!

When a small boy was asked to write what he had learned about the human body, this was the result:

"Our body is divided into three parts, the branium, the borax, and the abominable cavity. The branium contains the brain, if any. The borax contains the lungs, lights and heart. The abominable cavity contains the five bowels, a, e, i, o and u."

If God Wrote Your Obituary...

"And Samuel died; and all the Israelites . . . lamented him."—I Sam. 25:1.

Have you ever observed the striking way in which the obituary notices of the Bible are written? Often a single brief sentence gathers up the characteristics of an individual and flashes them upon the screen of our minds like a photograph of his soul.

Notice this one above of Samuel.

Here are others: Abner—"Died Abner as a fool dieth?"

Herod—"He was eaten with worms. . . . But the word of God grew and multiplied."

Stephen—"Looked up stedfastly into heaven, and saw the glory of God."

If God wrote our obituaries, yours and mine, how would He sum us up at the end of life's short day? Would ours resemble this picture?

> *He has done the work of a true man—*
> *Crown him, honor him, love him;*
> *Weep over him, tears of woman;*
> *Stoop, manliest brows, above him!*
>
> *For the warmest of hearts is frozen;*
> *The freest of hands is still;*
> *And the gap in our picked and chosen*
> *The long years may not fill.*
>
> *He forgot his own life for others,*
> *Himself to his neighbor lending;*
> *Found the Lord in his suffering brothers,*
> *Alike as in clouds descending.*
>
> *And he saw, ere his eye was darkened,*
> *The sheaves of the harvest-bringing;*
> *And knew, while his ear yet hearkened,*
> *The voice of the reapers singing. . . .*
>
> *He has heard the Master's blessing,*
> *"Good and faithful, enter in!"*

—J. G. Whittier, alt.

Home

An artist, wanting to paint a beautiful picture, asked a pastor, "What is the most beautiful thing in the world?"

"FAITH," answered the pastor. "You can feel it in every church, find it at every altar."

The artist asked the young bride the same question. "LOVE," she replied. "Love builds poverty into riches; sweetens tears; makes much of little. Without it there is no beauty."

A weary soldier said, "PEACE is the most beautiful thing in the world and war the most ugly. Wherever you find peace, you find beauty."

Faith, Love, Peace! How can I paint them? thought the artist.

Entering his door he saw Faith in the eyes of his children and Love in the eyes of his wife. And there in the home was the Peace that Love and Faith had built. So he painted the picture of the "Most Beautiful Thing in the World." And when he had finished, he called it, "Home."

—*First Baptist Beacon*

A LITTLE EXERCISE

Two women who were maneuvering their car into a tight parking space gave up after a valiant struggle when the driver shut off the motor and said to her companion: "This is close enough. We can walk to the curb from here."

"Just Show Him Your Hands!"

A little girl was left motherless at the age of eight. The father was very poor, making it necessary for the oldest child to help. There were four children younger than she was, so this little girl tried to care for all of them, tried to take her mother's place. She got up early every morning and worked all day until late at night. She cooked, and scrubbed the house. Her little fingers became hard and scarred, and her little body became thin.

When the girl was thirteen, her strength was all gone. When she became sick, she said to a neighbor, "I think I'm going to die. I'm not afraid to die, but I'm ashamed!"

"Why are you ashamed?" the neighbor asked.

"Since Mamma left us, I have been so busy I haven't had time to

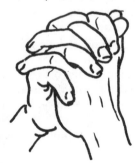

do anything for Jesus. When I get to Heaven and meet Him, I will be ashamed. What can I tell Him?"

The neighbor took the little girl's hands in hers, looked at the scars and calluses, then said, "My dear, you will not need to tell Him anything. Just show Him *your hands!* You have been living for Him every day, doing the work He has given you to do. You have been a little mother to your brothers and sisters! Jesus will understand."

Some folks occasionally say, "I'd die for Jesus!" He doesn't ask you to die for Him—He asks you to live for Him, and that's more difficult to do.

* * * * *

Not Quite Perfect

The plump lady stepped off the penny scales and frowned.

"What's the matter, Jenny?" asked her husband. "A little overweight?"

"No, not at all," said the wife, "but according to the height table printed on the front, I ought to be six inches taller."

▲ ▲ ▲ ▲ ▲ ▲ ▲

"God? Who's That?"

The following letter from a grief-stricken mother appeared in the Warsaw (Indiana) *Times-Union:*

"As I sat in a courtroom and heard the judge say, 'Twenty years,' my heart almost stopped! The sentence was punishment of my son for drinking, gambling and committing robbery which ended in the almost fatal shooting of a man. The sentence might have been less but for my son's sneering, defiant attitude.

"Before passing sentence, the judge asked, 'Young man, don't you believe in God?' My son laughed loudly and answered, 'God? Who's that?' I think everyone in the courtroom turned to look at me.

"I went to church and Sunday school when I was young, but after I married I attended only on special days. Regretfully I say, 'If only I had those years to live over, it would be different. I would go to God's house faithfully and take my children with me. So many say they do not believe in making a child go to church if he doesn't want to, but how many children would go to school if they weren't made to go?'"

Of all the words of tongue or pen, The saddest are these: It might have been!

> *Other books are given for our information; the Bible was given for our transformation.*

Dear Mr. God, Please Listen

Dear Mr. God, please listen,
  Since I had to give him up,
Please take good care of Tippy, Sir—
  He's such a little pup.

Mother says You called to him
  And he just had to go.
I wonder if he misses me,
  'Cause, oh, I miss him so.

I know You'll treat him awful nice,
  But he's really lots of care,
And if it's rainy out-of-doors,
  He'll track mud everywhere.

He'll sure get into everything,
  If You leave him just a crack.
But, Mr. God, if he bothers You,
  I'd be glad to have him back!

—*Pete Reed*

‡ ‡ ‡ ‡ ‡ ‡ ‡

• An old story tells of a man's approaching a slave about to be sold and asking, "If I buy you and take you to live and work in my home, will you be an honest man?"

The proud slave replied, "Sir, I will be honest whether you buy me or not."

FAITH TO FLY

It is said that John Wesley and Charles Wesley were in a prayer service together.

Charles said, "I feel so happy that, if the Lord should tell me to fly and I had wings, I would fly!"

John replied, "If the Lord should tell me to fly, I would fly whether I had wings or not!"

A COUNTRY BOY

I'm just a dumb old country boy
  That ain't so very smart;
And when I talk I get mixed up,
  My gears are hard to start;
It seems I don't have many brains
  Like other folks I know;
And when it comes to society,
  My dumbness there I show.
I found it don't take many brains
  The best in life to gain:
It's not your wealth or what you are
  Or prestige you might obtain;
It only takes just simple faith
  Eternal life to find;
No matter who you are or where
  you stand,
  There's grace for all mankind.

I went down to the jailhouse to see
  If I could witness for the Lord.

Once when a husband gently asked his wife what time dinner would be ready, he really got told off: "Don't bug me," she said testily. "Can't you see I'm in the middle of a good book on how to make our marriage work better!"

I told them how the Lord saved me,
  But they sure were mighty bored;
They nudged each other and
  smiled,
  Because they all know I was
  dumb;
But they stayed in, and I walked out
  When leavin' time had come.
I'm still a dumb old country boy,
  And I hope I'll always be
Just dumb enough to trust the
  Lord
  For all eternity;
So I'll just keep travelin' on,
  With Jesus in my heart;
Because I'm a dumb old country
  boy
  That ain't so very smart.

—From *Selah*

HOW TO COUNT

Count your garden by the flowers,
  Never by the leaves that fall.
Count your day by golden hours;
  Don't remember clouds at all.

Count your nights by stars, not shadows;
  Count your life by smiles, not tears;
And, with joy on every birthday,
  Count your age by friends—not years.

I don't like these cold, precise, perfect people who, in order not to speak wrong, never speak at all, and in order not to do wrong, never do anything.

—**Beecher**

When God Forgives, He Forgets

A little girl had been good for a whole week. When she asked some favor from her aunt, the child reminded her how good she had been all week. The aunt said, "I know you have been good all this week, but you were bad all last week."

The little girl exclaimed, "Oh, Auntie! You are not one bit like God. When He forgives, He forgets! He doesn't keep reminding us of our sins."

"God Doesn't Live at Our House"

Five-year-old Margaret was a frequent visitor in the home of a neighbor. One of the never-ending wonders of the neighbor's home was the prayer time. Little Margaret loved to be there at that time. The daddy in the home read out of a big, black Book. Afterwards he talked to God as if God were very near and dear to them all. Sometimes, the family would join in singing a song of praise.

One morning when little Margaret had been present at the prayer time, the mother in the home asked, "Margaret, don't you pray at your house?" Margaret shook her head sadly and said, "No. You see, God doesn't live at our house like He does at yours."

How sad that a little girl like Margaret had to go next door if she wanted to meet God, the Heavenly Father. God wasn't included in her family circle.

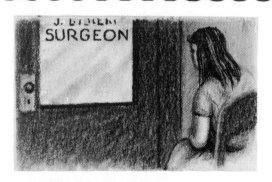

Watch Your Wait!

By June Critcher

How do you spend the 30 or 40 minutes in the doctor's waiting room? or the 30 minutes under the hairdryer? or the 10-minute waits for your children at school functions, music lessons, scouting activities, etc.? For an interesting experiment, count the number of waiting minutes you spend each week.

One of the best ways to gather up fragments of time is by reading. Many women complain that they are too busy with diapers, dishes and housework to read. So the busy woman should assimilate bite-size books for mental and spiritual nourishment.

Women who practice the art of reading find greater self-fulfillment. They achieve a better sense of balance in various areas of life. Christian women who read discover that the world is a fascinating place. The one who reads becomes a more interesting person through intellectual growth, which leads to self-confidence and self-respect. Reading helps one to make distinctions in new areas of development and become sensitive to them.

Reading Christian literature can give you new release and freedom, confidence and power in your witness. Getting a proper perspective on God's role and your role in evangelism can also have a dramatic impact on you.

God's Word is always at the apex of the reading list. Other materials that aid one's understanding of the Word should also occupy a spot of top priority on any reading list.

Many Christian bookstores have racks well-stocked with small booklets—about 5" x 3½"—just the ideal size for your purse or car's glove compartment. Why not make a note to visit your local bookstore this week and purchase a booklet for each purse and 2 or 3 for the glove compartment? Then when you find yourself waiting 10 or 15 minutes, reach for the booklet. Feed your soul while you stretch your mind. By reading during waiting minutes, you'll be amazed at the amount of reading you can do in just one month.

How you spend your waiting moments tells much about your basic affections. Do you sit idle, letting your mind wander aimlessly? Or are you bored while waiting for someone?

Reading is a matter of earnest commitment. After evaluating your commitment to what is really important in your life, determine to put good Christian reading at the top of your priority list this year.

Make your waiting moments count for God. Honor Him as you read Christian booklets.

—From *Contact*

Mama's Coat

Mama's coat was threadbare. The cuffs and collar were worn, and the elbows were thin. We children looked at it critically. "Mama," we said, "you have just got to have a new coat for this winter." "I will," she promised. "I'll begin to save for one."

All that depression summer mother dropped spare coins in her savings jar. Slowly, so slowly, the coins moved upward. She scrimped all summer to make our dream a reality.

Summer days passed and autumn nights grew cold. Chilling rains drenched the landscape. Snow squalls and icy winds blew. It was then we discovered our church roof was leaking. That meant the church had to have a new roof. Mother mended her coat again, and the church we knew was in good shape.

Again we discussed the coat situation. "The old one will last this one more winter," she promised.

Mother's jar began a slow collection. Few coins found their way into it that winter, but things were more hopeful in the spring. And by autumn the coins were near the top. We were excited as we emptied the jar and began the count. Indeed, there was enough for the new coat, and we envisioned her in it. We would all be so happy when the mail order coat arrived!

A church bulletin came that day stating a new missionary would be leaving for India. Would church members support her with prayer and offerings? Mother would! And so she exchanged the contents in the jar for a money order to the new missionary. When we challenged her liberality she responded, "It is such joy to share in God's harvest field. Don't ask me to forfeit my gladness. This year I promise you and myself to get a new coat."

Sometime in June we noted that the jar was filling with coins faster than in the previous years. July had several surprises. Now we knew the dream would be a reality. And as July slipped closer to August, Mother admitted to us that she was having times of weakness. Then suddenly and unexpectedly word came, "Mother has gone to Heaven."

No, she would not need a coat for winter. Wasn't she already clothed in shining garments of the redeemed? The winter coat wasn't needed after all.

—Asenath Box
(From *The Burning Bush*)

File It Away

If an unkind word appears,
  File the thing away.
If some novelty in jeers,
  File the thing away.
If some clever little bit
Of a sharp and pointed wit,
Carrying a sting with it—
  File the thing away.

If some bit of gossip come,
  File the thing away.
Scandalously spicy crumb,
  File the thing away.
If suspicion comes to you
That your neighbor isn't true,
Let me tell you what to do—
  File the thing away.
Do this for a little while,
Then go out and burn the file.

THE SEVEN AGES OF WOMEN

BABY GIRL
LITTLE GIRL
SCHOOL GIRL
TEENAGE GIRL
YOUNG WOMAN
YOUNG WOMAN
YOUNG WOMAN

—John Kendrick Bangs

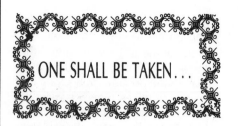

ONE SHALL BE TAKEN...

Dr. Gordon used to tell of two sisters who lay down to sleep one night in the same bed; the one, a Christian; the other, a scoffer. The Christian girl had just come from a religious service in which the preacher had quoted that phrase, "One shall be taken, and the other left," and had solemnly warned his hearers of the coming of the Lord.

Her heart was so filled with concern for her sister that she could not sleep. When she told her of the sermon and her feelings and earnestly begged her to think of her soul's salvation, she was only met with jests and rebuffs, and soon the thoughtless girl was fast asleep. The other could only weep and pray in agony until at last she was so distressed that she rose from her bed and, stealing into an adjoining room, she fell upon her face and poured out her heart in sobs and prayers for the salvation of her sister.

After a while the sleeper awoke and, missing her sister from her side, suddenly remembered the conversation of the earlier part of the night. Suddenly it flashed upon her: *What if the Lord had come, and she was left?* Then she broke down with alarm and sought her sister in the darkness of the room. At last she heard her sobbing in the adjoining room. Throwing herself on her knees by her side, she besought her prayers. She found the Saviour and, a little later, clasped in each other's arms, they rejoiced in the thought that if He should come, they would be together.

—*A. B. Simpson*

*   *   *

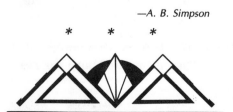

Seeing Heaven on Knees

Said the great and devout scientist, Sir Isaac Newton: "I can take my telescope and look millions and millions of miles into space; but I can lay it aside and go into my room, shut the door, get down on my knees in earnest prayer and see more of Heaven and get closer to God than I can assisted by all the telescopes and material agencies on earth."

"My Pop's Tops!"

By DAVID McCARTHY

A few years ago a Milwaukee newspaper invited young readers to submit short essays on the theme "My Pop's Tops!" The most interesting entries were published in the paper on Father's Day. The following excerpts from those letters are respectfully dedicated to dads everywhere.

● "My pop's tops. He lets me hoe the garden, even when I don't want to."

● "The first time he took me to church he was so afraid I would make a riot that he sweat all the way through the commercial."

● "Because I am not very good in arithmetic, he gave me a small adding machine. But it is not very good at arithmetic, either."

● "My pop is willing to help with the housework, although he complains about it a little—quite a bit, really. In fact, he hollers. Well, to tell the truth, he won't do no housework at all!"

● "My pop's tops! One time he took me to the lake and threw me in to see whether I could swim. I couldn't. My pop saved my life."

● "My pop is a farmer. He smells like a cow. And when I come in and smell a cow in the house, I know my pop is home; and I'm glad."

● "Right now I should be mowing the lawn; and if my pop sees me goofing off to write this letter on his being a top pop, why, then he'll holler at me. If he doesn't catch me and holler his head off, I'll send this letter; but if he does catch me and holler at me, he can finish the letter himself."

Sometimes it's useful to catch a glimpse of Dad through the eyes of a son or a daughter. We all need to remember that our daily lives are making an impression on those around us.

Maybe it's too much to expect a young boy or girl to write about a dad's relation to the Lord Jesus Christ, but someday—

Would anything mean more to you than the candid observation, "My dad lived for Jesus Christ and helped me realize that being a dedicated Christian is the greatest experience there is"?

GET-WELL CARDS HAVE BE-COME SO HUMOROUS THAT IF YOU DON'T GET SICK YOU'RE MISSING HALF THE FUN.

+ + + + +

Do not blame God for the harvest when you, yourself, do the sowing.

It is reported that a book publisher advertised in various newspapers: "Millionaire, young, good looking, wishes to meet, with a view to marriage, a girl like the heroine in M____'s novel." Within 24 hours, the novel sold out in every bookstore in the towns where the ad appeared.

BUILDING A HOME

A young girl watched her mother washing dishes; and thinking of how many times she did them along with all the other housework, she said, "Mother, don't you ever get tired of washing dishes?" The mother replied, "I'm not doing dishes: I'm building a home."

—Selected

"Just once I'd like to see you react like the cats in the TV commercials."

Every Thanksgiving the newspapers are full of diagrams showing how to carve a turkey. The trouble is that the birds we get never have dotted lines on them.

* * *

INSTEAD OF COMPLAINING BECAUSE YOU DON'T GET WHAT YOU WANT, BE THANKFUL YOU DON'T GET WHAT YOU DESERVE.

* * *

"I Have Lost My Faith in God!"

A small boy who attended Sunday school for the first time was greatly pleased with a picture card which was given him. On it was written the text, "Have faith in God."

On his way home, the precious card slipped from his fingers and fluttered from the open bus window. Immediately a cry of distress arose: "I have lost my faith in God! Stop the car!"

The good-natured driver signaled, the bus stopped, and the card was recovered while the passengers smiled.

How wise it would be if older people would call a *halt* when they find themselves rushing ahead on some road without faith in God!

Front-yard Christians! A boy had a red wagon that was a new possession and the delight of his heart. But when he brought it out to the front walk one morning he was told that he must play with it at the back of the house. "This is Sunday," added the father by way of explanation.

The boy obeyed; but he questioned wonderingly as he trudged away, "Isn't it Sunday in the backyard, too?"

—Selected

"Love...not provoked."

Someone apologized to a good-natured little woman for an occurrence at which she might have taken offense; whereupon she laughingly disclaimed any such thought. "I am honest, you know, so I never pick up things that don't belong to me—not even slights."

WHAT MATTERS

My mother says she does not care
About the color of my hair
Nor if my eyes be blue or brown
Nor if my nose turns up or down—
    It really does not matter.

And Mother says she does not care
If I am dark or if I'm fair,
Or if I'm thin or if I'm fat;
She does not fret o'er things like that—
    It really does not matter.

But if I cheat or tell a lie
Or say mean things to make folks cry,
Or if I'm rude or impolite
And do not try to do the right,
    Then that does really matter!

—*Juvenile Pleasure*

• • • •

Experience is always the hardest teacher because you take the test before you learn your lesson.

One friend to another: "You sure look worried." Second friend to another: "Man, I've got so many troubles that if anything bad happens today, it will be at least two weeks before I can worry about it."

Times Change!

Dear Mother used to sit and sew while listening to the radio. Our socks were darned, our buttons tight; neatly she mended every night.

Now, two buttons off Dad's shirt I see—for who can sew and watch TV?

• • • •

Is anybody happier because you passed his way?
Does anyone remember that you spoke to him today?
This day is almost over, and its toiling time is through.
Is there anyone to utter a kindly word of you?

Did you give a kind greeting to the friend who came along,
Or a churlish sort of "howdy" and then vanish in the throng?
Were you selfish, as you rushed along your way,
Or is someone mighty grateful for a deed you did today?

Can you say tonight in parting, with the day that's slipping fast,
That you helped a single brother of the many that you passed?
Is a single heart rejoicing over what you did or said?
Does a man whose hopes are fading, now with courage look ahead?

Did you waste the day or lose it, was it well or poorly spent?
Did you leave a trail of kindness or a scar of discontent?
As you close your eyes in slumber, do you think that God would say,
"You have blessed the ones around you by the work you did today"?

SITUATION WANTED

Will keep your children occupied for you. I guarantee they will learn from what I can teach them. I will show them how to drink liquor, smoke cigarettes, murder, rob and commit adultery. I will keep them up late on Saturday nights so they won't feel like church on Sunday morning, and I will offer exciting things on Sunday night to keep them home. Yes, I desire to sit with your child...you don't know me...but I live with you....

MR. T. V.

The greatest danger confronting the children today is the example set by adults.

* * * *

Dictated, but Not Read

"Now look here! I fired three girls for revising my letters, see?" said the boss to his new secretary. "All right; now take a letter and take it the way I tell you."

And the next morning Mr. C. J. Squizz of the Squizz Soap Co. received the following letter:

Mr. O., or A. J., or something, look it up, Squizz, what a name, Soap Company, Detroit, that's in Michigan, isn't it? Dear Mr. Squizz, hmmm. The last shipment of soap you sent us was of inferior quality and I want you to understand—no, scratch that out. I want you to understand—hmmm—unless you can ship—furnish, ship, no, furnish us with your regular soap you needn't ship us no more, period, or whatever the grammar is.

Where was I? paragraph. Your soap wasn't what you said—I should say it wasn't. Them bums tried to put over a lot of hooey on us. Whadda you want to paint your faces up like Indians on the warpath? We're sending back your last shipment tomorrow. Sure, we're gonna send it back. I'd like to feed it to 'em with a spoon and make 'em eat it, the bums. Now read the letter over—no, don't read it over, we've wasted enough time on them crooks, fix it up and sign my name.

What do you say we close up shop for the day?

A True Story

Once upon a time, they say, a man invented a mousetrap. He believed his fortune would be made by its sale if he could get President Lincoln to recommend it.

After a long, persistent effort, he secured an audience with the President and received the following recommendation, which will apply to many things besides mousetraps:

For the sort of people who want this sort of thing, this is the sort of thing that sort of people will want.

TRUST

*I oft' times think
I'd like to see
beyond my limit's view.
I'd like to know
the wondrous things
my gracious Lord will do.
But if I understood
and saw
as God sees from above,
I'd lose the privilege
and joy
of trusting in His love!*

—Ruth E. Narramore

If you want a jolt, write down what you accomplished yesterday.

Don't Waste Your Time "Fussing"

A dear old lady from the country went for the first time on a railway journey of about fifty miles through an interesting and beautiful region. She had looked forward to this trip with great pleasure. She was to see so much and enjoy it all so greatly. But it took her so long to get her basket and parcels adjusted, her seat comfortably arranged, the shades right, that she was only just settling down to enjoy her trip when the conductor called out the name of her station, and she had to get up and hustle out. "Oh, my!" she said, "if I'd only known that we would have been here so soon, I wouldn't have wasted my time fussing."

Dear friend, the wheels of time are flying; the last station is at hand; these things are so trifling. Get your mind on the main business of life. Live as you would wish to have lived when the porter calls out the last station, and don't waste any more time "fussing."

—A. B. Simpson

"I'll Wait"

John had been convicted of murder and sentenced to death. The last day of his life had come. The warden awakened him and said, "Since this is your last day, John, you can have anything you want to eat."

"I'd like some watermelons," he said.

"But," protested the warden, "they won't be ripe for six months."

"I can wait," he said.

But don't wait to turn to the Lord. You can count on fire to burn and ice to chill. You can count on fish to swim in the sea and birds to fly in the air. You can count on the sun to shine by day and the stars by night. But you can't count on tomorrow.

Our Lord says, "Come now." You will, won't you?

—Michael Guido

LIVE SO THAT WHEN MEN UNEARTH YOUR FOOTPRINTS ON THE SANDS OF TIME THEY WON'T FIND ONLY A HEEL.

Needed: A Rest

A shoe salesman who had dragged out half his stock to a woman customer: "Mind if I rest a few minutes, lady? Your feet are killing me."

Are there bicycles in Heaven?

I wondered, *Are there bicycles in Heaven?* as I reflected on the previous 24 hours.

It had been a hot August night in Bettendorf, Iowa. Hundreds of rosy-cheeked, wiggling boys and girls packed the church pews for a special Kids' Roundup Crusade.

Enthusiasm was high. "Cowboy" and Mrs. Smiley (Evangelist and Mrs. Paul Hild) held the youngsters spellbound with their gospel films and animated stories.

Now Smiley was concluding with his famous black-light painting of the three crude crosses on Calvary.

The 6-year-old lad with sun-bleached hair seated just ahead of me was giving wide-eyed attention. His big blue eyes were thoughtful as he whispered in my ear, "Jesus is dead, isn't He?"

"Yes," I replied, "He did die—but He's alive now. Remember on Easter Sunday—He arose for our salvation?"

"Oh, yes! That's right," Craig answered. "He is alive now, isn't He! Good!"

Moments later Craig followed other boys and girls down to the altar to accept Jesus Christ as his personal Saviour. His joyous face shone as bright as his beautiful blond hair.

Before leaving, he yelled, "I'm going home to ride my bicycle!"

He did.

But the following morning he rode it in the side alley by his home—not realizing the Davenport City garbage truck was also rumbling down the same narrow alley making its weekly rounds.

Before Craig noticed, tragedy struck. He and the big truck met on impact, and Craig was immediately crushed to death. The county coroner pronounced him dead at the scene of the accident.

Craig's words keep recycling through my memory: **"I'm going home to ride my bicycle!"**

Craig went to Heaven—his eternal Home. If there are bicycles in Heaven, then surely he is riding one there now.

What a beautiful Home the Lord has provided where there is no death, no pain, no tears. For the Bible says, "And God shall wipe away all tears from their eyes; and there shall be no more death, neither sorrow, nor crying, neither shall there be any more pain: for the former things are passed away" (Rev. 21:4).

All of us may enjoy that heavenly Home if we, like Craig, will accept the Lord Jesus as our personal Saviour. For "The Spirit and the bride say, Come. And let him that heareth say, Come. And let him that is athirst come. And whosoever will, let him take the water of life freely" (Rev. 22:17).

—Douglas R. Rose

If you could telegraph, telephone, or write to Heaven for information on how to be saved, you would get the same answer the Bible gives, "Believe on the Lord Jesus Christ, and thou shalt be saved" (Acts 16:31).

It Isn't Easy Being a Kid!

By Marlene Evans
Editor, *Christian Womanhood*

It wasn't easy being a kid—not during the 30's and 40's anyway.

No, sir! No matter how good a childhood I had, it was very difficult to figure out adults. I was always listening and watching to catch any clue I could, and I was still left groping in the dark.

My dad got insurance against Mom being sick, and she got sick anyway. Grandpa Zugmier was insured against an accident, but he fell in the flour mill where he worked and had to have his leg amputated anyway. Grandpa Fauver was insured against death, and he died in spite of the insurance policy.

Dad could write on pieces of paper, go into a building with bars in front of a man, give the paper to the man, and get money from the man. Then, Dad would tell me he didn't have enough money to get us ice cream cones. When I suggested writing on a piece of paper, he'd laugh and say, "Money doesn't grow on trees."

???? Solitary Confinement!

Adults always said, "Just ask a question when you don't understand." I'd ask and they'd say, "Find something to do, question box, I'm tired. Don't ask me one more question."

One time Mom and Dad took me to an Evangelical United Brethren Church Conference at a campsite in Milford, Nebraska, where they had a banner over the front of the auditorium and sawdust as a floor. Because of being allergic to sawdust at 4 and 5 years of age, I'd hack and then say, "Mom, what does that sign say?" Then a few minutes later I'd ask, "Dad, what does that sign say?" Each time they'd tell me the banner read, "Follow Thou Me."

Somehow I kept forgetting it. I guess my coughing distracted me. Finally, Mom marched me out to the ladies' restroom—all because I

asked a question, I guess. I didn't need to go to the restroom.

Teachers were infamous for nice words like, "If you need help, raise your hand, and I'll answer your question." I'd raise my hand whenever I needed help, and they'd say, "Marlene, just stay in your seat and figure it out yourself." I was isolated and put in solitary confinement.

World War II Was in Vanilla!

The war was really puzzling to a child. Part of the war was fought in vanilla. Mom had bottles of vanilla in the kitchen cabinet, but I really couldn't see a war being fought in them! Yet the newsmen on the radio kept talking about problems in vanilla in the Philippines.

That brings up another problem. At the very same time that there was trouble in vanilla in the Philippines, I was learning the books of the Bible. Mrs. Viola Krauss, my Sunday school teacher in the Blue Springs, Nebraska, Evangelical United Brethren Church, showed me the Philippines right after Ephesians. Can you beat that?

Sick in September

My mom often told me to keep my ears open and pay attention, and I'd learn without asking so many questions. In trying to follow that advice, I stumbled into a real brain teaser.

When visiting my great-grandma in Thayer, Kansas, I overheard my mom and great-grandma talking about an aunt who had gained a lot of weight in the stomach. My great-grandmother looked at me, winked at my mom, and told her that this aunt was going to be sick in September. Now, we were in the middle of the summertime, and my curiosity was truly aroused. I'd always been told if you planned on being sick on Sunday or on a test day, you weren't really sick. Yet here were these perfectly sane, reliable adults aiding and abetting in planning an aunt's sickness months in advance. Can you believe it?

People Laughed at Me!

Sometimes when I asked questions, people laughed at me. They didn't let me in on the joke, either. Grandparents who take time to explain could really help kids a lot.

It's rough being a kid, and don't you ever forget it!

—From *Christian Womanhood*

HOT DOG!
HOT DOG!
HOT DOG!

By DR. TOM WALLACE

My favorite illustration comes from my own pastoral experience. It took place on Sunday morning at Bible Baptist Church in Elkton, Maryland.

The Sunday morning service was just ready to begin when in came a man who had never attended our church before. He looked around with awe and amazement at the great number of people packed into the large auditorium. He had heard about these people; now he had come to see for himself.

He came slowly down the aisle looking from side to side and seated himself on the second row from the front.

As I preached he listened with the keenest of interest. When I gave a negative tone to my statements, he would shake his head from side to side showing agreement. When I asked, "Don't you think everybody ought to be saved?" he nodded his head up and down in definite approval. It was not hard to tell how he stood on any issue.

When the invitation time came, I said, "Every eye closed and every head bowed. Now how many of you are not saved, but you would

like to be, and you want us to pray for you? Will you raise your hand?" He shot up his hand and waved it back and forth persistently until he was sure that I had seen it. When I asked those who would claim Christ to come forward, he literally bounced out and darted to the altar. One of our men prayed with him and gave him assurance of salvation.

In a moment I asked him to stand. He stood stiff and erect; he was really into the matter with body, soul and spirit.

I asked, "Sir, do you believe that Christ died to save sinners?"

"Yes, Sir, I surely do!"

"Will you take Him and trust Him to be your very own Saviour?"

"Yes, Sir, I want to do just that," he said rejoicing, with a beam of triumph about him.

When he came into the baptistry, I dropped him into the water and drew him out again to walk in the newness of life. He came up out of the water clapping his hands and shouting, "Hot dog! hot dog! hot dog!"

Our people roared with laughter. I quickly asked them for silence as I explained that this poor man had not been around the church and didn't know about Amen! Praise the Lord! and Hallelujah! His word was "Hot dog," and he was praising the Lord with the only vocabulary he knew.

Make the Most of Time

So the sands of Time that slowly flow
From out my hourglass
Will all too soon have ebbed away,
My life will then be past.
So I must make the most of time
And drift not with the tide,
For killing time's not murder:
It's more like suicide.

—Unknown

Live for That Last Page!

God will set all things right in His good time. . . . If I look far enough ahead, everything clears up. I've read the last page! There may be some distressing chapters between here and there, but somewhere sickness and sorrow and grief and tears will disappear along with the Devil. I'm living for the last page!

What a dreary journey would this be if we did not have that last page in the Book! There is so much now that defies explanation. But one day everything will be fixed and final. . . .

Things do not add up now; but one day the facts will all be in, the accounts settled without appeal. Everything and everybody will be where they belong. Don't live for today. Live for that last page.

"My talent is to speak my mind," said a woman to John Wesley. To which Wesley answered, "I am sure, sister, that God wouldn't object if you buried THAT talent."

Margaret's Crutches

One day a minister received a request from a missionary society to preach a missionary sermon to be followed by a collection for a certain foreign field. The minister put his whole soul into the effort, encouraging the people to give cheerfully for the Lord's work.

After the sermon, the collection basket was passed as usual; but the minister watched the result with depressed feelings as only small amounts were dropped in. Evidently his words had not reached the hearts of his hearers. He noticed how those who were well able to give kept looking at the time, anxious to be out and about other things.

On the last bench, in the meantime, a battle was waging in the breast of a poorly clad little girl. Through an accident, she had become lame. She could not take a step without assistance. One day a kind lady procured a pair of crutches for her, and since then her life had been much happier. This Sunday she ventured for the first time to come to church. What a great blessing it was to be able to listen to the Gospel once more!

As the sexton came near with the basket, Margaret said to herself with a sad heart, *I have nothing to give—not a cent—and there in the foreign land the missionaries are expecting our gifts; they need so much to carry on their work. Oh, what can I do?* These thoughts went through her mind and made her shudder. *My new crutches could be sold for a sum of money, but I cannot spare them; I must have them; they are my very life.*

"Yes, your life," said a voice within; "but did not Christ give His life for you? If you give what is your life, some poor souls in Africa will hear that He is their Saviour, too. Oh, if you only would!"

Finally a shine came over her face. She pressed a kiss on the crutches and waited with a beating heart.

The collection basket came to where Margaret sat. The sexton knew her well. He gave a friendly nod and was about to pass on. To his astonishment, she made an effort to lay the crutches on the basket. The old man grasped the situation, took the crutches out of her hand, put them on the basket and carried them slowly through the aisle, laying them without a word on the altar.

Everyone watched him in breathless suspense. They all knew the little girl, and many eyes filled with tears. The minister, deeply affected, laid his hand on the crutches and repeated solemnly the words of Jesus: "She hath done what she could."

What a stir this incident made in the meeting! Suddenly the perspiration came on the banker's brow, and he wiped his face with his handkerchief and pulled out his pocketbook. The rich lady fumbled about for her purse. The rich merchant whispered something in the ear of the sexton, who passed the collection basket once more from bench to bench. This time money came like raindrops.

Quietly and solemnly the people left the church. One lady stepped up to Margaret and gave back her new crutches. She had redeemed them for the benefit of the missionaries for the sum of one hundred dollars.

The happy girl returned home little realizing how much she had done that day for her Master.

—Author Unknown

At Least an "Oh!"

An eminent clergyman sat in his study, busily engaged in preparing his Sunday sermon, when his little boy toddled into the room, and, holding up his pinched finger, said, with an expression of suffering, "Look, Pa, how I hurt it!"

The father, interrupted in the middle of a sentence, glanced hastily at him and, with the slightest tone of impatience, said, "I can't help it, Sonny."

The little fellow's eyes grew bigger; and as he turned to go out, he said in a low voice, "Yes, you could; you might have said, 'Oh!'"

—Selected

◀ ▶

Age and Attitude

Nobody grows old merely by living a number of years. People grow old only by deserting their ideals. Years wrinkle the skin, but to give up enthusiasm wrinkles the soul. Worry, doubt, distrust, fear and despair—these are the long, long years that bow the head and turn the growing spirit back to dust.

Whether 70 or 17, there is in every being's heart the love of wonder, the sweet amazement of the stars, and the starlike things and thoughts, the undaunted challenge of events, the unfailing childlike appetite for what is next in the game of life.

You are as young as your faith, as old as your doubts; as young as your Christ-centered confidence, as old as your fears; as young as your hope, as old as your despair.

"Marriage is honourable. . ."
—Heb. 13:4

One of the distinguishing characteristics of Christianity is the clear high system of ethics and conduct in the field of marriage relations. There is no set of religious teachings or precepts, aside from God's Word, which advocates and maintains so dignified and noble an attitude toward marriage as does the Book in which we believe.

It may be true that greater numbers of people believe the Koran than accept the Bible; but no sane woman would choose the marital standards of the Koran in preference to those of the Christian Book. The degraded status is so graphic a contrast to the enlightened liberty enjoyed by Christian women in any land that this one fact alone is sufficient to establish the superiority of *our* faith over the religion of Mohammed!

This ever has been true of the people of God in every age: they were admonished and required to treat their wives with kindness and honor. In Israel, during the times of apostasy, this rule was ignored; but Jesus sternly chided them for such conduct, saying it came from hardness of heart. "Have ye not read," He demanded, "that he which made them at the beginning made them male and female, and said, For this cause shall a man leave father and mother, and shall cleave to his wife: and they twain shall be one flesh?. . . What therefore God hath joined together, let not man put asunder."

In such stirring words did Jesus set His approval upon marriage, and even more so upon monogamous marriage.

The New Testament is replete with such suggestions. Seeking a figure for the clarification of the relationship that is to exist between Christ and His church, the realm of human marriage provided the Holy Spirit with the perfect figure. Hence the church is called "The Bride of Christ," and the greatest dignity is thus conferred upon the body of believers who constitute that church!

Again and again the Christian is urged, COMMANDED, to esteem his wife as his own body; and God condemns, in stern terms, marital infidelity. He goes so far as to state that a married man no longer owns his own body; it belongs to his wife. And in the same figure, the married woman must realize that her body, in turn, belongs to her husband.

No man can be guilty of the heinous and awful sin of unfaithfulness toward a partner in marriage, and attempt to find justification for such conduct in the Bible. Every paragraph that is remotely connected with the subject solemnly commands fidelity in this most sacred union.

How tragic, then, is the awful careless and callous attitude of our modern age toward the marriage vows, which is filling our courts with divorce proceedings and our land with broken homes! No nation with the sad divorce record that we possess can call itself a "Christian" nation. The frank and legalized adultery of our day and time is an offense against every law of God and a complete negation of all the teachings of Christ.

The most beautiful spectacle in the ordinary course of life is the sight of a man and woman who have grown old together, bound by the countless ties of love and life. It may be that births and deaths have molded their days, sickness and struggle have been shared in turn; laughter one day and tears the next may have been their portion. But because these things were *shared*, they had only a sweet and softening effect; and the married couple who *remain* true to each other really can say, "Every wedding anniversary is a GOLDEN wedding day!"

"Husbands, love your wives, even as Christ also loved the church, and gave himself for it," still remains the ultimate and highest commendation that can be written concerning the marriage estate.

"Marriage is honourable in all" is putting it mildly, indeed. When the world at large accepts the Christian view of marriage, both as regards its obligations and its privileges, the sorrows and troubles of broken homes will all be ended.

—Harry Rimmer

One preacher was known to be an ardent fisherman, but he also was forgetful. He asked the groom, "Do you promise to love, honor and obey this woman?"

"I do," the groom replied, meekly.

"Okay," said the preacher, turning to the bride. "Reel him in."

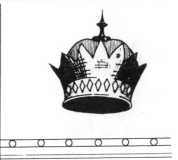

IN HEAVEN THERE ARE NO CROWN-WEARERS WHO WERE NOT CROSS-BEARERS HERE BELOW.

—*Spurgeon*

WHAT IS HEAVEN LIKE?

A class of third-graders was asked, "What is Heaven like?" The replies were:

A girl: "Heaven is where I will meet the man of my dreams."

A boy: "Heaven is where some very nice teachers and a nice principal will be found."

A boy: "Heaven is where you will get everything you want, but if you want everything, you might not go there."

A girl: "Heaven should be the happiest part of my dead life."

Joint Heirs With Him!

A forsaken old mother at close of day
With trembling heart would kneel down to pray.
  Her soul lifting Heavenward with sweet acclaim,
  Softly, so softly she whispered the name
Of JESUS.

A poor, ragged beggar, defiled and diseased,
Would pause each night when his troubles had eased;
  Then stretching himself right across his cot prone,
  He humbly, yet boldly, approached the throne
Of JESUS.

A fragile young stripling who dwelt in the street,
Running odd errands for something to eat,
  Each evening would pray with a childlike belief,
  Touching the heart (I'm assured, with his grief)
Of JESUS.

Though wretched, these souls could yet earnestly sing,
"Glory to God, I'm a child of a King!"
  Beggar and waif and forsaken old mother,
  All rightful heirs and claiming as Brother—
This JESUS.

Children of royalty at poverty's door?
Can regal splendor be theirs evermore?
  Yes! Not a one of them shall suffer a loss
  Since, searching, they found the old rugged cross
Of JESUS!

—*Lorraine Johnson*

What an Arrest Means

A youth was stopped for a traffic violation. The public safety official recognized the odor in the violator's car, and it was found that he had a few "joints" with him. He was convicted of marijuana possession, an automatic felony, and received a suspended sentence.

Maybe you think that is a pretty light sentence and something he could take in his stride and that he didn't lose much.

Well, all he lost was his right to vote, to own a gun and the right to run for public office.

He also lost the chance ever to be a licensed doctor, dentist, certified public accountant, engineer, lawyer, architect, realtor, schoolteacher, barber, funeral director or stockbroker.

He can never get a job where he has to be bonded or licensed.

He can't work for the city, county, state or federal government.

He cannot be admitted to West Point, Annapolis or the Air Force Academy.

That's what he lost.

—*The Railroad Evangelist*

(P. S.: Parents, show this to a teenager in your house. This may wake him/her up!)

Viewing his first American football game, the Englishman watched one of the teams go into a huddle. "It's not a bad sport," he observed, "but they have too many committee meetings."

There is a line on the ocean where you lose a day when you cross it. There's a line on most highways where you can do even better.

An announcer for a local radio station was interviewing a man on his 99th birthday. As the announcer was leaving he said, "I hope that I can come out and interview you again next year on your 100th birthday."

The old man cocked his head, studied the announcer, then said, "I don't see why you can't; you look healthy enough to me."

It is a privilege to look with anticipation toward tomorrow, to have the heart leap with the break of each new day. For the man of God there is a double privilege: the joy of belonging to God, which only the believer can feel, and the thrill of service as a man lends himself to godly tasks.

Read Ecclesiastes 3:10.

Learn to Piddle

Every financial retirement plan demands you start in your early 20's for the best return on your money. And I would suggest that you start preparing mentally, emotionally, spiritually and physically for retirement at that same age.

Most people come to retirement never having learned how to loaf. Now if you want to be a successful loafer, you have to learn how to loaf without feeling guilty about it. All our lives we have been told to work, work, work. Idle minds, idle hands, idle anything, become the Devil's workshop. And those "wise sayings" have guided us to the point that work and production are all we know.

But loafing is not being idle; it is changing gears, going from what you usually do to what is unusual for you.

For instance, I like to piddle. (That's another word for loaf.) Every time we have moved I have always made sure the house had a spare room in the basement for my workshop. I don't make many things there, but I do enjoy piddling around, repairing this and that. Oftentimes I fix things beyond repair, and I have a box full of things I've fixed—trash to my wife, but stored inventory for my cherished times of piddling.

I really pity the person who does not know how to piddle. Piddling takes place on any level. It is going from what you do for a living to what you like to do when not making a living. It is what you work at when you're not working.

Piddling is . . . putting around on a golf course . . . working out in a gym . . . poring over a good book in the library . . . doing handwork, drinking coffee with friends at unheard of hours, riding a bike and 101 other things the relaxed mind can come up with when allowed the freedom to piddle without guilt.

Fulfillment in retirement goes to those who have learned the art of piddling by training for it during those demanding, productive years when everything around us yells, "Don't drop a stitch in your work pattern." But everything inside quietly says, "Piddling, like happiness, cannot be retroactive."

It is now or never! ■

—*R. F. Smith, Jr.*
From *CONTACT*

Rejected by the college of his choice, the banker's son angrily accosted his father: "If you really cared for me, you'd have pulled some wires!"

"I know," replied the parent sadly. "The TV, the stereo and the telephone would have done for a start."

The hardest thing in all art is to be brief and full of content. Metternich once wrote, "Excuse me for the length of my letter, as I have not had the time to be brief."

—*Constantine Stanislavski*

Remember

Always remember to forget
The things that made you sad,
But never forget to remember
The things that made you glad.

Always remember to forget
The friends that proved untrue,
But never forget to remember
Those that have stuck by you.

Always remember to forget
The troubles that passed away.
But never forget to remember
The blessings that come each day.

God's Promise of Heavenly Real Estate! Too Good to Pass Up!

"He that overcometh shall inherit all things."—**Rev. 21:7.**

Fiske planetarium, on the campus of the University of Colorado, needed money, so its director dreamed up a gimmick. He printed brochures offering 1,000-acre lots on the planet Mars for only twenty dollars. Located in the Olympus Mons region, the land is a huge, extinct volcano more than twice as high as Mount Everest. The flyers read:

> This land features pink skies, unlimited rock gardens and not one but two moons. So peaceful, quiet and romantic—even the natives are friendly. At one-sixth the gravity of Earth, your golf game will improve immensely—drives will be six times longer. Mars will provide a world of adventure for the entire family.

The gag was surprisingly successful. People from across the country sent in twenty dollars for a deed, space flight insurance and a simulated sample of red Martian soil.

But better than any offer for property on Mars is God's promise of heavenly real estate. God is preparing it for Christians, not to make money, but to express His love for all who trust Jesus as their Saviour. "New World II" is a real place where the Lord Himself will live with His people. The additional features are beyond description. There will be no tears, pain or death, and the occupants will rejoice forever in God's everlasting goodness.

How reassuring to know that God's free offer of a home in the heavens is not just some promotional gimmick! It may sound too good to be true, but it isn't. It's too good to pass up.

—*M. R. DeHaan II*

* * * * *

Heaven is a prepared place for a prepared people.

Quite a Feat for Lincoln!

Little Hattie, determined to give her hero full credit for his achievements, wrote the following in a history examination:

"Abraham Lincoln was born February 12, 1809, in a log cabin he built himself."

Then Heaven Became Real!

When I was a boy, I thought of Heaven as a great shining City with vast walls, domes and spires and with nobody in it except white-robed angels who were strangers to me.

By and by when my little brother died, I thought of a great City with walls, domes and spires and a flock of cold, unknown angels and a little fellow I was acquainted with. He was the only one I knew at that time.

Then another brother died; and there were two that I knew. Then my acquaintances began to die, and the flock continually grew.

But it was not until I had sent one of my little children to his heavenly Parent that I began to think that I had gotten in a little myself.

A second went; a third went; a fourth went; and by that time I had so many acquaintances in Heaven that I did not see any more walls, domes and spires. I began to think of the residents of the Celestial City.

And there have been so many of my acquaintances gone there that sometimes it seems that I have more in Heaven than I do on earth.

—*D. L. Moody*

Bishop Hamline said: "When in trouble, my boy, kneel down and ask God's help; but never climb over the fence into the Devil's ground and then kneel down and ask help. Pray from God's side of the fence."

A small child received an "A" on her essay about mothers: "A mother," she wrote, "is the one who takes care of the children and gets their meals; and if she's not there when you come home from school, you wouldn't know how to get your dinner, and you wouldn't feel like eating it anyhow."

The difference between being ordinary and extraordinary is that little extra.

*   *   *

One day a young man found a $5.00 bill between the ties of a railroad. From that time on he never lifted his eyes from the ground while walking. In 30 years, he accumulated 25,916 buttons, 62,172 pins, 7 pennies, a bent back, and a sour, miserly disposition.

In "finding" all this, he lost the smiles of his friends, the songs of the birds, the beauties of nature, and the opportunity to serve his fellowman and spread happiness.

—*Unknown*

"Deep...all the way to the bottom!"

Karlyn was four years old. We were walking together through a beautiful part of Oregon where she lived.

She laughed and she jumped. She ran and she called. We looked at everything. Taking my cue from her, we curiously touched some things and wisely avoided others.

Conversation and questions just bubbled out of her about a most amazing variety of subjects—sticks and birds, tractors and frogs, rhubarb and flowers, Oregon people and China people, God and her family (including herself, Mommy,

Daddy, Baby George and four wonderful grandparents).

We walked beside a lovely stream. She stood between me and the water and asked solemnly, "Do you know how deep that is?"

I sensed that she had a better answer than I, so I did not guess. Her eyes widened and she said, "It's all the way to the bottom!"

The utter simplicity of true wisdom! I would have estimated the depth in feet and inches. It would have been a poor guess, I'm sure; but her answer fitted all the puddles and pools along the road —and in the whole wide world!

God speaks like that. He said, 'My grace is enough for you' (II Cor. 12:9). It goes 'all the way to the bottom' of our problems, our pressures, our sorrows, no matter who we are, where we are, nor what we face....

Remember that God's help "goes all the way to the bottom" of our need. And God has no favorites. We are all special to Him.

—From a Houghton, NY church bulletin

THE ONLY OBJECTION AGAINST THIS BIBLE IS A BAD LIFE.

***

"God Knows My Size"

Once I was a dinner guest in the home of a friend whose husband, a prominent lawyer, had recently died. During the meal my host looked intently at me, as if "sizing me up."

At the conclusion of the meal, she said, "I believe the suits of my deceased husband would fit you. The Lord has told me to give them to you."

I replied, "If the Lord has told you to give them to me, they will fit perfectly, for He knows my size!"

For years I wore those elegant suits.

How varied are God's methods to supply the needs of His children!

The preacher's little daughter had been sitting by him, watching him go over his Sunday morning's sermon. "Father," she asked after awhile, "didn't you tell me once that God tells you what to put in your sermons?"

"Yes, dear," the minister replied. "He tells me. Why do you ask?"

"Nothin'," she replied, "but I was just wondering why you scratch so much of it out."

"Read it loud enough so I can hear, too, Daddy."

It's queer the things you remember when life has crumbled suddenly and left you standing alone. It's not the big important things nor the plans of years nor the hopes you've worked on so hard. It's the little things you hadn't noticed at the time—the way a hand touched yours and you were too busy to notice; the hopeful inflection of a voice you really didn't bother to listen to.

John Carmichael found that out. All he could remember now was that his little girl had said something one evening, perhaps three weeks ago.

That particular evening he had brought home from the office the finished draft of the stockholders' report. Things being as they were, the report meant a great deal. He had to be sure it was right.

Just as he turned a page, Marge, his little daughter, came with a book under her arm and said, "Look, Daddy."

He looked briefly. "New book, eh?"

"Yes, Daddy; will you read me a story in it?"

"No, dear, not just now," he said.

Marge stood there and he read through a paragraph telling the stockholders about certain replacements of machinery at the factory; and Marge's voice with a timid, hopeful little inflection was saying, "But Mommy said you would, Daddy."

He looked over the top of his typed script: "I'm sorry, Marge. Maybe Mommy will read to you; I'm busy now, dear."

"No," Marge said politely, "Mommy is much busier upstairs. Isn't this a lovely picture?"

"Oh, yes, beautiful," he said, "but I have to work tonight; some other time, Marge."

Marge stood there with the book open at the picture. It was a long time before she said anything else. He read through two more pages explaining in full detail the shift of the market in the past twelve months, the plans outlined for the sales department in meeting these problems, and the advertising program which had been devised to increase the demand for the product.

"But it's a lovely picture, Daddy; this story looks so exciting," Marge said.

"I know," he said. "Some other time. Now just run along."

"Read some other time, Daddy?"

"Of course," he said, "sure, you bet!"

She put the book down on the stool at his feet and said, "Well, whenever you get ready, just read it to yourself, only read it loud enough so I can hear it, too."

"Sure," he said, "sure, later."

And that was what John Carmichael was remembering now—the well-mannered child had touched his hand with timid fingers and said, "Read it loud enough so I can hear, too." That was why he now put his hand on the book and took it from the table where he had piled some of Marge's things, picking them up from the floor where she had left them, and opened it to this lovely picture.

Reading the story, his lips moved stiffly with anguish to form the words. He didn't try to think anymore, and for a little while he even forgot the horror and the bitterness of his hate for the half-drunken driver who had careened down the street in a secondhand car and who was now in jail on manslaughter charges. He didn't even see his wife, white and silent, dressed for Marge's funeral, standing in the doorway trying to make her voice say calmly, "I'm ready, dear. We must go." He didn't see or hear any of this because John Carmichael was reading: "Once upon a time there was a little girl who lived in a woodcutters' hut in the black forest, and she was so fair that the birds forgot their singing looking at her." And then there came a day when he was reading it to himself, but loud enough for her to hear, too, just perhaps.

—Robert E. Edgar

Hardly Heartily

Employees in a Detroit business office found the following important notice on the bulletin board:

The management regrets that it has come to their attention that workers dying on the job are failing to fall down. This practice must stop, as it becomes impossible to distinguish between death and the natural movement of the staff. Any employee found dead in an upright position will be dropped from the payroll.

This situation finds a parallel in our work for the Lord. Like hollow people, we often go through the motions of obedience without any real heart involvement. Others may not sense anything different at first, but sooner or later they'll see that behind our business-as-usual appearance is a lack of enthusiasm for serving God.

Psalm 119:2 makes it clear that we can receive the benefits of happiness only if we remain intense in our desire to please the Lord. That is why Psalm 119:33-40 is so important. It is a prayer that expresses the desire of one who didn't want to settle for a casual religious experience. He longed for a total commitment to what God loves and hates as found in the Law. Furthermore, he sensed that, to carry out God's work in the world, he would have to give his whole heart, mind and strength to the task.

It's still true today that we will never accomplish anything for the Lord by shuffling our way through the motions of faith, knowledge and love. We must set our wills against the current world and the pull of our sinful nature. But that can't happen if our service is hardly done heartily.

—Dan Elliott in *Baptist Trumpet*

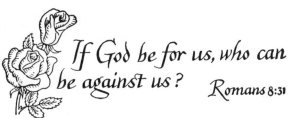

If God be for us, who can be against us? Romans 8:31

Old Is Wonderful

● Let us take note that it is the old apple trees that are decked with the loveliest blossoms;
● That it is the ancient redwoods that rise to majestic heights;
● That it is the old violins that produce the richest tones;
● That it is for ancient coins, old stamps and antique furniture that many eagerly seek;
● That it is when the day is old and far spent that it displays the beauteous colors of the sunset;
● That it is when the year is old and has run its course that the world is transformed into a fairyland of snow;
● That old friends are the dearest and that it is the old people who have been loved by God for a long, long time.

Thank God for the blessing of old age—its faith, its love, its hope, its patience, its wisdom, its experience, its maturity.

When all is said and done, OLD is wonderful!

—*M. Gemma Brunke*

"Boy, is that place organized!"

It seems that a private went to his sergeant to find out what he should do about a cut on his finger. The sarge recommended that he go to the dispensary.

The private thereupon ambled over to a door marked "Dispensary." He walked in and found himself in an empty room with two doors at the far end, one marked "Sickness" and the other "Injuries."

He figured the latter covered his case, so he opened that door, only to find himself in another empty room with two doors at the far end. These were marked "Head and Body" and "Limbs and Extremities."

He decided a cut finger would come under the latter category so he went through that door. Again he found himself in an empty room with two doors. This time one was marked "Major" and the other "Minor."

He figured his was only a minor injury, so he walked through that door, only to find himself outdoors.

Later the sergeant asked him if he got his finger fixed. "No," he said, "but, boy, is that place organized!"

CORRECT

"Some plants," said the teacher, "have the prefix dog. For instance, there is a dogrose, the dogwood, the dogviolet. Who can name another plant prefixed by dog?"

"I can," shouted a little redhead from the back row. "Collie flower."

Shhhhhhhhhhhhhhhhhhhh!!! SHHHHHHHHHHHHHH!!!

If all we have said this past year, and with never a word left out, were printed in clear black and white, 'twould make queer reading, no doubt.

And then, just suppose, ere our eyes would close, we must read the whole record through; then wouldn't we sigh, and wouldn't we try a great deal less talking to do?

And I more than half think that many a kink would be smoother in life's tangled thread, if one-half that we say along life's way, were left forever unsaid.

—Selected

IT IS NEVER TOO SOON TO BEGIN TO MAKE FRIENDS WITH DEATH.

***

No Reruns

Posted on the bulletin board in front of a Buffalo, New York, church:

ALL NEW SERMONS—NO SUMMER RERUNS.

Don't Forget the Paddle

By WENDELL E. KENT

I did a dumb thing the other day. We decided it was time to enjoy some homemade ice cream. At our house this is one sure way to liven up a dull day, for we all love it.

It's strange, isn't it, that in all the years people have been selling ice cream not one company has been able to market a product that even begins to compare with homemade ice cream. Brenda asked me why the other day, and I didn't know how to answer her. It just seems that this is one delicacy that requires the loving care of home folks. Some even argue that you have to turn the crank by hand really to get the best result, but we have gone electric at our house, perhaps to our loss.

Honestly now, can you think of any taste in this world more delightful than the first scrapings from the paddle after you pull it out of the freezer? It's a good thing the ingredients are so expensive, or I would be twice my present size, happily spooning my way to obesity.

Our freezer had been turning for half an hour when I stopped it to take a look. Something told me that all was not well. I lifted the lid, peered hopefully inside, and then to my chagrin, discovered my dumb mistake. I hadn't put the paddle in!

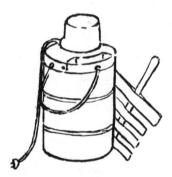

All that potential recipe was resting on the bottom, freezing to the sides, but not about to be converted into ice cream!

With some frantic maneuvers we managed to recover some of our loss, but I learned one important lesson: You can't make ice cream without the paddle. There must be something to stir up the ingredients.

Now, you're wondering what application I'm going to make of that. Isn't it obvious? There is still the need in Christian homes for the use of a paddle now and then. There is no other way, really, to take the delightful ingredients that make up a young child and to convert that child into the pleasing, satisfying, God-honoring adult we will be proud to present to the world. The Bible supports the idea of firm discipline given by loving parents. Many of our world problems today are undoubtedly partly because somebody forgot the paddle.

There is also this application we might suggest: Anything worth doing requires some constant stirring. The Apostle Paul told Timothy to stir up the gift that was in him. If the Lord has bestowed gifts upon us—and it is certain that He has—let's make sure we stir them up. Don't leave the paddle out.

Reverend Browne was asked by a parishioner why the local ministers were seen gathering at his house every Monday morning.

"To tell the truth," answered Reverend Browne, "we exchange sermons."

"Well, don't do it!" warned the lady. "You get stuck every time."

Unusual Translation

The old preacher stood up to preach. He read his text, Matthew 4:24, ". . . they brought unto him all sick people that were taken with divers diseases. . . ."

The preacher said: "Now, the doctors can scrutinize you, analyze you and sometimes cure your ills; but when you have divers disease, then only the Lord can cure.

"And, brethren, there is a regular epidemic of divers diseases among us. Some dive for the door after Sunday school is over. Some dive for the TV set during the evening services. Others dive for the car for a weekend trip, while others dive for their dimes and nickels to put in the offering, instead of tithing. Yes, it takes the Lord and the love of the church to cure DIVERS DISEASES."

—Bible Baptist Reminder

"Such a Little Way Together"

They were at the family supper table. Mary was telling of an exasperating experience she had had on the way home from work that evening.

"This woman got on the bus at 55th," she said, "and squeezed into a small space right beside me. There she sat—half on top of me, and her bundles always poking me in the face. I had to keep dodging most of the time so that the one bundle wouldn't knock my hat off."

At that point Mary's little brother piped up: "Why didn't you tell her that she was half on *your* seat—and that she should get up?"

"It wasn't worthwhile," replied Mary, "we had such a little way to go together."

Mary, of course, didn't realize it at the time, but in those words she had expressed a philosophical (yes, theological) thought which well might serve as a motto for all of us. "It wasn't worthwhile; we had such a little way to go together."

How relatively unimportant the vexations and irritations of the day become when, at eventide, we view them in their true perspective. The unkindness, the ingratitude, the lack of understanding on the part of our fellowmen—how much easier it is to bear them silently when we remember that "we have such a little way to go together"!

And how much more urgent does it become that we, on the other hand, show patience, forbearance and sweet reasonableness to those who are making life's journey hand in hand with us—whenever we remind ourselves that "we have such a little way to go together."

We have so little time to show forth the virtues of Him who has called us out of darkness into His marvelous light! so little time to demonstrate the love of Him who first loved us! so little time to *live* His Gospel!

What a different world this world would be, what a different church our church would be, what a different family most of our families would be, if each of us would always remember: we have such a little way to go together!

—Herman W. Gockel

Time

Time passes quickly. There is nothing we can do about it except to see, as far as possible, that it passes fruitfully. If, in passing swifter than a weaver's shuttle, it nevertheless lays up its store of good deeds done, noble ambitions clung to heroically, and kindness and sympathy scattered with a lavish hand, there will be given to it a permanence and enduring quality that nothing can take away.

The past has gone; the future has not yet come; the present is all we have. We cannot change the past nor can we draw upon the future, but we can use the present.

Take time to look—it is the price of success. Take time to think—it is a source of power. Take time to play—it is the secret of perennial youth. Take time to read—it is the source of wisdom. Take time to be friendly—it is the way to happiness. Take time to laugh—it is the music of the soul.

"It's this way, Doc!"

A seventy-five-year-old gentleman went to his doctor for a physical examination. He checked him thoroughly and said, "I have never seen anyone in such perfect condition at your age. Can you tell me what rules you follow and what exercises you take?"

"Well," said the old man, "my wife and I have been married fifty years. We agreed that whenever I lost my temper over any fault in her or with any of her people, she would keep quiet and not answer back. But whenever she lost her temper for a like reason, I would take a walk. I suppose my good health must be due to the last fifty years, for I have lived pretty much of an outdoor life."

A Cause to Weep

Some time ago a pastor's wife was called upon to substitute for a Sunday school teacher who was absent. In the process of her teaching, she asked, "How did Jesus die?" One of the boys immediately answered, "Why, He got shot, of course." Another boy in the class scorned, "Aw, you're crazy! He just got old and died."

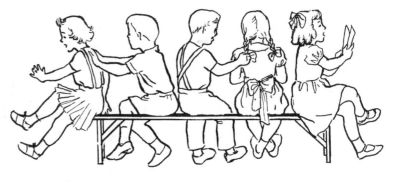

This was in a fundamental church!

Millions of children in America have never heard the true Gospel and have never had a chance to be saved! And some of them go to "church"—such as some are called.

And children are so easily won when told of the Saviour. They have a desire to be saved. Read this paragraph received from a mother:

> **My baby just put her arms around me this morning when I was talking about her being saved and said, "Mommy, if we just had a church where we could go, then I could be saved, too." Every time I talk and pray with her, she cries so hard. I just plead with you to intercede for her.**

The mother was written a letter instructing her how to lead her child to Christ.

Whose fault is it that only one-third of the children in America go to Sunday school? Whose fault is it that most of them never had a chance to be saved? Whose fault is it that most homes don't have any Christian instruction? Surely it is not the fault of the dear, innocent children! No, they are the victims of our own unconcern and sin.

Parents, how important it is that you indoctrinate your young ones in spiritual matters while they are yet tender in heart! Don't let your children grow up not knowing how and why Jesus died, as the boys mentioned above. Read Bible stories to them if they are too young to read for themselves. See that they get saved before they have to meet these worldly problems they will face.

It is hard today to know the difference between a boy and a girl because of their dress and hairdos.

A man at a party said to a stranger, "Isn't it awful the way kids look today? Look at that silly-looking girl over there."

"Sir," the stranger answered, "I'll have you know that isn't a girl. It's my son."

"Oh, I'm sorry," said the embarrassed man, "I had no way to know you were his mother."

"I'm not," the stranger answered angrily. "I'm his father."

A child's letter to God:

"Dear God,

"I would like to live 900 years like the guy in the Bible. Can this be arranged?

Love,

Chris."

SERVICE CAN NEVER BECOME SLAVERY TO ONE WHO LOVES.

—*J. L. Massee*

▲ ▲ ▲ ▲ ▲

They Had No Squeak!

Humorous incidents often happen on the mission field. In an African village a native Christian went to the village merchant to purchase a pair of shoes. He was fitted out with a suitable pair and went away happy.

Some weeks later he brought the shoes back. "Didn't they fit all right?" asked the merchant.

"Yes."

"But were they not good shoes?"

Again the answer was, "Yes."

"Then why are you returning them?"

The answer was, "They don't have any squeak."

It appeared that the man wanted a pair of shoes that would squeak when he walked up the aisle of the church. He wanted something that would draw attention to himself.

That type of Christian is as old as the church.

—*Christian Union Herald*

Ready for school, a little boy turned to his mother and said, "Mother, I wish Jesus lived on earth now!"

"Why, my darling?" asked the mother.

"Because I would like so much to do something for Him."

"What could a little fellow like you do for Him?" asked the mother.

The little boy replied, "I could run errands for Him."

"So you could, my child," said Mother, "and so you shall. I have a glass of jelly and some oranges that you can take to poor old Margaret. That will be doing an errand for Jesus. When He was on earth, He said, 'Inasmuch as ye have done it unto one of the least of these . . . ye have done it unto me' (Matthew 25:40). My darling, remember that when you do a kind deed for someone because you love Jesus, it is just the same as doing it for Jesus. You can run errands for Him every day!"

*   *   *

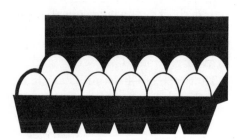

One man stayed at a new motel in Chattanooga where a guest jokingly wrote on the "Compliments and Complaints" card:

This morning at breakfast in your restaurant I ordered two eggs, one scrambled and one sunnyside up. And do you know—*they scrambled the wrong egg!*

"DON'T BE GROUNDED WHEN THE RAPTURE COMES."

"Walk a little plainer, Daddy,"
  Said a little boy so frail;
"I'm following in your footsteps,
  And I don't want to fail.
Sometimes your steps are very plain,
  Sometimes they are so hard to see;
So walk a little plainer, Daddy,
  For you are leading me.

"I know that once you walked this way,
  Many years ago!
And what you did along the way
  I'd really like to know;
For sometimes when I am tempted,
  I don't know what to do.
So walk a little plainer, Daddy,
  For I must follow you.

"Someday when I'm grown up,
  You are like I want to be—
Then I will have a little boy
  Who will want to follow me.
And I would want to lead him right,
  And help him to be true.
So walk a little plainer, Daddy,
  For we must follow you."

—Author Unknown
Christian Courier

"I Blowed Myself Out!"

A little girl asked her mother, "How can I shine for Jesus?" The mother replied, "You can shine for Jesus by being kind and loving in the home!" The little girl said, "I am going to shine for Jesus every day."

Things went well for awhile. The little girl was kind and loving. Then one afternoon she became angry and said unkind things to her little brother. He began to cry. Mother said, "I thought you were going to shine for Jesus." "Oh," said the little girl, "I was shining for Jesus, but I 'blowed' myself out!" She meant that her light had blown out. She was not shining for Jesus when she was unkind.

Are You Lost in the "Woulds"?

Some folks are lost in the "Woulds." We hear them say from time to time, "I *would* go to church, but it is my only day off; I *would* stay for preaching service on Sunday morning, but I have to eat lunch early; I *would* go to training union, but I have to get up early Monday morning, and I must have my rest; I *would* tithe, but I can't afford it; I *would* attend prayer meeting on Wednesday, but I always have another engagement; I *would* visit for our church, but I don't have the 'knack' for meeting strangers." And there are many more *woulds*.

If these people were lost in the woods, they *would* be very concerned about their condition; but too often they are complacent about being lost in the WOULDS. How sad it is that these people are not giving God their very best; and, too, they are robbing themselves of the joy of giving Christ all.

If you are lost in the "Woulds," our church will help you chart your course to the trail that leads to happy Christian living. Yes, we're on the trail, with joy, contentment, spiritual growth and rich rewards as our companions; and best of all—the trail leads to life eternal.

—Adapted

Parents' Imprints

When Woodrow Wilson was president of Princeton University, he spoke these words to a parents' group:

"I get many letters from you parents about your children. You want to know why we people up here in Princeton can't make more out of them and do more for them.

"Let me tell you the reason we can't. It may shock you just a little, but I am not trying to be rude. The reason is, they are your sons, reared in your homes, blood of your blood, bone of your bone. They have absorbed the ideals of your homes. You have formed and fashioned them. They are your sons. In those malleable, moldable years of their lives you have forever left your imprint upon them."

NO!

Learn to say "no"; it will be of more use to you than to be able to read Latin.

—*Spurgeon*

The words of an unknown author are clear and piercing:

What shall you give to one small boy?
A glamorous game, a tinseled toy,
A barlow knife, a puzzle pack,
A train that runs on a curving track?
A picture book, a real live pet . . .
No, there's plenty of time for such things yet;
Give him a day for his very own—
Just one small boy and his dad alone.
A walk in the woods, a romp in the park,
A fishing trip from dawn to dark,
Give the best gift to that bright lad—
The companionship of his dear dad.
Games are outgrown, and toys decay—
But he'll never forget if you
*   "Give him a day."*

• In olden days when dyes would not hold their colors very well, they were frequently used as illustrations. One such appeared on a tombstone, reading, "She fitted herself for heavenly reward with virtues that will not fade when washed."

Short-Order Lingo

Today's fast-food restaurants can't compare with the old-time soda fountain, contends Rose Heiberger of Lancaster, Pennsylvania.

Rose recalls that soda fountain waitresses and soda jerks had a lingo all their own. Do you remember hearing a waitress shouting:

"Need some lumber!" (toothpicks);

"Nervous Pudding" (Jell-O);

"Sinker 'n' Suds" (doughnut and coffee);

"Squash the lemon!" (lemonade);

"Black 'n' White" (chocolate soda and vanilla ice cream);

"Burn the Cheese" (grilled cheese);

"Burn Two" (toast);

"Fish in a Can" (tuna sandwich);

"Coney Island Chicken" (hot dog);

"Drown One, Hold the Hail" (Coke, no ice);

"Clean the Kitchen" (hash);

"Adam's Ale" (water);

"Fly Cake" (raisin cake);

"Break It; Shake It" (scrambled eggs).

In the town of Needham, west of Boston, Massachusetts, a street sign leaves no doubt in drivers' minds as to the rules of the road. The sign reads: "Don't even think of parking here."

That sign should be put up at certain places on the highway of life.

It should appear, for example, at the place we call "bereavement." "Don't even think of parking here." Sometimes people in their grief park for years at that point and as a result make no progress in moral and spiritual growth. A similar sign should be put up at the place called "defeat," and another one at the place called "ecstatic experience." These are no places to park. "Don't even think of parking here."

—*The Prairie Overcomer*

Close the gate behind you!

"Fear not...for thou shalt forget the shame of your youth."—Isa. 54:4.

Two men walking down a country road decided to take a shortcut home. They passed through a field where a number of cattle were grazing. Deeply engrossed in conversation when they reached the other side of the pasture, they forgot to shut the gate behind them. A few minutes later one of them noticed the oversight and ran back to close the gate. As he did, he remembered the last words of an old friend who summoned all his children to his bedside and gave them this wise counsel: *As you travel down life's pathway, remember to close the gates behind you."*

The man knew that problems, difficult situations, heartbreaks, and failures were inevitable; but he wanted his children to know that they didn't have to allow those things to follow them through life.

This is especially true for believers. Once we have confessed a sin and have done what we can to right the wrong, we must put the incident behind us.

The Apostle Paul told us to forget the things of the past that will hinder us and to reach forward to those things which are ahead. Then we will be better able to "press toward the mark for the prize of the high calling of God in Christ Jesus" (Phil. 3:14).

When it comes to the failures of the past, we can always close the gate behind us.

—*R. W. DeHaan*

If it were not for the legal abortions performed every year there would be almost 100 beautiful babies born in every state every day—seven days a week.

eeeeeeeeeeeeeeeeeeeeeeeeeeeeeeeeeeee

Live the Christian life! Men will **admire** you, women will respect you, little children will love you, and God will crown your life with success. And when the twilight of your life mingles with the purpling dawn of eternity, men will speak your name with honor and baptize your grave with tears, as God attunes for you the evening chimes.

—*Billy Sunday*

§§§§§§§§§§§§§§§§§§§§§§§§§§§§§§§§§§§§

I saw a woman lying on a stair,
Head down, flies crawling on her face and
   hair,
While lodgers came and went, nor looked
   at all.
She was a masterpiece of Alcohol.

I saw an old man lying on a bed,
Helpless for life, his weary old wife said.
His hip was broken in a needless fall—
Achievement credited to Alcohol.

I saw a man in death's stark whiteness
   lie,
A bullet through his heart. I heard the cry
Of wife and children sensing hunger's
   thrall—
Work of the all-efficient Alcohol.

I saw a lovely girl, clean-faced and fine,
But foolish, plied by men with gin and
   wine,
Till self-respect had tottered to its fall.
Another Magdalene. Hail, Alcohol!

I saw these things; you may have seen
   them, too.
The world is saturated with them through
   and through.
And there are those who claim it has a
   place—
A drug that does that to the human race.

—*Clarence Edwin Flynn*

Longing for Heaven

It's mighty tiresome layin' 'round
This sorrow-laden earthly ground;
And ofttimes I thinks, thinks I,
'Twould be a sweet thing jest to die
   And go 'long Home.

Home, whar the friends we loved will say,
"We've waited for you many a day;
Come here an' rest yourself, an' know
You're done with sorrow an' with woe
   Now you're at Home."

I wish the day was near at hand;
I'm tired of this grieving land;
I'm tired of the lonely years;
I wants to jes' dry up my tears
   An' go 'long Home.

O Master, won't You send the call?
My friends are there, my hope, my all;
I'm waiting whar the road is rough;
I want to hear You say, "Enough,
   Old man, come Home!"

·♡·♡·♡·♡

𝕷𝖔𝖛𝖊

Based on I Corinthians 13

Though in the glamour of the public eye I sway the emotions of man by my oratory or by my silver singing or by my skillful playing, and then go home and gripe because supper is late or because my clothes weren't made to suit me, I am become as sounding brass or a tinkling cymbal.

And though I am able to impress others with my vast knowledge of the deep things of the Word of God, and though I am able to accomplish mighty things through faith so that I become famous among men as a remover of mountains, and have not the love that reads the deep longings of the hearts around the family circle and removes the barriers that grow up in shy and tender hearts, I am nothing.

And though in the glamour of public praise I bestow all my goods to feed the poor, and though I win the name and fame of a martyr by giving my body to be burned, and yet close up like a clam at home, or behave like a snapping turtle, knowing nothing of the glory of giving myself in unstinted, self-denying service to those nearest and dearest, it profiteth me nothing.

Love is never impatient, but kind; love knows no jealousy; love makes no parade; gives itself no airs.

Love is never rude, seeks not her own nor fights for her own rights, is never resentful, never imagines that others are plotting evil against her.

Never brooks over wrongs; never exults over the mistakes of others; but is truly gladdened by goodness.

Love suffers silently, is always trustful, always cheerful, always patient.

Home is the acid test of the truly yielded life, for in all other phases of Christian service there is a certain amount of glamour; but in the home one is confronted with the bare facts of life, stripped of all glamour. The home is given to help every Christian "not to think of himself more highly than he ought to think." And it is in the home that we have the privilege of demonstrating that the Christian life is "faith which worketh by love."

·♡·♡·♡·♡

EASIER TO BE GOOD AROUND HER

In a cemetery, a little white stone marked the grave of a dear little girl, and on the stone were chiselled these words—

A CHILD OF WHOM HER PLAYMATES SAID, "IT WAS EASIER TO BE GOOD WHEN SHE WAS WITH US."

—one of the most beautiful epitaphs ever heard of.

"I helped to build that!"

When Milan Cathedral was finished, in the vast throngs of people assembled to witness the dedication was a little girl who was heard to cry out in childish glee, as she pointed to the great building, "I helped to build that!"

"What!" exclaimed one of the guards who was standing in brilliant uniform. "Show me what you did."

"I carried the dinner pail for my father while he worked up yonder," she replied.

Her part, though humble, helped to complete the plans of the architect.

In relating this story Bishop Leonard makes this comment: "Our part in life may seem small, but it should bulk large in our thought when we remember that it is helping to complete the plan of the Divine Architect."

Live Like a Sinner, Pay With the Sinners

A story is told of a North Carolina preacher who lived in the days when traveling preachers were entertained at hotels free of charge. This particular preacher put up at a hotel for a few days, where he was most hospitably entertained by the host; but as he was leaving, he was much surprised to be presented with his bill.

"Why," he said, "I thought preachers were entertained free."

"Well," said the innkeeper, "you came and ate your meals without asking the blessing; no one has ever seen you with a Bible; you smoked big cigars. While you were here you talked about everything but religion. Pray, how were we to know that you were a preacher? You have lived like a sinner, so now you will have to pay with the sinners."

—From *Missionary Baptist News*

A lady walked into a supermarket in a desperate attempt to get supper ready quick and asked one of the grocery clerks, "Do you have anything quicker than instant?"

God's Album

We may write our name in albums;
* We may trace them in the sand;*
We may chisel them in marble,
* With a firm and skillful hand.*
But the pages soon are sullied,
* And inscriptions fade away.*
Every monument will crumble,
* And our earthly hopes decay.*

But, dear friends, there is an album,
* Full of leaves of snowy white,*
Where no name is ever tarnished,
* But forever pure and bright.*
In the book of life, GOD'S ALBUM,
* May our name be penned with care,*
And whosoe'er hath written,
* Write it forever there.*

—Author Unknown

A recent visitor to our country from India, after many weeks of travel through our great nation, was asked by a newspaper reporter to give his number one impression of America. His unhesitating reply was this: "The size of the American garbage cans."

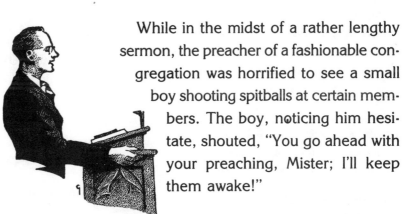

While in the midst of a rather lengthy sermon, the preacher of a fashionable congregation was horrified to see a small boy shooting spitballs at certain members. The boy, noticing him hesitate, shouted, "You go ahead with your preaching, Mister; I'll keep them awake!"

Love is the one treasure that multiplies by division. It is the one gift that grows bigger the more you take from it. It is the one business in which it pays to be an absolute spendthrift. You can give it away, throw it away, empty your pockets, shake the basket, turn the glass upside down; and tomorrow you will have more than ever.

—*Author Unknown*

"Something that won't work"

"Good morning, ma'am," said a caller. "I'm from the gas company. I understand there's something in this house that won't work."

"Yes, sir," she answered. "He's upstairs."

The world is enriched most by men who labor, not by those who loaf.

A pint of effort is worth a gallon of excuses. An ounce of example is worth a pound of exhortation. An inch of cooperation is worth a yard of cheering. A foot of work is worth a mile of wishing.

Our Lord Jesus said, 'My Father has never yet ceased His work, and I am working too.'

Shouldn't you?

—From *Sowing & Reaping*

†   †   †

I Live to DYE

In a city he visited during one of his many journeys preaching the Word of God, A. C. Gaebelein noticed this sign in a small dyeing establishment:

**I Live to Dye, I Dye to Live.
The More I Dye, the More I Live;
The More I Live, the More I Dye.**

Read these words aloud, and you will hear a great spiritual truth. The more there is death to self, that much more fully is the Lord Jesus Christ able to live His life in us. "I am crucified with Christ: nevertheless I live; yet not I, but Christ liveth in me" (Gal. 2:20). This kind of living is possible to every believer by full appropriation of all that is his in Christ. "Likewise reckon ye also yourselves to be dead indeed unto sin, but alive unto God through Jesus Christ our Lord" (Rom. 6:11).

The World According to Parents:

"Bring me the change."

"Call us when you get there."

"I hope I'm alive when you kids turn sixteen."

"Stop doing that—you might poke out your eye."

"Shut up and eat."

"How did you know your brother had his eyes open during the prayer?"

"Sit up and look at the scenery."

"How many times have I told you...?"

"Why is it that you remember to eat, but you never remember to take out the garbage?"

"All you had to do was pick up a phone and call us."

"If you break your leg, don't come running to me."

"You *will* have fun."

"Because I said so."

"Next time wait until I get off the phone."

"That milk is going to be awfully chocolatey."

"This is going to hurt me a lot more than it's going to hurt you."

"If Johnny jumped off a bridge, would you?"

"Do it to make your mother happy."

"Wait until your dad gets home."

"No, I'm not sleeping. I'm just resting my eyes."

"When I was your age, I walked twenty-six miles to school one way through blizzards, hail storms and 110 degree heat. NOW GO!"

"Don't do as I do, do as I say."

GOSSIP'S WAY

*Gossip should, as I was told
By Father and by Mother
When I was very young, go in
One ear and out the other.*

*And so perhaps it should; but I,
Who've listened through the years
With studied concentration and
Alert, attentive ears,*

*Have learned that gossip mostly takes
A detour to the south—
By which I mean that it goes in
One ear and out the mouth.*

—Richard Armour

WE LOVE HIM SINCE HE LOVED US

After Mother had finished a task, she said to her little girl, "You may come now, dear."

The child said, "I'm so glad, for I wanted to love you so much." "But I thought you were happy with your dolly," said the mother.

"Yes, Mother, I was, but I soon get tired of loving her, for she can't love me back."

There is profound wisdom in the answer of the wee philosopher. God could have stopped His creative work with an inanimate creation; but, no; He wanted to be loved back! And so He made man. Then He revealed to man His sacrificial love on the cross, and sinful men who see that love trust God and love Him back.

So God will have in Heaven, not mere "dolls," machines; but He will have redeemed men who will love and serve Him for all He has done for them!

"We love him, because he first loved us."—I John 4:19.

Things You Never Regret:

Showing kindness to an aged person; destroying the letter written in anger; offering the apology that saves a friendship; stopping a scandal that is wrecking a reputation; helping a boy find himself; taking time to show consideration to your parents; remembering God in all things.

—The Echo

A four-year-old attended prayer meeting not long ago with his parents. When he knelt to say his prayers before going to bed upon his return, he prayed: "Dear Lord, we had a good time at church tonight. I wish You could have been there."

—Christian Advocate

Miss Me but Let Me Go
by George R. Monseur

*When I come to the end of the road
and the sun has set for me,
I want no rites in a gloom-filled room;
why cry for a soul set free?
Miss me a little...but not too long,
and not with your head bowed low.
Remember the love that was once shared,
Miss Me...but Let Me Go.*

*For this is a journey we all must take,
and each must go alone.
It's all a part of the Master's plan,
a step on the road to home.
When you are lonely and sick of heart,
go to the lonely and sick of heart,
go to the friends we know,
And bury your sorrows in doing good deeds...
Miss Me...but Let Me Go.*

"The Sun Is Up!"

An old saint of God lay dying. At his request the friend who was sitting with him turned on all the lights in the house.

Time passed, and the old man became weaker and weaker.

Finally when the night was darkest outside, the old pilgrim lifted his head, looked around and said, "Put out the lights; the sun is up," and he was gone to the place where the sun never sets.

Telling of it later the friend said, "Wasn't that strange?" No, it was not strange, for there is a light in the valley of the shadow for God's people.

Be Still and Listen

Years ago a man who operated an icehouse lost a good watch in the sawdust on the floor. He offered a reward. Although many went through the wood-sawings with rakes, they were unable to find the lost treasure.

When they left the building for lunch, a small boy entered and came out a few moments later with the treasured timepiece. When asked how he had found it, he replied, "I just lay down in the sawdust and quietly waited *until I heard the watch ticking!*"

Many of us have lost much more than a watch. If we will just be still and listen quietly, the Lord will speak to us and show us where we lost our power and testimony.

Let us "study to be quiet" when God takes us aside, for only thus will we know the miracle of His grace and the peace of His blessing. Listen like Elijah for the "still small voice."

—H. G. Bosch

◆ ◆ ◆ ◆ ◆

Can you explain it to the lady?

A lady with only a dollar to spend went to town to get some aspirin and some Vaseline. She found two stores: one advertised Vaseline at 40¢ and aspirin at 60¢. Across the street she saw Vaseline advertised at 45¢ and aspirin at 55¢. So she went to the first store and bought their 40¢ Vaseline, saving 5¢. Then she went to the second store and bought their aspirin at 55¢, saving another 5¢. But she had only 5¢ left out of her dollar; as she had saved 5¢ on each purchase, she thought she should have 10¢ left.

The two merchants were unable to convince her that neither had shortchanged her. Can you explain it to the lady?

If the "Gay life style" is normal, why did God destroy Sodom and Gomorrah from the face of the earth because of it, and continue to use this as an example of His wrath? And why does Paul say three times in Romans 1 that "God gave them up"?

A very good illustration of forgiveness was given by a little boy who, on being asked what forgiveness of injuries was, gave the answer: "It is the scent that flowers give when they are trampled on!"

"I'm sorry, dear, but your remote control doesn't work in church!"

*   *   *

> IF EACH HUNG UP HIS PACK OF TROUBLES ON A WALL AND LOOKED AROUND AT THE TROUBLES OF OTHERS, HE WOULD QUICKLY RUN TO GRAB HIS OWN.

OPEN-MINDED OR EMPTY-HEADED—IT DEPENDS ON WHETHER YOU'RE DEFINING YOURSELF OR SOMEONE ELSE.

Where to Find Gratitude

A businessman said, "People are ingrates. It took me 61 years to find it out. I have 175 employees, men and women. At Thanksgiving, I sent them 175 choice turkeys. Only four thanked me. Two thanked me by notes, and two said 'Thank you' when they chanced to meet me in the hall. Because of their thanklessness, I've decided never to go out of my way to be nice again."

Someone has said, "If you want to find gratitude, look for it in the dictionary. The reward of giving comes from the good feeling it gives the giver. Don't expect any other returns."

—*W. B. Knight*

÷   ÷   ÷   ÷

They Come Out Right

Some little girls were told the story of Abraham and his sacrifice of Isaac. The teacher, with a dramatic touch, made it live.

Suddenly, as the story approached its climax, a nervous little girl burst out: "Oh, please don't go on—this story is too terrible."

But a second little girl spoke up at once: "Oh, Mary, don't be so silly. This is one of God's stories, and they always come out right."

—*Gerald Kennedy*

Why Tommy Couldn't "Say Grace"

Tommy, nine years old, loved Jesus with his whole heart. He also loved his Bible and tried to follow its teachings.

One day Tommy and his father and mother were invited to the home of a relative for dinner. Grandfather was present. He was getting old and had many aches and pains. A friend had told him to take a bottle of beer to "pep" him up a little, so Grandfather brought a bottle of beer to the table with him.

When the family was seated, Tommy was asked to say the blessing. He had never "said grace" over a beer bottle before, so he was troubled.

All bowed their heads. Tommy couldn't say a word. Finally he raised his head and, looking over to his mother, said, "Mom, I can't ask God to bless us or the food on this table, with that beer bottle sitting there!"

Grandfather grabbed the bottle and started for the back door. He put it in the garbage can and returned to the table. Then Tommy said grace, and the meal was eaten.

Grandfather vowed right then never again to touch strong drink.

LIFE

Life is currently described in one of four ways: as a journey; as a battle; as a pilgrimage; and as a race. Select your own metaphor, but the finishing necessary is all the same. For if life is a journey, it must be completed. If life is a battle, it must be finished. If life is a pilgrimage, it must be concluded. And if it is a race, it must be won. Live every second of your life.

—*Capital Voice*

"My Pastor Aims at Me"

My pastor shapes his sermons
From A to final Z
In clear and forthright language,
  And aims them straight at me.

And when he gets to preaching,
  I look around to see
If there might be another
  Deserving more than me.

But every soul looks saintly—
  Their hearts to Heaven turn—
While I, in my conviction,
  Can only sit and squirm.

You know, I often wonder,
  If I should miss a day;
Would he, without his target,
  Have anything to say?

—*Author Unknown*

Lettered!

A young man left the farm for New York and after several months wrote to his brother back in the cornfield: "Thursday we autoed out to the country club where we golfed until dark. Then we motored to the beach for the weekend."

A few days later, he received the following reply from his rural brother: "Monday, we buggied into town and baseballed all afternoon. Then we went to Ted's and checkered until morning. Tuesday, we muled out to the cornfield and geehawed until sundown. Then we suppered and fiddled for a while and then staircased up to our room and bedsteaded until the clock fived."

We Christians forget so easily that we are not citizens of earth en route to Heaven but citizens of Heaven temporarily residing on earth. The wild duck is not too attached to a northern lake; he knows that he will be leaving at summer's end.

God's people, sit loose to this world, for you are leaving at the close of the season.

A LIAR WILL NOT BE BELIEVED EVEN WHEN SHE SPEAKS THE TRUTH.

No one is so old that he cannot live yet another year, nor so young that he cannot die today.

—**F. De Rojas**

Two little teardrops were floating down the river of life; one teardrop said to the other: "Who are you?"

"I am a teardrop from a girl who loved a man and lost him. Who are you?"

"Well, I am a teardrop from the girl who got him."

Life is like that. We cry over the things we can't have; but if we only knew it, we would probably cry twice as much if we had received them.

Paul had the right idea when he said, "I have learned, in whatsoever state I am, therewith to be content."

Iky and Izzy were separating after an evening together. Iky said, "Au revoir."

"Vot's dat?" asked Izzy.

"Dot's good-by in French."

"Vell," said Izzy, "carbolic acid."

"Vot's dat?" asked Iky.

"Dot's good-by in any language."

"I'm a magician."

"That's interesting. What's your best trick?"

"I saw a woman in half."

"Is it difficult?"

"It's child's play. In fact, I learned it while I was a child."

"Are there any more children at home yet?"

"I have several half sisters."

Bear in mind that children of all ages have one thing in common—they close their ears to advice and open their eyes to example.

REJECTING THINGS BECAUSE THEY ARE OLD-FASHIONED WOULD RULE OUT THE SUN AND THE MOON.

REVENGE. A little girl was making faces at a bulldog. Her mother reprimanded her. "Well, he started it," said the girl.

No doubt the girl was right, for it is no trouble for a bulldog to look ugly. The weakness was in the girl's conclusion drawn from the dog's face. The dog was probably innocent; but if not, the girl gained nothing by competing with him in making faces.

The person who proceeds on the theory that he must return every ugly act which is directed toward him will have a never-ending and profitless job. Hate has injurious effects on the person who resents, so that he is the chief sufferer.

—*Telescope*

Shouting Time in Glory

When we see the Saviour coming,
When His shout shall split the air;
*It'll be **Shouting Time in Glory**,*
The time to meet Him there.

He shall split the graves wide open,
Much to this world's surprise.
*It'll be **Shouting Time in Glory**,*
When His call comes from the skies.

The living saints will answer;
The dead shall hear His cry;
*It'll be **Shouting Time in Glory**,*
When we bid this world goodbye.

Then upward into Heaven
The saints of God will go.
The Lamb of God will lead us,
The One who loved us so.

Then it'll be, "Welcome Home, My children,"
We'll hear our Father say.
*It'll be **Shouting Time in Glory**,*
When He wipes our tears away.

—*F. M. Riley*

An Advertisement of Heaven

An ad from the Bible:

FREE
BEAUTIFUL HOMES
to be
GIVEN AWAY
in a
PERFECT CITY!
with:

- *100% Pure Water Free*
- *No Light Bills*
- *Perpetual Lighting*
- *Permanent Pavement*
- *Nothing Undesirable*
- *Everything New*
- *Perfect Health*
- *Immunity from Accidents*
- *The Best of Society*
- *Beautiful Music*
- *Free Transportation*

SECURE A CONTRACT TODAY FOR THE NEW JERUSALEM.

—*The Bible Friend*

Her small son was sent off to his first day of school. When asked upon his return how many children were in his class, he replied, with all the dignity of his age, "There are 14—7 boys and about a million girls."

"And the Lord called him home!"

Dr. Tom Wallace tells of a pastor visiting a home. Suddenly the door flew open and little Willie came racing in yelling, "Ma! Ma! Look what I've got!" He was holding aloft a dead, bloodied rat of no small size.

Excitedly, the lad began giving the gory details of his triumph, saying, "I found this old rat and grabbed a big stick and beat him and clubbed him. Then I got a rock and smashed him and beat him some more. Then. . . I," and for the first time he glanced up and saw the preacher listening intently. Suddenly the lad's fierce, scowling countenance became meek, and his manifestation of toughness melted like fat in the fire. His voice lowered to a tone of tenderness and piety as he concluded his story, ". . . and then the Lord called him home!"*

Be as careful of the books you read as of the company you keep, for your character will be influenced as much by the one as by the other.

Enough

I praise Thee, Lord, and I am ever thankful
　To know my flour barrel ne'er shall empty be;
And I am grateful that my cruse of oil
　Shall ne'er run dry, for 'tis supplied by Thee.
Grant me assurance, Lord, that when supplies are lowest,
　When in my heart I need so much to know
That every time I go unto my barrel
　There'll be enough, even though it may be low.

And when I lift my little cruse of oil
　But fear to tip it o'er lest it be dry,
Teach me to trust and simply turn it over
　To see once more Thy bountiful supply.
Help me, O Lord, to never, never doubt Thee;
　For Thou dost graciously supply my need,
And every day my barrel is replenished,
　And I have flour and oil enough indeed.

—*Choice Gleanings*

The Last Slur

A man who had given his wife a black eye was hauled into court for assault. The judge listened to his sob story and let him off on probation.

The next day he was back before the same judge, having blacked his wife's other eye. "Well, Judge, it was this way," he explained to the boiling-mad magistrate. "Yesterday was a difficult day for me—here in court, surrounded by all these lawyers. Judge, my nerves were shot. I thought a little drink might help —and another and another. When I finally made it home the little woman was waiting for me. 'You good-for-nothing drunk,' she said.

"Judge, I didn't do a thing then. I thought about the condition I was in, and I could see maybe she had a point. Then she said, 'You lazy no-good bum,' and, Judge, I thought about the way I'd let my job go and the rent being due. And again I didn't say a word or do a thing. Because I could see that maybe she had a point.

"But then, Judge, she said, 'If that nincompoop of a judge had any backbone, you'd be behind bars right now.'

"And, Judge—that slur on our judiciary was more than I could bear."

Modest Model

The photographer peered thru his viewfinder.

"Lady," he asked, "why are you tying that string around the bottom of your dress?"

The little old lady replied, "You can't fool me, young man. I know you can see me upside-down in that camera."

Mother-love: abuse cannot offend it; neglect cannot chill it; time cannot affect it; death cannot destroy it. For harsh words it has gentle chiding; for a blow it has beneficent ministry; for neglect it has increasing watchfulness.

Oh, appreciate a mother's love. If you could only look in for an hour's visit to her, you would rouse up in the aged one a whole world of blissful memories. What if she does sit without talking much; she watched you for months when you knew not how to talk at all.

What if she has ailments to tell about; during 15 years you ran to her with every little scratch and bruise, and she doctored your little finger as carefully as a surgeon would bind the worst fracture.

You say she is childish now; I wonder if she ever saw you when you were childish.

You have no patience to walk with her on the street; she moves so slowly. I wonder if she remembers the time when you were glad enough to go slowly.

—*T. DeWitt Talmage*

A LITTLE BOY BY HIS MOTHER'S GRAVE

"I don't understand it," the little boy said.
"What do they mean when they say, 'She is dead'?
John's got a Mom—and Bob's mother's there
To kiss them good night and rumple their hair.
What did my mom do that she should be here
And not back at home...warm...near?

"Was the driver who killed her so full of hate
That he wouldn't brake until 'way too late?
Had she harmed his family—or maybe him?
Was he drinking and driving on some sort of whim?
Did he have a mother...kids and a home?
Doesn't he know how it feels—all alone?

"The Lord says 'forgive,' my daddy said.
It's kinda hard when they say, 'She is dead.'"

A WOMAN'S FONDEST WISH IS TO BE WEIGHED AND FOUND WANTING!

How to Make a Scandal

Take a grain of falsehood, a handful of running about, the same quantity of nimble tongue, a sprig of herb backbite, a teaspoonful of "don't you tell it," six drops of malice and a few of envy. Add a little discontent and jealousy and strain through a bag of misconception; cork it up tight in a bottle of malevolence and hang it out on a skein of street yarn; keep it in a hot atmosphere; shake it occasionally for a few days, and it will be fit for use. Let a few drops be taken before walking out, and the desired results will follow.

—Selected

"I'M REVERENT—AND YOU'D BETTER BELIEVE IT."

Sixty-second Sermon

A schoolteacher asked the pupils to bring their birth certificates so she might check up on their correct age. The next day, a little girl brought the certificate to the teacher, saying, "Here is my excuse for living."

She had confused the document with excuses, absences or tardiness; but, as one pointed out, we ought to ask ourselves what excuse we have for living. Is there a real purpose to our lives?

Paul's "excuse" was, "For to me to live is Christ."

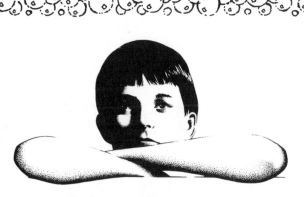

Being a Kid Is Tough

One of the great puzzles in my life is when Daddy whips me for smoking a cigarette butt he threw away. And Mommy sometimes washes my mouth out with soap for saying a word that I learned from her.

Ever since I can remember, my parents have taught me not to tell lies, but the other day Mother sent me to the door to tell a salesman that she was gone.

Maybe when we get big and our folks get little, we can enjoy the privilege of telling "whoppers." You know, being parents must be fun . . . but being a kid is tough, with so many restrictions.

Remember that every word spoken before our children and every action observed contribute to the formation of their character.

—Selected

The salesman after gaining entrance to the prospect's home put on his personality act. "My, what a lovely home you have," he gushed. "And what is in that beautiful vase on the mantel?"

"My husband's ashes," said the young wife.

"Oh, I'm so sorry. How long has he been dead?"

"He's not. He's just too lazy to find an ashtray."

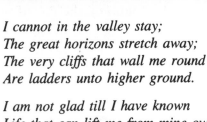

I cannot in the valley stay;
The great horizons stretch away;
The very cliffs that wall me round
Are ladders unto higher ground.

I am not glad till I have known
Life that can lift me from mine own;
A loftier level must be won—
A mightier Strength to lean upon.

—Lucy Larcom

FACE POWDER MAY HELP CATCH A MAN, BUT IT'S THE BAKING POWDER THAT HOLDS HIM.

‡   ‡   ‡   ‡

"I didn't come to see you to be told I'm burning the candle at both ends," said the lady patient to her doctor; "I came for more wax."

Perfect Marriage Is Extremely Frustrating

Washington (UPI)—My wife and I have a wedding anniversary coming up this week, and I don't mind saying I am under a terrific strain.

The trouble is that we seem to be ideally mated.

After all these many years I still regard her as a perfect wife, lover and mother of my children. She, in turn, continues to appreciate my many sterling qualities, which grow more numerous as the years roll by.

In all of our married life there has never been a shot fired in anger, and seldom even a discouraging word. This is extremely frustrating, to say the least.

For one thing, it makes it difficult to plan a proper anniversary celebration.

The custom is to treat a wedding anniversary as a special occasion.

The husband takes his wife out to dinner at a place he can't afford and that sort of thing.

In our case, however, just being together makes every meal ambrosia. Consequently, there isn't much point in trying to gild the lily.

Another big frustration stems from the fact that the largest single body of humor in America is built around marital friction.

Guys are forever coming up and telling me jokes of the Maggie-and-Jiggs type. But since I am unable to relate them to my own experience, I miss the punch lines.

I have said, "I don't get it," so many times that people have begun to regard me as a hopeless square.

Then there is the matter of party conversation, which is based in large measure on the battle of the

sexes. I find myself unable to participate and as a consequence am rapidly becoming a social outcast.

In short, I have started to wonder whether there is any longer a place in America for a well-adjusted couple. And the other evening I spoke to my wife about this.

"Sweetheart," I said, "what's wrong with us anyway? We have become total misfits. Our marriage has worked out so well it's almost unbearable."

"I know," she said, being ever understanding. "Every day that passes without a quarrel makes it more difficult to hold the marriage together."

Apparently, however, we are stuck with each other. My lawyer says it's impossible to obtain a divorce on grounds of compatibility.

—*Dick West*

A woman who had received a remarkable healing in her body wrote to a minister to tell him of this wonderful experience. In concluding her letter, she wrote, "Do you think God would do anything about my overweight?"

He wrote back, "This kind goeth out only by fasting."

We need not expect God to do for us what we can do for ourselves. Prayer is not a crutch but a clutch—putting us in gear with God.

What you have in this world will be found on the day of your death to belong to others; what you are will be yours forever.

—Henry Van Dyke

* * * * *

Grandmother's "Receet"

—Nadine Mills Coleman in the 65 Magazine

Years ago when my mother was a bride, my Kentucky grandmother gave her "receet" for washing clothes. This treasured bit of writing now hangs above my gleaming automatic washer.

1. bild fire in back yard to het kettle of rain water.
2. set tubs so smoke won't blow in eyes if wind is peart.
3. shave 1 hole cake lie sope in bilin water.
4. sort things. make 3 piles. 1 pile white. 1 cullord. 1 pile werk briches and rags.
5. stur flour in cold water to smooth then thin down with bilin water.
6. rub dirty spots on board. scrub hard. then bile. rub cullord but don't bile just rench and starch.
7. take white things out of kettle with broom stick handle then rench, blew and starch.
8. spread tee towels on grass.
9. hang old rags on fence.
10. pore rench water in flower bed.
11. scrub porch with hot sopy water.
12. turn tubs upside down.
13. go put on cleen dress—smooth hair with side combs, brew cup of tee—set and rest and rock a spell and count blessins.

Bloopers From Church Bulletins

How's That Again??

1. This afternoon there will be a meeting in the south and north ends of the church. Children will be baptized at both ends.

2. Thursday at 5 p.m., there will be a meeting of the Little Mothers Club. All wishing to become little mothers will please meet the pastor in his study.

3. This being Easter Sunday, we will ask Mrs. Brown to come forward and lay an egg on the altar.

4. Ladies of the church have cast off clothing of every kind, and they can be seen in the church basement on Friday afternoon.

5. On Sunday, a special collection will be taken to defray the expense of the new carpet. All wishing to do something on the carpet, please come forward and get a piece of paper.

6. Tonight's sermon: "What is Hell?" Come early and listen to our choir practicing.

7. Another marriage-encounter weekend is being offered. It's a chance for a weekend away for just you and your souse.

Seventeen Secrets to Success

* Keep your temper to yourself.
* Give your enthusiasm to everybody.
* Be yourself, forget yourself, become genuinely interested in the other guy.
* Be fair, honest, friendly—and you'll be admired and liked.
* Make other people feel important.
* Count your assets and stamp out self-pity.
* Meet the other person at his/her own level.
* Put your smile power to work.
* Keep moving.
* Keep trying.
* Give the gift of heart.
* Get off to a good start in anything you do.
* Forgive yourself if you fail.
* Be lavish with kindness.
* Overwhelm people with your charm, not your power.
* Keep your promises.
* Be an optimist.

THE WARMTH OF A HOME IS NOT NECESSARILY DETERMINED BY ITS HEATING SYSTEM.

* * *

Our children are our only earthly possessions we can take to Heaven.

* * *

"The best and most beautiful things in the world cannot be seen nor even touched, but just felt in the heart."

—*Helen Keller*

* * *

● *Most homes nowadays seem to be on three shifts: Father on the night shift; Mother on the day shift, and the children shift for themselves.*

One writer tells of an old lady who always began her testimony at prayer meeting by saying, "Forty years ago. . . ." The writer says, "I felt like asking her, 'Lady, hasn't anything happened since?' "

We thank God for the happy day that fixed our choice on Him our Saviour and our God, but there should be more happy days all along. Christian lives sometimes become like some married lives that get to where there is nothing left but anniversaries.

—*Vance Havner*

Calling All Grandmothers

One Sunday little Johnny went to a new Sunday school, and so naturally his parents wondered how he liked it.

"Real good!" he said.

"Who was your teacher?" Mother probed.

"I don't know her name, but I think she must have been Jesus' grandmother."

"Why do you say that?" asked the father.

"Well, she sure bragged about Jesus, so she must be His grandmother," he said seriously.

"Only a Piece of Paper," They Say

Some whose lifestyle is contrary to the norms of a well-regulated society, speak lightly and self-excusingly of procuring a marriage license and a minister to consummate the sacred marital bond. "A marriage license is only a piece of paper. Why bother?"

So also is a birth certificate, a driver's license, a high school diploma, a degree in medicine and law, a passport, a divorce decree, and a ticket on a bus, train and airplane.

Nameless confusion would ensue in our society without pieces of paper. When the divinely regulated marital relationship is contemned and debased, moral and spiritual suffering are inescapable.

Forced Labor!

A salesman knocked on a door of a house where just inside and plainly visible was a boy painfully practicing his piano lessons.

"Sonny, is your mother home?" he inquired.

"What do you think?" snapped the boy.

Five Keys for a Happy Home

1. Give God the first hour of each day (Mark 1:35). Pray in the morning.
2. Give God the first day of the week (I Cor. 16:2). Serve in your church to save your community.
3. Give God the first portion of your income (Prov. 3:9). Keep books on what you give to be sure you do not think you are giving more than you actually are.
4. Give God the first consideration in every decision (Matt. 6:33). This includes your choice of house, close friends, work, church, school, etc.
5. Give God's Son first place in your heart always (II Cor. 8:5). Live in His presence as though He were the unseen Guest in your house—He is, you know!

—*Ord L. Morrow*

◆　　◆　　◆　　◆

Can I Marry an Unbeliever?

No. One of the most important decisions in a Christian woman's life is whom she marries. Yet it is an all-too-frequent tragedy that at this point specious reasoning will make the most earnest of women myopic.

She is doing all right, when along comes Henry, and he is not a Christian. But "I want Henry!" she wails, and "I must have Henry; I cannot go on without Henry!"

So she marries Henry, who is still not a Christian, in the hope that he will become one. But she is asking God's blessing on her disobedience to His explicit command:

"Be ye not unequally yoked together with unbelievers . . . what communion hath light with darkness? . . . or what part hath he that believeth with an infidel?"—II Cor. 6:14, 15.

God's will is sovereign; and He may still bless the marriage, and Henry may be saved—but the point is, she has no right to hold God to a promise He never made.

No Christian, man or woman, should voluntarily go into such a union.

—*Ethel Barrett*

Married to a BUZZARD

Mother Dove and Father Dove were more than just proud of their little teenage daughter. She was all they had, and their lives not only were centered around her, but all of their attention and devotion had been applied to her upbringing.

They had taught her the value of a good, clean nest! They took her each Sunday morning to the Bible class run by the Right Reverend Hoot Owl. They had taken great pains to see that she was exposed to the finest of culture and to the most honorable Ringneck sons of their friends.

But one day their little teenage daughter told Mother and Father that she was old enough now to fly in the woods by herself! "All of my friends are laughing at me, the way I've become a little homebody!" she complained.

So she took to flying, first in the neighborhood, then farther out each day, until finally she came across the carcass of a three-day dead rabbit. Above the carcass she saw young Cock Buzzard. "Why do you stoop so low at mealtime as to eat an old dead rabbit?" she cried, filled with horror!

"Well, sweet thing," he replied, "I have never had a chance in life like you. My daddy was an old buzzard. My mamma was an old buzzard. In my neighborhood, all I had to run with were buzzards. I have been pushed back in the corner of culture so long that I find myself doing things like this just from force of habit, and for survival."

"But do you have the desire to change?" she asked.

With eyes of lust he peered at her and croaked, "Oh, if only I had someone like you to watch over me and teach me and encourage me, I know I would change!"

And with such words the old buzzard swept little dove off her twig.

Mother and Father Dove were horrified at the news! "But, daughter," cried Father Dove, "you hardly even know the young man! And besides this—he is a BUZZARD!"

"But, Daddy, that's just the thing; he has been treated like a buzzard all his life! He hasn't had  a chance to be anything else. He has made efforts, so he told me, to fly with other birds; but they will have nothing to do with him. Whenever he tries to perch on the same limb as other birds, they all flee in horror! Don't you see, Father and Mother, he just

needs love! And I love him. I am going to marry him and take him to my little love nest and make a new bird out of him!"

The wedding day was set. Of course, Mother and Father Dove were not there! Nor were Cousin Turtledove and Uncle Ringneck Dove. Even the black sheep of the Dove family, Nephew White Wing, refrained from attending.

But the wedding was supplied with many guests! All the buzzards were there! And as buzzards do, they had invited their close friends to attend. There was the Raven family and the Bluejay clan along with old Amos Magpie.

The best man, Billie Butcherbird, adjusted the tie of young groom Buzzard, and the procession began.

Two crows seated the relatives present, and two members of the branch water kin sang, "I can't give you anything but love, baby!" as the lovely bride walked down the aisle!

They stood before Judge Bald Eagle, who turned to little Miss Turtle Dove and said, "Do you take this . . . er, ah, buzzard . . . to be your lawful wedded husband?"

And the silly little thing cooed, "I do!"

"And you, Buzzard; do you take this sweet little dove to be your lawful wedded wife?"

And with eyes filled with lust, and with a wing crawling with lice wrapped around his lovely little bride, he croaked, "I do!"

Rice was thrown, and as they flew off for their honeymoon, little Mrs. Buzzard was heard to whisper to her bridesmaid, "I will take him to my little love nest now, and you just wait and see the change in a week or two!"

All went well for a few days; then one night Mr. Buzzard failed to come home. Little Dove waited anxiously. Hours turned into a day. Frantically she flew here and there looking for him! She went to their old dating tree and seeing an old acquaintance she cried, "Have you seen my darling buzzard? Have you seen him? Have you seen him?" was her cry all that day, but each cry received no answer. He was nowhere to be found!

Then in desperation, Little Dove flew out to the old haunt where she had first met Mr. Buzzard; and to her horror, there he was! He and several of his cousins were perched on the carcass of an old dead horse, pulling rotten meat from its bones with their hooked beaks! With maggots crawling on his feet, there stood her husband, fighting for his share!

"Oh, you promised me, darling, that you would never go back to this kind of life! You promised me! Haven't I been a good cook? Haven't I given you the love you lacked? And haven't I pulled you out of the corner and given you a chance?"

But the greedy eyes of the buzzard glanced her way just long enough to say: "Head for home, you silly dove you. I got what I wanted when you married me; now I want what I had besides! Go home to your mother if you want. Go on back to your church and their silly religion. Leave me alone. I'm hungry and am satisfying myself with the kind of food I was made to eat!" And with the smell of putrefaction on him, he dug his beak into the sorry rotten flesh of the carcass and ate deeply, stopping only long enough to sigh and belch before eating again.

And with weary wing, languished heart and a broken spirit, Little Turtle Dove wept her way back to Mother, crying, "You were right...you were right, he's just a sorry old buzzard."

Take note, dear reader: YOU JUST CAN'T REFORM AN OLD BUZZARD!

—*Phil Shuler*

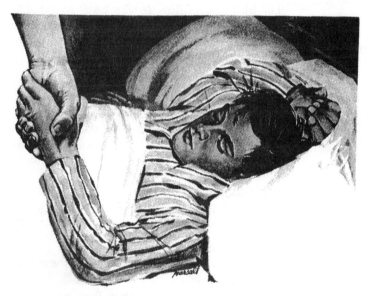

Christians Die Well

During the past few years I have been privileged to be present at the deaths of several people. These experiences have taught me one mighty, thundering fact: we Christians die well.

No matter what the circumstances—in a violent car wreck, a hospital bed, a sickbed at home or a lingering death in a nursing home—a Christian dies with the Saviour standing at his or her side. Christ holds the dying believer's hand and gently leads that trusting one into the last great earthly experience.

Their faces may be bloodied; they may be wracked with pain; but there is a period of grace bestowed upon them. It may last for a few months, several days or only a few seconds.

But as John Wesley proclaimed concerning the early Methodists, "Our people die well."

—*Selected*

IF YOU TRAIN A CHILD UP TO GIVE PENNIES, WHEN HE IS OLD HE WILL NOT DEPART FROM IT.

■ ☐ ■

She met an old flame and decided to high-hat him. "Sorry," she murmured when introduced by the hostess, "I did not get your name."

"No," the old blade countered dryly, "but you tried hard enough!"

☐ ■ ☐

Someone said we spend the first three years of a child's life teaching him to walk and talk, and the next fifteen teaching him to sit down and be quiet!

■ ☐ ■

God has wiped my slate clean. He cannot see my sin because it is covered by His blood. He gave me a white robe of righteousness, which is kept clean by a special detergent called FORGIVENESS.

Clothes Don't Make the Marriage

L. C.'s son Jerry asked his father to wear a tuxedo and be best man at his wedding. Reluctant to get that dressed up, and allowing as how the groom ought to be the best man at his own wedding, L. C. said:

When me and your mama got married, I 'jest' put on a clean pair 'uv' overalls, jumped on Old Blue [his mule] and went down to Beach Flatt after her. She swung up behind me, we rode by the preacher's house, and he married us standing under 'tha' big oak tree in his yard. We got us a drink 'uv' cool well water, got back on Old Blue, went to Mama and Papa's and stayed till the crops wuz gathered—and it's lasted 35 years.

Fifteen years later at his mother and dad's fiftieth wedding anniversary celebration, Jerry had already been married and divorced. When he announced plans to marry again, L. C. said, "Son, this time you better wear a pair of overalls and go get her on a mule."

—Ibbie Ledford

Something went out with that old telephone

The day of fancy telephones in diverse colors carries me back to the old box on the wall of my childhood home. It was operated by a crank, and we were on a party line up and down that country road, so we could listen in on some gossip from the neighbors! One could really keep up with the local news, good and bad. Some of those rural housewives could put modern teenagers to shame in long-winded conversation!

But those party-line days had their compensations. Today we hibernate in mammoth apartment towers of Babel and do not even know who lives next door or overhead. People are born, marry or die all around us; and we are unaware of their joys and sorrows. We were a great deal closer in the old days, when we were miles apart, than we are now living under the same roof.

Then there was concern and interest. And when a neighbor died, there were many gentle ministries performed by the neighbors that are now left to the morticians.

It is one of the ironies of this congested world that physical proximity has not brought us nearer in our hearts. We are far greater strangers to each other as we lessen the distance between us.

We do not know anybody up and down the street. Then it was a personal concern what happened to the Smiths' cow or how old Granny Johnson's rheumatism was doing. If farmer Brown's barn burned down or one of the Doe boys broke his arm, we were interested.

Something went out with that old telephone. Something more precious than gold left us. The old telephone is a fitting symbol of it. Something went out of our souls, and that will be difficult to replace.

I am thankful for all the true progress that has been made since those good old days, but I would turn time backward in its flight if that were in my power.

Viola Walden

She Died Free!

I came upon Mary Kellogg's gravestone in the cemetery at Oberlin, Ohio, while searching for the grave of the renowned revivalist, Charles G. Finney. The unusual epitaph caught my attention:

> MARY KELLOGG
> BORN
> A SLAVE—
> DIED FREE
>
> Sept. 23, 1862
> Aged 15 years

Who was Mary Kellogg? I don't know. But her story, if it could be told, might be quite interesting. Oberlin, a little town near Cleveland, was one of the underground delivery points for slaves during the Civil War, so I imagine Mary came from the South. Probably she was one of the slaves who fled from their masters and found refuge in the free states.

The "underground railroad," as it was called, had its widest development in Ohio. Begun in the 1830's, it comprised a network of "stations" (hiding places) for fugitives from slave labor. By day the escaping slaves would hide in homes or barns where abolitionists would furnish them with food; by night they would move on to the next station on their route to freedom.

Perhaps Mary Kellogg was one of the hundreds of slaves who escaped into freedom through this "underground railroad."

We do not know how old she was when she fled from bondage nor how long she enjoyed her new freedom. She was only 15 when she died.

But those who knew Mary wanted everyone to know that, although she was born a slave, she died free. That's the important thing. It's a privilege to be born free, but it's vastly more important to die free.

We like to think that slavery is a thing of the past, but is it? *Webster's New Collegiate Dictionary* says a *slave* is "a person who has lost control of himself and is dominated by something or someone."

Millions are "dominated by something or someone" today. They are not free but are slaves to sin and sinful habits.

"Born a slave"—that describes all of us. And some have been running a long time, trying to stay ahead of the haunting feeling this slavery brings.

Ever since Adam and Eve sinned in the Garden of Eden, men and women have been slaves to sin and have been suffering the uncomfortable feeling sin brings. Worst of all, many die without ever fleeing to freedom.

"Everyone dies because all of us are related to Adam, being members of his sinful race, and wherever there is sin, death results. But all who are related to Christ will rise again. Each, however, in his own turn: Christ rose first; then when Christ comes back, all His people will become alive again.

"Then cometh the end, when he shall have delivered up the kingdom to God, even the Father; when he shall have put down all rule and all authority and power. For he must reign, till he hath put all enemies under his feet. The last enemy that shall be destroyed is death."—I Cor. 15:24-26.

Dying a slave must have given a person a miserable feeling. What frustration there would be! Never to have been able to accomplish what he wanted to accomplish! Forced to do what his owner demanded at all times! What a bitter situation!

My friend, sin does this. It squeezes and presses until you

MARY KELLOGG

BORN
A SLAVE —
DIED FREE
Sept 23. 1862
Aged 15 Yrs

SHE DIED FREE (Cont.)

lose control of your life and are in bondage. Don't you want to be free? Jesus said you are slaves of sin, every one of you. And slaves don't have rights, but the Son has every right there is! So if the Son sets you free, you will indeed be free (John 8:34-36).

I urge you to come to Christ, the Son of God, and let Him set you free today. If you will confess your sins to Him, He will forgive every one of them, and you will not be dominated by them any longer.

Then your epitaph can read: "Born a slave [to sin], died free [in Christ]."

—*Ed Eliason*

No Mourning When I Go

As you love me, let there be
    No mourning when I go;
No tearful eyes,
    No hopeless sighs,
No woe, nor even sadness.
    Indeed I would not have you sad;
For I, myself, shall be full glad,
    With a high, triumphant gladness
Of a soul made free,
    Of God's sweet liberty.

No windows darkened;
    For my own
Will be flung wide as ne'er before
    To catch the radiant inpour
Of Love, which shall in full atone
    For all the ills that I have done
And all the good things left undone.
    No voices hushed;
My own, full flushed
    With an immortal hope, will rise
In ecstasies of newborn bliss
    And joyful melodies.

—*John Oxenham*

Talk It Out With God

*If your heart beats faint from struggling
With the problems and the cares
That confront us as we walk this mortal sod,
    There is just one way to rally—
    Just one way to win the day:
Find a quiet place and talk it out with God.*

*If your heart is sad and lonely
Longing for companionship,
If you seek an outstretched hand, a cheery nod;
    If you'd like an introduction
    To the greatest Friend of all,
You only need to talk it out with God.*

*For there is no sweeter solace,
No relief that can compare
With the joy of winging where His feet have trod.
    Trouble comes—and you can't bear it?
    All you have to do is share it
On your bended knee—just talk it out with God!*

—*M. Kathleen Haley*

In this dark world of sin and pain
We only meet to part again;
But when we reach the heavenly shore,
We there shall meet to part no more;
The joy that we shall see that day
Shall chase our present griefs away.

Some people can
TALK Christianity
by the yard,
but they can't
WALK it
by the inch.

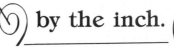

How We Keep Kids Out of the Ministry

By Duane A. "Dewey" Roth

The chairman of the elders approached the platform with a prepared statement in hand:

"Brothers and sisters of the congregation, after much prayer and considerable discussion, the elders have unanimously agreed to appeal to our youth to consider any career they desire except full-time, vocational ministry. Please, dear teenagers, with every ounce of strength within us we beg you... don't grow up to be missionaries, preachers or youth ministers!"

Now, to the best of my knowledge, this has never actually taken place. However, we do use some methods that, considering the possibility of adolescent rebellion against such a direct approach, are probably more effective at keeping kids out of ministry work.

These methods generally fall into one of two categories: what we say or what we do.

What We Say

"Shouldn't you study something you can fall back on, just in case?" I can understand saying this to someone who wants to be an actor or a singer or a professional athlete. But what sense does this advice make for a young person who feels the call of God to give his or her career over to the spreading of the Gospel?

Would you say this if your son wanted to be a doctor? No! You would encourage him to work hard and study well and assure him of your support. Shouldn't we do at least the same for the young person who wants to save souls as we would for the young person who wants to heal bodies?

"You know, you'll never make much money doing that." Consider the impact this statement may have on the young person who has expressed an interest in going into the ministry.

If the teen is really convinced of the world's need and that the Lord wants to use him or her, maybe

you'll get a rebuke for placing something like prosperity in a higher priority than saving souls, and I say, "Amen!"

But if the young person is merely testing the waters and considering the possibilities, your negative comment may hold him or her back from really giving God a chance to speak.

Of course, another aspect of this "not much money" approach is that usually the person who makes the comment is in the position to do something about it. Do you think ministers are underpaid? Then speak up in favor of raising your minister's salary!

Would you be ashamed to have your son and his growing family try to live on what your congregation pays your youth minister? Then do something about it! Would you worry about your daughter's becoming a missionary because they are undersupported? Then cough up some support!

What We Do

Recruitment: Just say, "No." Different ministry positions have different responsibilities, but almost universal is the need to recruit members of the congregation to perform certain duties or fulfill certain functions.

How We Keep Kids Out of the Ministry

(Cont.)

While this can be an exciting time of plugging people into areas of service that utilize their God-given gifts and abilities, it usually is more aptly described as shaking the bushes and finding arms to twist.

"So what's the problem?" you ask. "Anybody interested in the ministry should know that comes with the territory."

While that may be true, it is also true that, more and more, people are willing to serve only when it meets *their* needs and is convenient to *their* increasingly restrictive time schedule.

The creative twists of reasoning that some use to justify making themselves unavailable are also increasing.

It reminds me of the story about one farmer who wouldn't lend his neighbor a rope because he said he was using it to tie up some milk. The neighbor replied, "But you can't tie up milk with a rope."

"That's true," said the farmer, "but when you don't want to do something, one excuse is just as good as another."

The point is, our young people are aware of the pressures involved in being expected to run a program but unable to find willing workers. They hear their parents beg out of doing this or that when asked by the preacher or youth minister. They know it's not because their folks are unqualified. (Why would they be asked if they couldn't do it?) It is simply because they don't *want* to. Their reasoning goes, if a minister has to go through all that in order to do what's expected, why bother?

Politics: the art of getting even. The longer I'm in the ministry, the more I hear of church after church treating minister after minister like so much bulk beef. Use up what you can, but if things get a little sour or stale, throw it out.

When we have a problem or point of irritation with a member of the church staff, why do we insist on trying to rally support for our position? Why do we talk to everybody about *the problem* except the person we've got the problem *with?* Why do we refuse to obey Christ's commands in Matthew 5:23, 24 and Mark 11:25?

How discouraging it must be for the tenderhearted teen to catch wind of secret confidence votes and private pow-wows aimed against his or her youth minister or preacher. No wonder many of today's young people turn away from even considering a life of specialized ministry.

...So What?

So, we can either read this article and comment on how true it is and say, "Well, that certainly is something to think about," or we can firmly resolve to be part of the solution instead of part of the problem.

We can censor our negative responses to a young person's indications of interest in the ministry (including, may I add, "That's fine for most kids, but not my boy").

We can pay our church staff and support our missionaries the way we would want our own family members to be paid and supported.

We can willingly volunteer to be used in the church however God directs.

We can refuse to be part of a gossip chain or lynch mob without going directly to the person involved.

The choice is ours. Heal or hurt? Help or hinder? The growth of God's kingdom on earth depends on our decisions.

> *Lord, when we are wrong, make us willing to change. And when we are right, make us easy to live with.*

DYING DAILY

Young folks are sometimes supersensitive to public opinion. The approval of others, especially their own peers, carries a good deal of weight. Conformity with the group is "in." Even nonconformity is conformity with the nonconformity group.

Are you confused? You're not alone, son!

A young lady wrote wanting to know my opinion about currently popular music. She did not care for it. Instead, she had what seemed to be a good start on a fine library of sacred music as well as semi-classical and classical.

Her problem was trying to answer the questions of her teenage friends who wanted to know why she had no time or taste for the "in" music. She was a little afraid that they would not understand that, because she was a Christian, her tastes in music ran to something more stable than the Beatles and the Animals and other such refugees from the local zoos. "Tell me a good answer," said the letter.

Okay. Just tell them that you are one Christian young lady who just does not care for the popular music of the day. Now help them pick up their eyeballs and the teeth that have popped out and go on your way.

Who said you have to like what the crowd likes? Who said you have to fit into the same little mold as every other teen in the school? Who said you cannot break out of the pattern and be healthy, happy and normal?

Sure, some kooks will think you are kooky. Sure, some oddballs will think you're odd. Some may even voice their thoughts loudly and in your presence. What then? Easy. Die!

You read it right! Haul right off and die! Paul did. He wrote in I Corinthians, "I die daily." No, he didn't mean that he stretched out on a slab and quit living. He meant that the old Paul died every day and what people saw walking around was the new Paul. It is the same thing he was talking about in Galatians 2:20: "I am crucified with Christ: nevertheless I live; yet not I, but Christ liveth in me: and the life that I now live in the flesh I live by the faith of the Son of God, who loved me, and gave himself for me."

A wise preacher once answered a young man troubled by the criticism others leveled at him by telling the young man to go to the new grave of a recently deceased saint and say every bad thing he could think of about that man. The boy returned and was asked: "What did Brother S_____ say?" He replied, "Nothing. He's dead."

He was then urged to return to the grave again and this time to say everything good he could imagine about that man. When he returned, the preacher asked again, "What did Brother S_____ say?" Once more the youth replied, "Nothing. He's dead."

But he had no more than got the words out of his mouth when he saw the lesson the preacher was trying to teach. Those who are dead care not a thing for what is said about them, whether good or bad.

Colossians 3:3 says, "For ye are dead, and your life is hid with Christ in God." Christian teenagers, you are dead. That should mean dead to sin, dead to selfish ambition, dead to worldly desires and habits, dead to false accusations and criticisms, dead to false flattery. Your life is hid with Christ in God. Only what you do for Christ is going to count. What He says and what He thinks are the things that really matter to you. Just be sure that what you do pleases Him. Be sure that what you love is what He would love.

You had better get used to facing your critics. There will be plenty of them as time goes on. Be kind toward them. Do not answer them sharply. Just show them and tell them that you have something inside that has brought satisfaction that nothing else can bring and nothing can take away.

—*Dr. Bud Lyles*

AMUSEMENTS!

By R. A. TORREY

Young people need recreation. Our Saviour does not frown upon wholesome recreation. He was interested in the games of the children when He was here upon earth. He watched the children at their play (Matt. 12:16-19), and He watches the children at their play today and delights in their play when it is wholesome and elevating.

In the stress and strain of modern life, older people too need recreation if they are to do their very best work. But there are recreations that are wholesome, and there are amusements that are pernicious. It is impossible to take up amusements one by one, and it is unnecessary. A few principles can be laid down.

1. Do not indulge in any form of amusement about whose propriety you have any doubts. Whenever you are in doubt, always give God the benefit of the doubt. There are plenty of recreations about which there can be no question. "He that doubteth is condemned: for whatsoever is not of faith is sin" (Rom. 14:32, A.S.V.). Many a young Christian will say, "I am not sure that this amusement is wrong." Are you sure it is right? If not, leave it alone.

2. Do not indulge in any amusement that you cannot engage in to the glory of God. "Whether therefore ye eat or drink, or whatsoever ye do, do all to the glory of God" (I Cor. 10:31). Whenever you are in doubt as to whether you should engage in any amusement, ask yourself, *Can I do this at this time to the glory of God?*

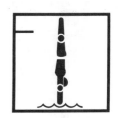

3. Do not engage in any amusement that will hurt your influence with anybody. There are amusements which perhaps are all right in themselves, but which we cannot engage in without losing our influence with someone.

Now every true Christian wishes his life to tell with everybody to the utmost. There is so much to be done and so few to do it that every

Christian desires every last ounce of power for good that he can have with everybody and, if any amusement will injure your influence for good with anyone, the price is too great. Do not engage in it.

A Christian young lady had a great desire to lead others to Christ. She made up her mind that she would speak to a young friend of hers about coming to Christ.

While resting between the figures of a dance, she said to the young man who was her companion in the dance, "George, are you a Christian?"

"No," he said, "I am not; are you?"

"Yes," she replied, "I am."

"Then," he said, "what are you doing here?"

Whether justly or unjustly, the world discounts the professions of those Christians who indulge in certain forms of the world's own amusements. We cannot afford to have our professions thus discounted.

4. Do not engage in any amusement that you cannot make a matter of prayer, that you cannot ask God's blessing upon. Pray before your play just as much as you would pray before your work.

5. Do not go to any place of amusement where you cannot take Christ with you, and where you do not think Christ would feel at home.

Christ went to places of mirth when He was here upon earth. He went to the marriage feast in Cana (John 2) and contributed to the joy of the occasion. But there are many modern places of amusement where Christ would not be at home. Would the atmosphere of the modern stage be congenial to that holy One whom we call "Lord"? If it would not, don't you go.

6. Don't engage in any amusement that you would not like to be found enjoying if the Lord should come. He may come at any moment. Blessed is that one whom, when He cometh, He shall find watching and ready and glad to open to Him immediately (Luke 12:36, 40).

A friend was one day walking down the street thinking upon the return of his Lord. As he thought, he was smoking a cigar. The thought came to him, *Would you like to meet Christ now with that cigar in your mouth?* He answered honestly, *No, I would not.* He threw that cigar away and never lighted another.

7. Do not engage in any amusement, no matter how harmless it would be for yourself, that might harm someone else.

(More next page)

Amusements (Cont.)

Take, for example, card playing. It is probable that thousands have played cards moderately all their lives and never suffered any direct moral injury from it. But everyone who has studied the matter knows that cards are the gamblers' chosen tools. He also knows that most, if not all, gamblers took their first lessons in card playing at the quiet family card table. He knows that, if a young man goes out into the world knowing how to play cards and indulging at all in this amusement, before long he is going to be put into a place where he is going to be asked to play cards for money, and if he does not consent, he will get into serious trouble.

Card playing with regular playing cards is a dangerous amusement for the average young man. It is pretty sure to lead to gambling on a larger or a smaller scale. And one of the most crying social evils of our time is the evil of gambling. Some young man may be encouraged to play cards by your playing, who will afterwards become a gambler, and part of the responsibility will lie at your door.

If I could repeat all the stories that have come to me from brokenhearted men whose lives have been shipwrecked at the gaming table; if I could tell of all the brokenhearted mothers who have come to me, some of them in high position whose sons have committed suicide at Monte Carlo and other places, ruined by the cards, I think that all thoughtful and true Christians would give them up forever.

For most of us the recreations that are most helpful are those that demand a considerable outlay of physical energy. Recreations that take us into the open air, recreations that leave us refreshed in body and invigorated in mind are best. Physical exercise of the strenuous kind, but not overexercise, is one of the great safeguards of the moral conduct of boys and young men.

There is very little recreation in watching others play the most vigorous game of football, but there is real health for the body and for the soul in a due amount of physical exercise for yourself.

Do what you can, being what you are;
Shine like a glowworm, if you can't be
    a star.
Work like a pulley, if you can't be a crane;
Be a wheel-greaser, if you can't drive the
    train.

****

Play It Safe...
Keep Electric Appliances
Away from the Tub

The Destiny of Your Child Lies in Your Hands...

From $1,100,000 to ZERO!

A few years ago a magazine gave some interesting statistics of two families who once lived in the state of New York. Max Jukes did not believe in Christianity, and he married a girl of like character.

From studies made of 1026 descendants of this union, 300 died prematurely; 100 were sent to the penitentiary; 190 sold themselves to vice; 100 were drunkards; and the family cost the state of New York $1,100,000.

Jonathan Edwards was a Christian and believed in Christian training. He married a girl of like character.

From this union they have studied 729 descendants. Of this family, 300 were preachers; 65, college professors; 13, university presidents; 6, authors of good books; 3, U. S. Congressmen; and 1 was Vice-President of the United States. This family did not cost the state a single dollar.

You see the great difference between these two families.

THE DESTINY OF YOUR CHILD LIES IN YOUR HANDS. YOU CAN MAKE OR MAR IT.

STOP ME IF YOU'VE HEARD THIS ONE!

☺ AN INDIAN was telling his doctor about his chronic insomnia. To the doctor's amazement, the Indian added that 499 fellow tribesmen also had the problem.

They're known as the Indian napless 500.

☺ *While riding a bus and reading a newspaper article on life expectancy, a man said to a lady seated beside him, "Did you know every time I breathe, someone dies?" She replied, "That's too bad. Have you ever tried a good mouthwash?"*

☺ **THE BIG JUMP**

The troops were being taught to jump from a plane:

"What if my parachute doesn't open?" asked one rookie.

"That," said the instructor, "is known as jumping to a conclusion."

☺ WHAT'S THE MATTER?
Found on a schoolboy's exam paper: "Matterhorn was a horn blown by the ancients when anything was the matter."

☺ A Sunday school teacher asked her young class how Noah spent his time on the ark. There were no answers, so she asked, "Do you suppose he did a lot of fishing?"

"What?" responded a six-year-old. "With only two worms?"

☺ *Employer: "Look here! What did you mean by telling me you had five years' experience when you've never even had a job before?"*

Young man: "Well, you advertised for a man with imagination."

☺ *Two morons were helping a carpenter nail siding on a new house when one noticed that the other would throw away a nail every now and then.*

"Hey! Why throw away the nails?"

"Why not? They ain't no good. They've got the head on the wrong end."

The first moron laughed and laughed, then said, "You must be crazy...those nails are for the other side of the house."

☺ **Farmer:** "Don't you see the sign, 'Private, No Fishing Allowed'?"

Fisherman: "I never read anything marked 'Private.'"

☺ Teacher: "Johnny, give me a sentence containing the words, deduct, defeat, defense and detail."

Johnny, after some thought: "Defeat of deduct gets over defense before detail."

☺ *Before boarding a plane, a man took out an accident policy for $50,000; then on his way to the boarding gate he stepped on a weight-and-fortune scale. He was taken back a bit when he discovered his fortune card read, "Your recent investment will soon pay off."*

The Porch Light

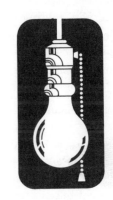

"Mother, why is the porch light on?"
  My son, it shines for you
Through the weary hours before the dawn
  As I wait the long night through.
My thoughts go back to the bygone days
  To my innocent little child;
Dear God! How quickly his baby ways
  Have been by the world defiled.

  "Mother, how long will the porch light burn?"
    Dear son, until you come home,
  For my aching heart will forever yearn
    Till your feet no longer roam.
  My fervent, pleading, unceasing prayer
    Is for God to protect my son;
  And I hear His answer, "My child, I care,"
    As I murmur, "Thy will be done."

  "Mother, is God's light burning still?"
    Oh, son! He loves you yet!
  To draw you close is our Father's will,
    To rest without care or fret.
  And God in His mercy will set you free
    To serve Him in peace and joy;
  To be the man that He made you to be,
    My son, my beloved boy.

—Source Unknown

God's Fiddle

By DR. BOB JONES, SR.

Many years ago when Bob Jones University was still Bob Jones College and we had 300 or 400 students, a young lady came into my office one day. She was a freshman, and had just returned from taking her music lesson.

She put down her violin and music books and said, "Dr. Bob, I want to talk to you. I don't have the joy I ought to have as a Christian. I wonder if you can help me find the trouble."

Now, frankly, I was amazed. The school was small enough in those days so that I got pretty well acquainted with every student; and if I had been asked to name two or three of the most spiritual girls in the freshman class, I would have named Dorothy as one.

I said, "Dorothy, is there any sin in your life?"
"No, Dr. Bob, not if I know my heart."

"Are you holding back anything from God?"

"No. Do you remember what I wrote you when I applied for admission last summer?"

I remembered. She had written something like this from her home in North Carolina:

Dear Dr. Jones:

I was saved last week in a meeting one of your preacher boys held in my home church. I have been playing in a dance band. Now I have given my violin to the Lord, and I want to play it for Him.

I want to come to Bob Jones College because I know you have a Christian student body and a godly faculty, and I know you have a good music department. I want to be the best possible musician for Christ.

My family is unsaved and doesn't want me to go. They say I can stay here in town and go to a state school. It is going to mean a complete break with my family, but I believe the Lord wants me there.

Dorothy had been in school about three months the day she sat in my office. I asked, "You are not holding anything back?"

"No."

"What about the fiddle?" I asked.

"Don't you know I told you I was going to play it just for the Lord? It is the Lord's now."

"That's fine, Dorothy. This is God's violin. You are going to play it for Him. But suppose God tells you to keep your fingers off His fiddle? How about that?"

"You mean not play?"

"Yes, I mean never play another note."

"Dr. Bob, you don't think God wants me to give up my music, do you?"

"I don't think so, Dorothy. God gives us talent to be trained and used and invested; but it may be He wants you to lay this 'idol' on the altar. It may be He knows you love music too much; it may be that music is taking His place. Suppose it is more for His glory for this instrument to be mute than to be breathing out melody. How about that, Dorothy?"

She began to cry. She said, "Dr. Bob, I could not live without my violin. I will use it for the Lord, but I just couldn't give it up!"

"Dorothy, I think we have found your trouble," I said.

I watched Dorothy the next day at chapel. When you stand on the platform and watch the students sing, when they are at their best, it is like looking into the sun at noonday; but looking at Dorothy that day was like looking at a cloud in an otherwise cloudless sky—miserable and unhappy. I watched her, and I prayed for her. The next day and the next she looked that way.

But the following day I could hardly see her face for her mouth—she was smiling all the way across. I thought, *She has settled it.*

Later that day she came into my office with her violin, put it on my desk, and said, "Dr. Bob, I want you to see God's fiddle. If He wants me to play it, I will play it for His glory; but if He says, 'Don't touch it again; don't ever play another note,' that is all right, too. I love Him more than I love music or anything else."

That is what it means to forsake all and follow Him. That is the test of our love for Christ—to have no plans except the plans of His making, no friends except the friends of His choosing, no husband, no wife except the husband or wife of His ordaining—no will except the will to do His will. "He that doeth the will of God abideth for ever."

I Gave My Fat to Missions

I had a battle with excess weight from my teen years. At 180 pounds I went to a doctor due to shortage of breath.

"You're just too fat," he told me. I managed to slim down to an average size; but after I married, I became less careful. At the end of our first year together, "we" weighed the same. My husband had lost 10 pounds, and I had gained 10 pounds.

By the time our five children arrived, I was back to 180.

But that was mild compared to the 240 pounds I reached later!

Our youngest son earned a Royal Rangers award, and I was called to the platform. Going up the steps I nearly lost my balance. Our pastor had to take my hand quickly to avert the congregation's attention from Big Fat Mama.

I looked pregnant. When I climbed stairs, I felt it. That wasn't so bad when I was youngish (after all, I *was* married); but when the gray hairs appeared, there was no excuse to hide behind.

After the children left the nest, our grocery bill was still our chief expense. I loved to cook—and a cup of coffee was never complete without "something to go with it." I was always living up to my name!

Of course, being fat has a few advantages. If your friends pick you up in a compact car, you always get preferred treatment—the front seat.

But as a Christian I knew I was not adorning the Gospel by my rotundity. I knew I should lose weight for three reasons.

In the first place, Jesus lived and taught self-denial, not self-indulgence. I knew I was desecrating the Lord's temple (I Corinthians 6:19).

Second, I was endangering my life. My blood pressure was too high. Actuarial statistics tell us overweight people are subject to more strokes and heart attacks than slim ones.

Third, my appearance should have shamed me into cutting down. My husband is slender and dislikes obesity. Surely his love has been strong, for many pounds did not quench it.

One day we received a touching letter about Christian believers in foreign lands who were suffering for lack of nourishing food. The photographs moved me to pity.

Then I read a quote by William Duckworth in *Alive Now.* It was a modern adaptation of Jesus' words in Matthew 25:35:

"When I was hungry, you were obese; thirsty, and you were watering your lawn; a stranger, and you called the police and were glad to see me taken away...."

That hit me right in the stomach. How unfair for some to suffer hunger and others to glut! Those words bugged me. I decided to give the Lord a "fat offering." You know, all the fat from the Old Testament sacrifices was the Lord's (Leviticus 3:16).

So I approached my husband. "Honey, I've finally found the answer. Will you give a dollar for missions for every pound I lose?"

He is a born comedian. He went out of the house holding his head and moaning, "Oh! Oh! Oh!" as though it might mean bankruptcy.

But warmhearted fellow that he is, he went along with the idea. And it worked.

When I gave the Lord my "fat offering," I felt so good. I thought of the hungry Christians in other lands, and I said to myself, "I'm losing; they're gaining."

No, we're all gaining. If you're overweight, why don't you try this idea? You really can't lose!

—Selected

If you're overweight, here's an idea that might work for you, too!

> Speak kindly today; when tomorrow comes, you will be in better practice.

Are You Sending Mixed Signals?

—By LAVENA CROOKS

What is that you are saying? Do I hear what you intend to be saying? Psychologists and fashion designers tell us that our code or standard of dress communicates the message of the inner person. With so much emphasis on fashion and style, we need periodically to take a look at our dress ethics.

So you ask: "Standards—again? Who wants to hear about them? Who needs them?" As a matter of fact, we all do. Nearly every aspect of our life is guarded by some type of standard or behavioral guideline.

For instance, how can you be sure you are receiving full measure when you buy a pound of sugar? How can you be sure that you have a gallon of milk? a pound of margarine? a yard of cloth? a board foot?

The National Bureau of Standards is a federal agency which employs scientists to set up standards for all weights and measures. The bureau specifies the weight of a pound as well as the length of a yard and the volume of a quart container. The bureau helps manufacturers design scales and containers that give correct weights and measures.

Other government agencies set up guidelines for just about every area of our lives—whether we like it or not! Consider for a moment what our world would be like if there were no standards—no regulations for weights and measures, no guidelines for operating automobiles or no criteria for determining pure foods. Problems arise when each person, business, institution or industry decides to do its own thing, riding roughshod over all restrictions and boundaries (or "standards," if you please).

The integrity of a business or individual is, to a great measure, based on codes or standards, including behavior, dress styles, ethics, etc. Thus, as Christians, we should be concerned about every area of our life, including dress codes. The basic codes for morality are in the Word.

Paul prayed an extraordinary prayer for the believer in I Thessalonians 5:23: "I pray God your whole spirit and soul and body be preserved blameless." A. M. Hills explains:

The body means our physical organization with all its natural appetites and passions and necessary functions. The soul means the animating principle of the body connected with the senses. The spirit is the higher soul to which the influences of the other world address themselves.

It is by this faculty that we know God, and feel His power and presence, and recognize our duty to love and obey Him . . . . This is all there is of a man—body, soul and spirit. There is nothing else about him but his clothes. And the dress question will easily be settled when . . . the heart is right with God (*The Secret of Spiritual Power*).

"Clothes are the vesture of the soul," said James Labor in a former edition of *Encyclopedia Britannica.* He went on to explain: "Clothes are the outward expression of what you are in your soul."

(More next page)

James T. Malloy, the expert in teaching people how to dress for success, says, "I can design a [person's] wardrobe to elicit just about any effect. If you want to look like a successful businessman, I can dress you to communicate that message . . . . If you want to look honest . . . to look sexy . . . I can dress you to convey that image."

Fashion, as we know it, has become a scientific technique. Those who are acquainted with TV techniques say:

> If you are skeptical about the impact clothes have on [the viewer] . . . consider how television producers use clothes to establish a character on a show.

> Since air time is limited, what a character wears helps to very quickly identify that personality. Producers consider clothes so crucial that they continually confer with wardrobe people to discuss each "look" (*Dress With Style* by Joanne Wallace).

Wallace goes on to say:

> I know a woman who always wears tight dresses with slits that extend to her hips. Perhaps she only wants to convey the message that she is "fun, confident and attractive." But when the message is received and decoded, it may read, "I'm available. Your place or mine?"

The basic principles which control fashions are outlined by James Labor in *Britannica*. (1) *The utility principle*—taking care of legitimate needs for warmth, comfort, covering, etc. (2) *The hierarchical principle*—asserting pride. Society recognizes that there are steps of authority or importance. This principle reveals a thirst to put oneself on the top of the totem pole. (3) *The principle of autonomy* (added by Professor Rich, Yale University)—the desire to be independent, to be free from authority. (4) *The principle of seduction*—sex appeal.

As one writer observed, regarding the principle of autonomy, "In an attempt to be autonomous . . .

[rebels] actually do not realize that they are listening to a subtle kind of authority!"

Recall the Hippie movement. Wanting to break with "the Establishment," they became so alike that they were identifiable nationwide!

Years before the Hippie days, fashionists discov-

ered slacks and "pants suits" for women. It was an appeal to the desire for autonomy—the break with authority—to be like the man, a practice specifically condemned by God. Much of the runaway fads and styles are geared to the woman. (Could that be part of the autonomy principle carried over from Mother Eve?)

The fashion industry apparently has discovered a way to get this principle through, even to rebels. They design clothes or create hair styles for the rebel so that he can feel, "I'm independent. I'm doing my own thing," while at the same time he is actually buying the fads which the fashion industry has designed for him!

The appeal to the desires of the opposite sex is the most powerful of all and the greatest factor in determining what most people of the world wear.

Though not speaking from a religious point of view, these experts have stated a shocking parallel between the Word of God and these principles. In determining our personal dress codes, we should ask ourselves how these principles, as given by the researchers, measure up to the Word and what God expects of His children.

Paul describes the hierarchical principle in people who are "boastful" and "proud." Peter says they are "self-willed." John indicates that one of the manifestations of this world mindset is the "pride of life."

The principle of autonomy (rebellion) is addressed in II Timothy 3:1-7: "This know also, that in the last days perilous times shall come. For men shall be lovers of their own selves . . . disobedient to parents . . . incontinent, fierce . . . heady, high minded."

Peter also describes such individuals as despising government (authority), being "presumptuous . . . not afraid to speak evil of dignities" (II Pet. 2:10).

In the seduction principle, the Word describes our generation as one that has been given over to many lusts, or strong fleshly desires. Peter says they are shameful, given over to the lusts of uncleanness, "having eyes full of adultery" (II Pet. 2:14). John says they are controlled by the lusts of the flesh and the lust of the eyes (I John 2:16).

Paul uses the forceful word "lasciviousness,"

(More next page)

...Mixed Signals (Cont.)

meaning: characterized by or expressing lust or lewdness; tending to excite lustful desires. He says, "Now the works of the flesh are manifest, which are these; Adultery, fornication, uncleanness, lasciviousness...they which do such things shall not inherit the kingdom of God" (Gal. 5:19, 21).

He reiterates: "Walk not as other Gentiles walk...being alienated from the life of God...because of the blindness of their heart...have given themselves over unto lasciviousness" (Eph. 4:17-19).

Thus many of the principles which guide the fashion industry are the things which God's Word condemns. We need to be firm in asserting that Christians should not be guided by the motives which control the world but by the standards given by the immutable Word of God. They are for our protection and eternal benefit and are as contemporary as today's news.

Tragically, many Christians appear to be naive or totally unaware that they are often following fads and fashions which were hatched in the hearts of the "heady and highminded" men who have no standards of morality, much less of godliness.

Even the writer in *Britannica* says, alluding to I John 2:15-17:

> Fashion has been looked at askance by moralists of all ages, who see in it an encouragement to the lust of the eye and the pride of life.... The early fathers of the church and the later Puritans were perfectly correct: Those are the purposes of fashion. They were correct in denouncing new fashions as harlotry. Why? Because they appeal to the lust of the flesh.

So how does fashion get its message across? Fashion psychologists indicate that it is by what they call the "shifting erogenous zones." That is, fashions are believed to be daring when they focus

attention on a part of the body that has been hidden long enough to accrue "erotic capital" (sex appeal), thus giving it the impact of novelty.

According to this philosophy, various parts of the body have a certain amount of sex appeal. It is called erotic capital that can be "spent," so to speak. Therefore, fashions

play up one part of the body and emphasize that part until people become accustomed to it. Then they change the fashions and cover that part of the anatomy, only to expose another, in perhaps a new or more exotic way. (A portion of the above is adapted from a message by G. R. French.)

While analyzing the miniskirt rage, we found that the knee had been discovered! The knee, which had always played a minor part among erogenous zones, was suddenly bared and created a new special interest.

The writer continues discussing the erogenous zones:

> The peek-a-boo dress was just the beginning. We will probably see more daring and imaginative necklines, that will hardly justify the term any longer! (*The Psychology of Fashion* by Michael Solomon).

Solomon goes on to describe a painting from the 18th century:

> Judith stands with her bare foot on the severed head of Holofernes and the slit side of her tunic reveals the sensual splendour of her leg—a weapon as powerful as her sword.

Hear what another writer from the secular world says:

> It is clear that most of the design community has become obsessed with promoting overt seductiveness (*New York Times*, "Will Sexy Sell?" 12/6/87).

> Legs. They are what's left to look at when the skirt vanishes (*New York Times*, 5/2/88).

The *Times* also describes a Paris fashion show:

> Now come the first suits.... Some have pants cropped at the ankles; others, skirts just above the knee.... The model begins to walk, and that's when the slit appears. The neat, tailored skirt is slashed—to the top of the thigh.

> Then they keep coming.... On almost all of them the skirts are slashed higher and higher, sometimes in evening dresses reaching the waist. The fabrics of many of the blouses and most of the evening gowns are sheer, revealing the breasts and often other parts of the anatomy .... Watered-down versions of Laurent's sexy, high-powered suits, slash-slit skirts, the V-vamped necklines, the revealing wrap dresses— all will be copied and interpreted.

Sad to say, many well-meaning people follow

(More next page)

the styles like well-trained dogs or mechanical robots. Scooped or plunging necklines, slit skirts, sheer or skin-tight garments—if its on the market, buy it!

Though some say we are off track when we mention the word "standards" and that it is no longer palatable to the Christian community, we are really on firm biblical as well as psychological grounds.

The stylistic movement that has dominated [this century] can be called modernism. It represents a conscious break with the past....In the rejection of the past cultural traditions and creation of the new ones, two features are important: the split between representation of communication and the dissolution of the unity of self. This fragmentation of the self is easily seen in [all the arts: literature, surrealist art, and fashion, including hair styles] (M. Solomon).

Psychologists say that we will either practice what we say, or we will finally speak what we practice. The personality cannot long endure the "dissolution of the unity of self."

Speaking from a purely business success rule, Malloy asserts, "No sensible woman who wants to make a success in business will ever wear new fashions [based on seduction] to the office."

Why does he say so? Because to dress for success in business one wants to convey the message of integrity, honesty and uprightness. The principle of seduction cannot be mixed with them!

Just as the setting and keeping of standards is vital to an orderly society, so the keeping of biblical standards is vital to maintaining the purity of Christianity and the heritage we pass on to our children. Adopting the world view of hierarchy, rebellion or seduction must be guarded against. We dare not blindly follow the social customs around us—dress styles, business practices, entertainment—without determining where they come from and what they were planned for.

The Christian must keep these two propositions in mind: (1) Clothes communicate the message of the inner person. (2) The fashions of society communicate the message of the fallen world. It is our duty to communicate integrity, holiness, purity, honesty and uprightness—the image of our God.

If we say that is what is in our heart, then the way we dress must communicate that message. If we don't want to bear the image of the rebel, homosexual or a Jezebel, then we cannot dress like one. When we dress like what we profess, then we add authority to our message.

Respect, restraint and discipline are the roots and

foundation of civilization; and those principles are expressed in all areas of our life, including simplicity of dress.

Simplicity can be a beautiful elegance. It is not slovenliness or shoddiness. It is not necessarily wearing styles that were in vogue forty years ago. The word for holiness, so we're told, comes from a word which means harmonious or harmony. The presence of the Holy Spirit within should radiate a beauty in our countenance, our dress code and our behavior. Indeed, our entire life style will reflect the simplicity and beauty of the inner harmony.

What do your clothes say about you?

(Permission obtained)

The Grieving Hen

(Dr. Bob Shuler—"Fighting" Bob—was for 33 years pastor of the large Trinity Methodist Church, Los Angeles. He was a splendid example of a type of Methodist ministry that was dominant among Southern Methodists 75 to 100 years ago. Dr. Shuler died in 1965. His splendid *I Met Them on the Trail* is intimate stories of 42 people who influenced his life and ministry.

One man was T. B. Sewell, a professional piano tuner. For many years, he belonged to Dr. Shuler's church. At last Mr. Sewell died. Dr. Shuler tells this story.)

*   *   *

My secretary phoned me that he was dead. I arrived at the little cottage where they lived just a few moments after the undertaker had taken the body away. Mrs. Sewell met me at the door. . . . I sought to say a consoling word, but found Mrs. Sewell seemingly forgetful of her own loss in her deep sympathy for a third party, of whose existence I had not known until that morning.

"It's just killed Tootsie. She'll never get over it," moaned Mrs. Sewell.

I confess that having been the pastor of this couple for almost 20 years and not knowing of any near relative, I was forced to proceed cautiously. I had never heard of "Tootsie." I did not dare say so, lest I offend in this hour of deep grief.

I looked at a neighbor appealingly, but her face registered a perfect blank. Just then I glanced over in the corner; and there, sitting on the edge of a wooden box in which there was straw, was an old hen. I confess that I immediately identified "Tootsie," for I think I have never seen such grief registered by any eyes as I saw in that chicken's pitiful gaze at me.

"You can't comfort her any way at all," sighed Mrs. Sewell. "She loved him so. She laid an egg for him every day in that box. But she didn't lay this morning. She goes over to his shoes and takes on until it almost breaks my heart."

Possibly my readers think that I saw something ludicrous in the incident and the conversation. I confess that I did; but a second glance at the old hen, her feathers ruffled and her head drooped as though she herself were sick unto death, brought me face to face with something altogether new to pastoral calling! That old hen was the very picture of grief and dejection!

Somewhere I have read that when a man has that something in him that causes dumb creatures to love him, he has within his soul a genuineness that need not be otherwise tested. Mr. Sewell must have had that.

While we were talking, the old hen got down from her perch, walked sadly over to where I was sitting and  began to peck my shoe laces. Mrs. Sewell insisted that she wanted me to get up and go with her. I did go with misgivings. The old hen gravely led me into the room where Mr. Sewell had died. There by the bed were his shoes. The hen walked up to those shoes; and, honestly, I could not have been much more surprised had she shed real tears, as human beings do. Her grief seemed real. At least she "had me going"! She would look down at the empty shoes, then up at me, as much as to say, "*That's all I have left of him!*" I know chickens are not intelligent. But I confess to a strange feeling that day.

Through this whole episode, Mrs. Sewell did not express any personal sorrow or give way to grief. She told me afterward that she did not want the old hen to see her weep, lest it intensify the grief that seemed so evident in this dumb friend. . . .

The next Wednesday night at prayer meeting, I asked Mrs. Sewell to tell this story to my daughter-in-law (a doubting Thomas). After she had related the facts recounted above, she added, "That hen never laid an egg after the day Mr. Sewell died; and, though we fed her and did everything for her we could, she soon died—I believe of a broken heart. She would sit for hours by the side of Mr. Sewell's shoes with that awful hurt look in her eyes."

As a pastor for many years I have had all kinds of experiences. Here was a new one. The grief of a chicken was something rather "spooky" to me. It still is. I certainly do not undertake to explain what I saw, but one thing is sure: I have never doubted the gentleness, the patience, the tenderness and the goodness of T. B. Sewell. When a chicken becomes chief mourner at the passing of a man, it is far more than ridiculous. It is indicative. It denotes that there was something in that man that selfish, greedy human beings are entirely devoid of.

When I see squirrels racing about over some fellow in a park or a man feeding wild birds out of his hand, I take off my hat to that fellow. I've prayed for that something that such a man undoubtedly has.

It is said that General Robert E. Lee so loved his horse Traveller, identified with his leadership of the armies of the Confederacy, that horse and man were almost inseparable and their love for each other clearly discernible.

John Wesley owned a horse and rode him thousands of miles over England. He and that horse became so attached that Wesley actually tried to make a horse heaven fit into Methodist theology.

There are thousands of stories of men and horses, even of men and dogs, that make you have a feeling that something finer than the fiber of common human clay was in the makeup of those men. But a man and a hen—that's a different matter!

Well, is it?

"What is the matter, darling?" asked Mrs. Smith, when her small son came to her in tears.

"Papa was hanging a picture and it fell on his toe," responded the child between sobs.

"But that is nothing to cry about," replied Mrs. Smith cheerily, "you should have laughed at that."

"I did," said the boy.

∽ ∽ ∽ ∽ ∽ ∽

It is easy enough to be pleasant when
*   life flows by like a song,*
But the one worthwhile is the one who
*   can smile when everything goes dead*
*   wrong;*
For the test of the heart is
*   trouble, and that always*
*   comes with years;*
But the smile that is worth
*   all the treasures of earth*
*   is the smile that shines*
*   through tears.*

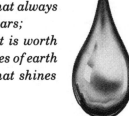

—*Ella Wheeler Wilcox*

Good or bad—we love 'em!

We love our children when they're good,
*   But when they're bad, in trouble,*
For reasons barely understood
*   We love them almost double.*

We love our children when they want
*   Affection and expect it,*
And even more, those times they taunt
*   Our loving and reject it.*

We love them when they make us cry
*   And when you'd think we daren't,*
And no one knows the reason why,
*   Except another parent.*

—Richard Armour

- Smooth wrinkled garments by placing them on hangers on shower curtain rod and running hot water from shower for a few minutes with bathroom door closed.

- Clean canvas shoes with rug shampoo. Use a toothbrush to get into tight places and around trim.

- To clean a glass flower vase, use toilet bowl cleaner, allow to stand ten minutes, then rinse well.

- Leather shoes or purses can be shined quickly with a light application of furniture polish.

- To get gelatin out of the mold easily, before filling, rinse the mold in cold water and coat inside with salad oil. The oil will leave a nice glaze on gelatin.

Ideas to Make It Easier...

MAY THE ROAD RISE UP TO MEET YOU,
MAY THE WIND BE ALWAYS AT YOUR BACK,
MAY THE SUN SHINE WARM UPON YOUR FACE,
AND THE RAINS FALL SOFT UPON YOUR FIELDS,
AND, UNTIL WE MEET AGAIN,
MAY GOD HOLD YOU
IN THE HOLLOW OF HIS HAND.

"What has become of our Little Boy Blue?"

The little toy dog is covered with dust,
But sturdy and staunch he stands;
And the little tin soldier is red with rust,
And his musket molds in his hands.

Time was when the little toy dog was new,
And the soldier was passing fair;
And that was the time when our Little
Boy Blue
Kissed them and put them there.

"Now don't you go till I come," he said,
"And don't you make any noise!"
So, toddling off to his trundle bed,
He dreamed of the pretty toys.

And as he was dreaming an angel song
Wakened our Little Boy Blue—
Oh, the years are many, the years are long,
But the little toy friends are true!

Aye, faithful to Little Boy Blue they stand
Each in the same old place,
Awaiting the touch of a little hand,
The smile of a little face.

And they wonder—as waiting these long
years through
In the dust of their little chair—
What has become of our Little Boy Blue
Since he kissed them and put them there.

—Eugene Field

The Haunted House for Friendly Ghosts

For half a century sightseers have visited the most bizarre private residence ever built—and left wondering what it was all about. The house has 160 rooms, 10,000 windows, 40 bedrooms, 13 bathrooms, 47 fireplaces, 40 staircases and 9 kitchens. It has had only one resident, Sarah Pardee Winchester, heiress to the Winchester Arms fortune.

For thirty-eight years workmen toiled around the clock to add to the sprawling house where the mysterious recluse lived until her death in 1922, allegedly having been told by a spiritualist that she would live as long as work continued on the residence. She died there, however, at the age of eighty-five.

It is said that she spent $5.5 million of her $20 million in building and furnishing the mansion.

Why did this eccentric oldster spend millions of dollars in building and furnishing this bizarre private residence? A Boston spiritualist claimed she warned Mrs. Winchester that vengeful ghosts of the thousands of men, women and children killed by her husband's guns would never leave her alone, but that she would come to no harm if she built a haunted house for friendly ghosts who would ward off the unfriendly spirits.

A bell in one of the towers was tolled by one of her servants each midnight to welcome incoming flights of good spirits, and again at 2:00 a.m. as the ghosts returned to their graves.

Rejecting the eternal Word of God, unorbed, fear-craven multitudes are the easy victims of "seducing spirits, and doctrines of devils" (I Tim. 4:1).

—Author Unknown

"I did it because my mother did it."

A bride of several months was sawing away at the end of a ham. "Why," asked a neighbor, "are you sawing off the end of that ham?"

"Because my mother always did it," was the bride's reply.

A few days later the neighbor met the bride's mother. "Your daughter tells me you always saw off the end of a ham before you bake it; I wonder why."

"Frankly," the mother replied, "I do it because my mother did it. Why not ask her?"

The neighbor phoned the grandmother who lived in the same town. The grandmother let her in on her secret: "I never owned a baking pan large enough to hold a ham. Why do you ask?"

The influence of Mother over child is reflected in the ancient proverb, "As is the mother, so is her daughter" (Ezek. 16:44).

What power a mother possesses! What influence she bears!

Not only has a mother the privilege of living close to her children, inspiring them toward high cultural ideals, teaching them right from wrong, but she is her children's spiritual counselor and chief example. What a divine calling!

A mother who lives a wicked life—what can she expect of her offspring?

A mother who laughs at the Bible may have started her child on the way to becoming a champion agnostic.

A mother who ridicules the moral standards of the Scriptures may have given her son a good start on the road to debauchery.

On the other hand, the mother who illustrates by life the importance of truth, the wrong of a lie, the loveliness of compassion and the rewards of self-denial, will be sowing the seeds of a life of value.

An old Spanish proverb says, "An ounce of mother is worth a pound of clergy." Many a son or daughter, about to tumble over the precipice of temptation to destruction, has been rescued by a piece of Mother's apron string which caught on something and held them safely.

Charles Dickens said, "The virtues of the mothers shall be visited on their children as well as the sins of the fathers."

Mother, what kind of an example are you setting before your children? Are you directing an inquiring mind into spiritual truth? Do you echo the words of Scripture which say, "I have no greater joy than to hear that my children walk in truth" (III John, vs. 4)?

The Apostle Paul wrote from his prison cell in Rome to his son in the faith Timothy:

"Greatly desiring to see thee, being mindful of thy tears, that I may be filled with joy; When I call to remembrance the unfeigned faith that is in thee, which dwelt first in thy grandmother Lois, and thy mother Eunice; and I am persuaded that in thee also."—II Tim. 1:4, 5.

To this he added the following statement:

"But continue thou in the things which thou hast learned and hast been assured of, knowing of whom thou hast learned them; And that from a child thou hast known the holy scriptures, which are able to make thee wise unto salvation through faith which is in Christ Jesus."—II Tim. 3:14, 15.

Believing mothers like Eunice and grandmothers like Lois produced godly men like Timothy.

LOST:

 Dog with 3 legs, blind in left eye, missing right ear, tail broken and recently spayed. Answers to the name of "Lucky."

The English language has made many a student's head swim dizzily. The lover is never far from acting or being a fool—only the distance of a few words. If he says to his affinity, "Darling, I must tell you! When I look at you, I forget the clock—time ceases to exist!" she falls on his neck with passionate kisses. But let him say it this crude way, "Listen! I must admit your face would stop a clock," and she'd fly on his neck with a club!

—L. V. Cleveland

Of Kitchens and Doghouses

It looks like I'm in trouble again. I hear Mrs. Preacher in the kitchen clanging and banging her pots and pans around. That's how I know it's serious. While I'm in the doghouse, she bakes.

Married folks settle their spats in a variety of ways. Normal ways. We lived next door to a couple once who would argue well past midnight. Others use the silent treatment. Some women are exceptional criers, while their husbands major in pouting. We even knew a couple once who threw things at each other. Not so with us. I've got a baker.

When we were newlyweds, I thought I'd intrude, once, when she was "cookin' mad." I peeked around the corner of the door and changed my mind. She body slammed a big batch of dough on the counter. She slapped it

all around the edges and then punched in its middle. Hard. She picked it up, flipped it, and smashed it onto the counter in a way that would make Hulk Hogan envious.

After she beat it up real good, she pinched a chunk and twisted it off. It caused me to envision the Pillsbury Dough Boy losing his ears. I retreated quietly to the living room.

I hate it when she bakes like this. I wish she would just get it over with. Do something sane like yell, cry or pout. But no! she has to come in and thrust a steaming blueberry muffin in my face!

What a predicament! To be madder than blue blazes and have a blueberry muffin under your nose!

"I'll show her. I'm tough! I don't have to eat her stinking muffin," I think as I push it aside.

"What's the use," I sigh a few moments later as I polish off the last of it. "I love the woman. She may not know how to fight, but she is an awfully good cook."

I get up and go to the kitchen to tell her so. We eat a muffin together, and the world is right again.

So if we run into you at the grocery store, and our cart is full of baking stuff, and you think we're putting on a little weight . . .well, as Paul Harvey would say, "Now you know the rest of the story."

"Page two."

'But if your enemy is hungry, feed him, and if he is thirsty, give him a drink; for in so doing you will heap burning coals upon his head.'—Rom. 12:20.

—*Chuck Terrill*

Be Still, My Heart

You've heard it said that all the world loves a lover. Don't you believe it. This world is geared mostly for young people, whether we're talking about romance, clothes, jobs or whatever. Everything revolves around folks who are thirty or under.

I know whereof I speak. Being over 60 and happily married for 46 years I should have known better than to try some suggestions in an article I saw the other day, which gave ten ways women could re-introduce romance in our marriages. It said letting our bodies speak for us can bring back romance.

I'm all for that. It's worth a try. I'll do it!

First, the article said, while talking to your man, turn an open palm toward him. Don't try that unless you're prepared to duck. Tom thought I was going to hit him, so he popped me first.

Number two said lick your lips. Better pick summer for that one. I licked mine in December until they became raw and cracked before he noticed. Then he asked if I had some kind of disease.

Three: This suggestion was to play with your hair. Flip your hair back and forth. He noticed and kept brushing dandruff from my shoulder.

Four: Now the article said, "Don't ever show him your back or the back of your head." That one was a real disaster. I backed out the front door ahead of him, fell off the four-foot porch onto a concrete walk, and it took twenty stitches to close the wound in my head.

Number five said twist your body to show off your curves. No use for us over 60's to even try that one. What curves?

Six: Touch his thigh. He said, "What are you doing? You've seen too many football games."

Seven: Try slipping off your shoes or earrings. I don't wear earrings, so I took off my shoes. He said my feet stunk.

Eight: Give him a special

look. Lean back, sigh and close your eyes. Let the eyelids flutter slightly. That bit of body language landed me in the hospital. He thought I was having a heart attack.

Nine: Touch an inanimate object as you talk to him. Slowly fondle the edge of a wine glass. We don't drink alcohol, so I filled my prettiest glass with apple juice, sidled up to him and said in a husky voice, "Hi," and ran my fingers along the edge of the glass. He said, "Oh, that reminds me, while your fingers are walking, look up a phone number for me in the yellow pages. I must call a shrink for you."

You'd think nine failures would be enough, wouldn't you? Not so. I decided to omit their tenth suggestion which was, caress your own body. I sure didn't want him to say, "You're fat."

I just had to try one more idea of my own, though. Maybe the helpless woman approach would do the trick.

The next time we went out to eat I tried it. Normally I hop out of the car, walk up to the restaurant door, grab the handle and go on in. This time I waited for him to open the door for me. He got halfway to the building before he noticed me still sitting in the car. With a frown, he motioned me to come on. He did wait for me.

I walked over to him, decided to combine all the magazine suggestions. I turned and backed up to the door; so as not to let him see my back. When we reached the door, I stepped back, licked my lips, fluttered my eyelids, flipped my hair, and turned my palms up.

He shook his head sadly, went on in leaving me standing there wondering what went wrong. If I ever get out from under this net the boys from the funny farm threw over me, I'll go back to my comfortable old rut. Tom will be glad.

—Johnnie Countess, in
From the Heart

HORNS OF A DILEMMA

"Okay. If I went out tomorrow and decided I must have one of the brand new models just because they had hit the market yesterday, for me that would be coveting."

That was still too theoretical. "God promises to supply all our needs. Isn't that so?" I was thinking aloud, hunting an answer.

"Right. Philippians 4:19 says that."

"Honey, we have hundreds of things in our home that go way beyond our 'needs.' We have a blender, a freezer of food, plenty of dishes, clothes to spare...." I ticked them off on my fingers.

"I don't think it means that," he said.

"All right. What are our basic needs? Enough food to subsist, enough heat to keep from freezing, a suit of clothes for decency. Just think how much more we could give to support missionaries if we did without half our food. We could survive, and nearly every missionary we know needs more support."

"Oh, come on. We give to missions."

"Okay. Let's bring it closer home. I want a new living room rug. Is that a sin?" I couldn't help it; the tears came.

"How can it be a sin when we need it?"

"Do we? Maybe we just need to refurbish the one we have and redirect that money."

We entered the house and walked into the living room. We surveyed the floor—mellow old pine boards protected by a set of brown-toned braided rugs. They seemed to fit the vintage flavor of our home, and we'd chosen them partially for that reason. Also they were cheaper than carpet.

"Maybe we could get them cleaned," I said.

Thou shalt not covet," the teacher said.

It disturbed me. When did "wanting" become "coveting"? I didn't want to sin.

We had been looking at those verses in James 1 which say: "Every man is tempted, when he is drawn away of his own lust, and enticed. Then when lust hath conceived, it bringeth forth sin." From these verses we established that yielding to temptation is sin.

Sunday school was dismissed; worship service started. I sang in the choir, sat through the sermon, and fulfilled my responsibility at the door in greeting people as they left.

Only part of my mind, however, was occupied with these activities.

The rest of it was busy churning over that problem of covetousness. I managed not to bring it up till we were halfway home.

"When do you think it's sin?" I asked.

"What?" my husband asked. He hadn't been in the class, so I filled him in on the details. By then we'd pulled into our driveway. He shut off the ignition, but neither of us moved. Perhaps he read the note of distress in my voice.

"What it boils down to," I said, "is this: When is wanting something a sin?"

"We have a perfectly good car here. Agree?"

I nodded. It was nice—comfortable seats, shiny, ran smoothly.

(More next page)

Horns of a Dilemma
(Cont.)

He laughed. "They'd fall apart."

They might at that. I'd used an upholstery needle to sew broken threads in them. But what about the hole through to the floor boards? With the toe of my shoe I pressed the fibers down as I did each time I swept, hoping the boards would remain invisible.

The new rug came up for discussion and kept cropping up in prayers.

To add to the dilemma I knew just the rug I wanted and where to get it on sale. And the sale was due to end. Earlier we'd never seen a braided rug big enough to fit our overlarge living room and so had assumed we'd have to use again a set of smaller ones or settle for broadloom; but this one, a lovely large oval in multitones, would be ideal.

I couldn't let it rest. I picked up the phone and ordered the rug. They said it would have to be shipped.

I'd started my housecleaning the week before. Perhaps because of my disturbed state, I worked with zeal.

My cleaning had progressed to the living room. The rug problem still was unresolved. Should I clean and wax the floor and put the old rugs back down again? I took down the draperies for a starter.

It was 10 a.m. when I called my husband. "Honey, did you hear the phone ring? The rug is in."

"Good. I'll pick it up while I'm in town."

With the old rugs out of the way, the room echoed hollowly as I moved about. I cleaned the walls, the woodwork, the windows. Then came the floor. The wax had barely dried when the car pulled into the driveway.

The rug was beautiful—just the right blend of colors. Furthermore it fit with a perfection that could not have been calculated. The wide oval swept along the sides of the room, just clearing the edges of the registers. When the furniture was in place, we sat and admired it.

"The Lord gave it to us!" I said it positively and with a lump in my throat. "Somehow it means more now than if I'd never agonized over it."

I suppose there are different theories as to when wanting becomes coveting. It may be eternity before I have a real answer. For now, when I'm not sure if my desire is legitimate, I'll just present that "want" to my Lord for examination. He knows my "needs" better than I do, and I'll trust Him to work out the details in His will. I know He does "exceeding abundantly above all that we ask or think" (Eph. 3:20).

—Reva Joy Harris

IN MEMORY OF TWO SONS

Somewhere upon a battlefield,
  In a war of bygone years,
One of our nation's brave sons fell
  And brought a mother's tears.
An unsung hero of our land
  Died so we might be free:
I'd like to take his hand in mine,
  Say, "Thanks, you died for me.
Though some may soon forget, by one
  You shall remembered be."

Somewhere upon a lonely hill,
  On a rugged cross of wood,
Another Son laid down His life—
  The precious Son of God.
Somewhere in Heaven up above
  It brought a Father's tears,
And so He knows that mother's heart—
  Oh, yes, He knows and cares.
Did He not soothe her deepest grief
  And calm her anxious fears?

And through the death of His dear Son,
  By the sacrifice He made,
Our freedom from all sin was won;
  The debt was fully paid.
I'd like to take His hand in mine,
  Say, "Christ, You died for me;
I thank You for Your suffering
  Upon the cruel tree.
Though others may perhaps forget,
  I give my all to Thee."

—Russell Stellwagon

A parable of a busy housewife

A dog named Sport started to chase a bear. Just as he came within a few yards of the bear, a fox suddenly crossed his path.

This turned his attention away from the bear, and immediately he set out in chase of the fox. When he was getting close to the fox, a rabbit ran out from a clump of bushes near him, and he began to chase the rabbit.

By this time Sport was panting hard. But just as he was about to catch the rabbit, a mouse ran into his path. And so he forgot about the rabbit and began to chase the mouse. Up and down the field for nearly half a mile he chased—then suddenly it disappeared into a hole.

Completely exhausted, poor Sport stood at the opening of the hole and barked—until he collapsed from exhaustion.

The story is only a parable, of course—but what a parable of the busy housewife today! How often at the end of what started out as a perfect day, you found yourself exhausted, panting down a rathole!

Something, someone got you off track. Like poor Sport, you started out to catch a bear and then switched your attention to a fox, then a rabbit, then a mouse; and finally you found yourself "done in" and barking down a rathole.

It is my hope that this volume has helped you better get through a "normal" day. If so, it will have been worth all the labor put forth.

God bless you and keep you, and cause His face to shine upon you, and give you peace.

—Miss Viola

At Journey's End:

Index of Prose Articles

Index of Prose Articles
(Cont.)

Index of Prose Articles
(Cont.)

Index of Prose Articles
(Cont.)

Index of Poetry

Index of Poetry
(Cont.)

Index of Authors

Index of Authors
(Cont.)